THE FORMULATION OF IRISH FOREIGN POLICY

THE FORMULATION OF IRISH FOREIGN POLICY

PATRICK KEATINGE

INSTITUTE OF PUBLIC ADMINISTRATION
Dublin

© Institute of Public Administration 1973
57–61 Lansdowne Road
Dublin 4
Ireland

ISBN 0 902173 52 9

Type set in 12 on 13 pt. Monotype Bembo, footnotes set in 9 pt. Monotype Bembo. Printed and bound for the publishers by Task Print & Packaging Limited, Naas, Co. Kildare.

FOR SUE

CONTENTS

TABLES

DIAGRAMS

PREFACE

RELATIVELY little has been written about the substance of Irish foreign policy, and even less about the political and administrative setting in which it is made. The purpose of this book is to start, at least, to remedy the second omission; to examine the way in which foreign policy issues are treated in the Irish political system, as well as the principal attitudes of Irish political figures towards their country's external relations.

The first draft appeared in the form of a thesis in the summer of 1968. In the succeeding years, the growing literature on the foreign policies of other states and on their decision-making processes suggested alternative and often more satisfactory approaches to a topic of this kind. Nevertheless, I have maintained the structure and most of the content of the original version, rather than engage on the lengthy business of re-casting the work in the interests of academic refinement. The principal reason for this decision lies in the transformation of Ireland's role in international politics which has occurred since 1968. At that time, foreign policy, no matter how broadly defined, was still a peripheral concern in Irish politics; but during the following five years, with the continuing crisis over Northern Ireland and accession to the European Community, it has come to make unprecedented demands on the country's political system. The reappraisal of that system in the light of this new situation is a matter of urgency. Consequently, in the hope of making some contribution to such a reappraisal, I have kept basic modifications of the original text to a minimum, though I have tried to keep up-to-date with the subsequent events where possible.

The preparation of this work owed a great deal to the assistance of those who read a part or all of the typescript, and who offered not only their time and patience, but often detailed and constructive suggestions. I am particularly indebted to Professor Basil Chubb, who shepherded me through the first draft and encouraged me to persist with later revisions. Other helpers, in the public service, must remain anonymous, but they may rest assured that their assistance is no less appreciated for that – and that responsibility for errors of fact and statements of opinion lies with the author. Completion of the final text owed much to Jonathan Williams, and I should also like to thank Geraldine O'Dea, Mary Ruane and Doreen Morehead for their quick and accurate typing.

INTRODUCTION

THE IRISH STATE AND FOREIGN POLICY

THERE is no single phrase which can be more tellingly applied to Ireland's position in the world than that of the French writer who referred to *"une île derrière une île."* [1] It conveys remoteness and even isolation, but at the same time a measure of shelter and protection from external events; all of these characteristics suggest an intermittent and marginal involvement in the mainstream of world affairs. Few states in western Europe can boast of a similar degree of good fortune. To have survived fifty years of this turbulent century, untouched by international wars and unconcerned by the obligations of alliance systems, is to have experienced what other peoples have only despairingly and vainly hoped for. Yet it seems as if the Irish people have often taken this condition for granted, and have appeared to dismiss the need to establish relationships with other states — to evolve a foreign policy — as an irrelevant luxury or, at best, something which will somehow happen, without the intervention of any human agency.

Geopolitical considerations, of course, lie at the root of this dismissive approach to foreign policy in Ireland. In ancient and medieval times, the British Isles were "at the end of the world — almost out of the world," [2] but the voyages of discovery profoundly altered this feeling of isolation. In so far as they were a political and economic unit, the islands became one of the centres of the new Atlantic civilisation, the focus of shipping routes and a point of departure for the New World. However, the most summary investigation reveals that this new position only marginally affected Ireland, the most westerly of the two large islands. The growth of the great ports — London, Liverpool and Bristol — demonstrates how essentially English was

---

[1] Jean Blanchard, *Le droit ecclésiastique contemporain d'Irlande* (Paris, 1958), p. 11.
[2] H. J. MacKinder, *Britain and the British Seas*, 2nd ed. (Clarendon Press, Oxford, 1907), p. 1.

1

the eventual development of the British Isles as the headquarters of world trade and finance in the nineteenth century, and this was hardly surprising in view of England's happy position in relation to the European mainland. "*Of* Europe, yet not *in* Europe," [3] England was close enough to the Continent to serve it as an entrepôt and financial headquarters, and yet sufficiently isolated from the disruptive effects of European power-struggles to build a relatively stable political base, the prerequisite for further economic expansion.

The fortunate paradox of England's situation, a combination of insularity and universality, was not enjoyed by Ireland. Indeed, Ireland's isolation from both commercial development and world politics was emphasised by her proximity to England, for a similar development on her shores would have provided an unnecessary duplication of effort, amounting to a harmful rivalry in the eyes of English mercantilists. Thus, as long as Ireland remained part of the British political unit, she remained, as a distinct region within this unit, isolated from the main developments of world trade. Very much 'John Bull's Other Island', she served to provide foodstuffs and human talents for Britain; for most other countries she appeared to be 'almost out of the world'. As a geographical unit, Ireland was a green isle of quaint and gloomy mystery but of little importance in international politics; even as a means of threatening the security of the British state, she had offered little to French and German invaders alike. Such is the image, and to a large degree the fact, with which Irish governments have had to contend since 1921, when the greater part of the geographical unit became an accepted member of international society. In war an advantage, in peace a barrier to economic development, Ireland's geographical isolation is a constant and salient factor to be heeded by policy-makers.

This isolation has been further accentuated by the nature of Ireland's economic resources. Not only was she ill-placed to take advantage of the commercial revolution of the fifteenth and sixteenth centuries, but when the Industrial Revolution developed in the eighteenth and nineteenth centuries, Ireland derived relatively little from it. Quite apart from adverse political and social conditions, the island lacked

[3] ibid., p. 12.

appreciable amounts of the raw materials, notably coal and iron, on which the British Industrial Revolution had prospered. Industrialisation, therefore, largely bypassed the Irish economy, which remained predominantly agricultural, able to support a relatively low standard of living and excessively sensitive to fluctuations in the world price of foodstuffs, its single important export. The exception to this, the north-eastern region around Belfast, remained part of the United Kingdom. Thus, when political independence was achieved, the new Irish state was comparatively under-industrialised. "It found itself without industries to supply such essential items as boots and shoes, clothing, furniture and other household goods".[4] Since 1921, Irish governments have attempted, by protectionist measures and encouragement, to reduce the economy's dependence on the agricultural sector. Accordingly, the volume of industrial production rose from 33.6 in 1926 to 104.0 in 1957[5] and, subsequently, following the impetus of the first programme for economic expansion (1958–1963), industrial development played an increasingly important role in the economy as a whole. This development has been accompanied by a marked reduction in the size of the agricultural working force, both absolutely and relatively, from being just under half of the total labour force in 1926 to under 30 per cent. at the beginning of the nineteen seventies.[6]

However, although the imbalance between agriculture and industry is becoming less pronounced, the fact remains that Ireland is still an industrialising rather than an industrialised state. The agricultural sector is relatively large by western European standards[7] and still enjoys considerable political influence. The total population, at just 3 million at the beginning of the nineteen seventies, is small by any standards, and economic expansion has to be achieved mainly through increased exports because of the small domestic market. A low marriage rate and constant emigration have persistently held back economic development and, although these and similar problems decreased in importance throughout the nineteen sixties, they continue

---

[4] *Economic Development* (Stationery Office, Pr. 4803, Dublin, 1958) p. 150.
[5] ibid., Appendix 8, p. 246. The index is expressed in real terms: base 1953 = 100.
[6] In 1969, employment in agriculture, forestry and fishing was 28.4 per cent. of the total labour force. See J. S. Oslizlok and K. Barry 'Ireland and the EEC — assorted comparative statistics', *Report of the Central Bank of Ireland* 1971, p. 92, table 2.
[7] ibid.

to influence public policies and affect the psychological climate in which specific decisions are made.

Ireland, then, is not only an isolated and sheltered state; it is a small and weak state. This particular combination of circumstances is perhaps chiefly responsible for the minor place which foreign policy holds in Irish politics. On the one hand, there is little incentive to become consistently and deeply concerned, for external threats often seem remote and diffuse; while on the other hand, there is a certain fatalism about the ability of the state to resist any threats that might arise. Yet although this attitude exists, it must be subjected to two qualifications, one concerning the meaning attached to 'foreign policy', the other concerning Ireland's relations with her nearest neighbour.

The term 'foreign policy' may be used in a narrow, specialised sense to denote those activities often referred to as 'high politics': issues relating to peace and war, the security and survival of the state in the face of external threats, and the negotiations, alliances and other attempts to exert influence which are associated with such issues. However, foreign policy also has broader connotations; it has even been defined as consisting simply "of decisions and actions which involve to some appreciable extent relations between one state and others".[8] Following this definition, it is appropriate to include economic, social and cultural relations between states in addition to the more dramatic concerns of traditional diplomacy, even at the risk of crossing the indistinct lines between 'foreign' and 'domestic' policy or 'political' and 'non-political' considerations.

In Ireland's case, the broader interpretation is particularly appropriate, for no matter how politically isolated she might be, the importance of external trade to her economy and the importance of social and cultural links with *émigré* populations in other states represent significant limitations on the range of objectives which may be pursued in relation to what are popularly thought of as 'political' issues. Thus, if it is possible to identify a general attitude of indifference towards foreign policy in the Irish political system, this pertains mainly, though not solely, to the restricted area of 'high politics'. In so far as this indifference does exist, however, it represents a failure to perceive the essentially

[8] J. Frankel, *The Making of Foreign Policy* (Oxford University Press, London, 1963), p. 1.

broad and varied nature of the range of activities which Ireland pursues outside her frontiers, and the ways in which these seemingly unrelated activities are so often interdependent.

An exception to this, or rather *the* exception, is the question of Ireland's relations with the state behind which she has sheltered from so much of world politics. These relations pervade every level of Irish public life.[9] Britain has always been by far Ireland's most important single trading partner, receiving well over half of her exports and supplying around half of her imports. It has been the principal labour market for Irish emigrants unable to find work at home. Geographical proximity has encouraged a continual movement of people between the two countries and has led the Irish to absorb many British values and expectations, in addition to the legacies of hundreds of years of British rule. All of this has been facilitated by the use of a common language and the absence of any serious restrictions on the freedom of movement between the two states.

The relationship between Ireland and the United Kingdom is not, however, a balanced one. The contrast between the two states in population, economic development and international influence is marked, to say the least. British influence on Ireland is pervasive; Irish influence on the United Kingdom is, more often than not, negligible. Moreover, while the relationship is close, in the area of 'high politics' it can occasionally be irritatingly close for Britain and suffocatingly close for Ireland. A politically independent Irish state has posed a strategic problem for successive British governments, concerned to protect their Atlantic flank; and the proximity of such a powerful neighbour is a constant source of unease for their Irish counterparts. Thus, the historical experience of the prolonged and often bitterly contested British dominion over Ireland is inevitably perpetuated beyond the point where the former British possession achieved political independence.

A more specific feeling of tension between the United Kingdom and Ireland has resulted from the unresolved issue of Northern Ireland. After the partition of the island in 1920, Irish nationalism remained unfulfilled and, like most irredentist nationalisms, has been of a bitter

[9] See F. B. Chubb, *The Government and Politics of Ireland* (Oxford University Press, London, 1970) p. 44.

and sometimes violent nature. This has meant that a large part of the content of Irish foreign policy has been concerned with a readjustment of relations with Britain, a readjustment which has demanded both acts and gestures of independence and sometimes opposition towards the state upon which Ireland is so economically dependent. The emotionalism, ambivalence and confusion associated with this persistently frustrating situation have helped to make Anglo-Irish relations an obsession of Irish politics. This obsession has contributed towards the restricted view of foreign policy which has generally prevailed in Ireland.

The relationship with Britain, particularly with regard to the partition of the island, often seems to be too vital to be lumped together with other questions of external policy. The nationalist ideologue will even deny that the main bone of contention — partition — is an external question, and sees the irredentist claim as a political reality. The politician may prefer to distinguish and elevate the purely 'political' aspects of Anglo-Irish relations by referring to them as 'constitutional', and to subsume the economic and social aspects under the general heading of economic and social policy. It can be argued that this fragmented terminology is of more than semantic interest, for it reflects a way of thinking in which the interdependence of the components of the relationship between the two states is all too easily ignored.

What has generally been accepted as foreign policy in the Irish context has been reduced to a mere residuum of what is normally implied by that term in other countries. The more obsessive the attitude towards Anglo-Irish relations, the greater the indifference towards other issues and towards Ireland's role in the world as a whole. Although developments in world politics have for some time undermined this lack of concern about the world outside Ireland, the fact remains that, apart from those few individuals with some responsibility for making policy, Irish politicians are essentially inward-looking. In short, "if Ireland now has a more wide-ranging foreign policy, it is a policy formulated and conducted largely without benefit of public commentary or public interest".[10] This, in part at

---

[10] ibid., p. 315.

least, explains why comparatively little academic attention has been paid to Irish foreign policy during the fifty not altogether uneventful years since 1921, and indeed it may also explain why the study of international politics in general has not yet been established in Irish universities, a situation not experienced in most western European states.

Yet, in spite of the peripheral role consigned to foreign policy in Irish public affairs and in spite of the tentative nature of Ireland's involvement in world politics, the substance of Irish foreign policy does include a wide range of objectives. In addition to those problems associated with the relationship with Britain, some Irish governments have demonstrated an interest in broader spheres. Security, for example, has been a problem with a European dimension and has been approached through such varied means as the League of Nations and a policy of military neutrality. Membership of the European Community may prove to be a counterweight to an exclusively British influence on both economic and political issues.

Nor has policy been confined to Europe. As a member of the League of Nations and of the United Nations Organization, Ireland has been concerned with world issues. The development of international cooperation through UN Agencies, disarmament schemes and peace-keeping operations have called for decisions by Irish governments. So too has the question of policy towards the states of the Third World, whether it has to do with the acutely political question of decolonisation or with practical attempts to provide aid to developing countries. It may be argued that in some instances Irish foreign policy has been no more than declaratory — a mere expression of attitudes without any consequential action — but the fact remains that many of the decisions taken have been, and still are, important to the existence of the Irish state.

This study of the political processes employed in the formulation of Irish foreign policy has been written with such considerations in mind. Its main concern is not to provide an historical account of the developments of policy but rather to examine the ways in which policy is made. The Irish political system (derived directly from that of Britain and, in spite of differences of scale, more noticeable for its similarities than for its contrasts to that system) does not offer insuperable obstacles to the pursuit of such an aim, especially since in recent years serious research into Irish politics has at last been undertaken.

However, serious problems do arise. At the best of times the study of the foreign policy of any state poses its own peculiar difficulties, occasioned by the lack of any widely accepted or fully developed theoretical approach. Foreign policy encompasses the politics both of the nation-state itself and of the community of nation-states, and in so doing falls, at times uneasily, within the scope of two academic disciplines—political science and international relations. In neither discipline, and particularly in the latter, are there any established guidelines to follow.[11] The comparatively limited material at the disposal of the student of foreign policy further hinders research.

In international politics, it is governments, not other groups, which place their states' relations somewhere on a line between the extremes of intensely constructive peace and totally destructive war. So foreign policy tends to be the preserve of those elements of government which reflect the unity rather than the diversity of the state, since the vital need to protect the state's existence demands a freedom of action and a measure of swift response and confidentiality which are not always compatible with the well-publicised partisan discussion found in domestic politics. Foreign affairs is therefore an area of government where we may expect the executive rather than the legislative institutions to play a more prominent role than is otherwise usual, and foreign policy is notorious for its secretive resistance to critical analysis.

This phenomenon is more pronounced in Ireland for several reasons. In the first place, the lack of concern about international politics and Ireland's role in the world has coincided with an unwillingness to reveal information about foreign policy; governments have been permitted to act while disclosing the briefest explanation about their actions. Furthermore, their reticence has been encouraged by the lingering suspicions and divisions following the brief but bitter civil war of 1922–1923, and the policy of neutrality has sometimes provided the reason, and often the excuse, for keeping the Irish public in a state of innocence.

---

[11] For a concise introduction to these and associated problems, see W. Wallace, *Foreign Policy and the Political Process* (Macmillan, London, 1971).

Consequently, participants in the policy-making process have been reluctant to write personal memoirs. Parliamentary debates and newspapers provide at best an intermittent and incomplete source of material, and case studies relating to specific issues or events are scarce and rarely comprehensive in scope. Above all, even for the early years of the Irish state, official documents that have been revealed to public scrutiny show only the tip of the iceberg and the student of Irish diplomatic history is still best advised to work in London rather than in Dublin. This paucity of material makes for an excessively general and superficial treatment of the subject-matter, but now that Ireland, as a member of the European Community, is starting to become more involved in international politics, there is an urgent need to make even the most modest contribution towards reducing the back-log of ignorance and indifference which have been so evident.

The making of foreign policy tends to be the concern of a relatively small area of government, although it necessarily involves the participation of a wide range of governmental institutions and political groups. A basic distinction may be made between those parts of the political system for which the making of foreign policy is a primary or direct concern and those other elements within the system which, although contributing to the making of foreign policy, do so in a less sustained and direct way. It would be misleading to equate these broad categories with the formal, constitutional role attributed to various institutions, for in practice the role played by these institutions varies widely, and some of them are less important as policy-makers than their constitutional status suggests. For example, as far as foreign policy is concerned, the legislature may be constitutionally treated as a policy-making body by virtue of its power to approve international agreements and to overthrow governments; however, in practice, the range and effectiveness of its powers are so limited that it can be argued that it influences rather than makes policy.

A similar difficulty in classification is found in the case of Ireland's President who, as head of state, has certain reserved powers which in times of crisis could impinge on foreign policy, but who, in practice, is not regarded as a significant element in decision-making. But there can be no doubt about the authority of the executive side of government to formulate policy; politically, the role of the cabinet and especially of its leader and foreign minister is paramount, while on the administrative level, the advice and information supplied by the government departments in general and particularly by the department directly responsible for foreign affairs are also important. The executive does in fact provide the core of policy-making, or what is referred to, in Part II of this study, as "the policy-making machinery".

In the second broad category of institutions and groups, whose participation in foreign policy tends to be indirect and incidental to their main functions, the emphasis is on influencing policy-makers rather than on making policy; this may be described as the policy-maker's 'domestic environment'. It includes not merely the formal parliamentary institutions, but the party organisations which operate both at the parliamentary level and at the electoral level. It also includes interest groups which attempt to influence the government's foreign policy and which express their views through the communications media.

However, foreign policy is not simply the consequence of the decisions, attitudes, perceptions and misconceptions of policy-makers acting in response to demands from the domestic environment. In all states, and especially in small and weak states like Ireland, it is the consequence of demands and pressures from outside the state — from the 'external environment'. The external environment cannot be so readily divided into separate components nor can it be fully understood, since the continuing influence of past decisions and a tendency to look to the past for guidelines to the present and future, are essential constituents of the uncertain and shifting arena of international politics.

PART I

THE EXTERNAL ENVIRONMENT

"All that we do, or can hope to do, in this country is materially conditioned by the state of the world in which we live".

James Dillon, 1944

(Dáil Debates: 94, 1338)

Chapter 1

INDEPENDENCE, ISOLATION AND PARTICIPATION

"We are outside the whirlpool of European politics."

John A. Costello, 1934
(Dáil Debates: 53, 262)

THE first fifty years of Ireland's statehood coincided with a period in international history when the world was often said to be 'shrinking', as states became increasingly interdependent both in peace and in war. The focus of world politics moved away from Europe, as the dominance of the old European empires was challenged by the colonial peoples and replaced by the less direct imperialism of the superpowers. It became possible to speak of a world economy and to think of world destruction. Never in human history has the pace of change been so great or its effects so widespread.

When the Irish state was established, following the ratification of the Anglo-Irish Treaty in January 1922, these changes were already taking effect and the tensions associated with them were already painfully evident to those who cared to look. Yet many of the assumptions underlying the old European-centred order were still unquestioned and it was to take further dissension on a global scale before they were seen in a clearer perspective. The darker shadows of the international environment did not, therefore, fall across the new state, and the more immediate preoccupation of the Irish government was not with the world as a whole but with the neighbouring government of the United Kingdom.

Quite apart from the comparative and deceptive lull in international tension in the mid-nineteen twenties, it is hardly surprising that, in the years immediately following independence from British rule, Irish external policies were above all else concerned with the state's relations with Britain. This is a pattern common to most newly

13

independent states as they part from their former rulers: the reconciliation of the elements of continuity with those of independence, the persistent need for economic or administrative help, and the necessity to find a new political relationship are matters of the most urgent priority. In general the new state, in spite of its independent gestures, leans most heavily on the former occupying state which, acting on a nice mixture of moral obligation and enlightened self-interest, will undertake the responsibility to help the new state overcome initial difficulties.

So it was, up to a point, in the case of Anglo-Irish relations. However, two features of the new relationship made the Irish policy-makers' task a complex and important one. First, the issue of partition had descended like a mist, obscuring and distorting each country's view of the other. The existence of the regional government of Northern Ireland, subordinate to the Westminster government, had a destructive effect on domestic politics in the Irish Free State; not only did it aggravate the divisions of the civil war of 1922–1923, but the issue of partition was responsible for the bitter and often violent nature of partisan politics throughout and beyond the period under consideration. Two emotionally distinct attitudes towards Ireland's relations with Britain evolved, and while the view of the Mr W. T. Cosgrave's Cumman na nGaedheal government prevailed (implying a temporary acceptance of the implications of the Anglo-Irish Treaty of 1921, and a cautious constitutional approach to foreign policy), this approach was severely criticised by opponents of the government and was vulnerable to doctrinaire nationalist claims.

A second striking feature of Anglo-Irish relations at this time was the fact that, on the whole, they developed in the context of the British Commonwealth rather than in a simple bilateral sense. Although provision had been made for a Council of Ireland in the original Anglo-Irish settlement, as a means of reconciling the two parts of the island and resolving the issue of partition, the failure of the Boundary Commission in 1925 to effect any significant change in the *status quo*, reduced the Council of Ireland to a dead letter. This experience traumatically underlined for Irish policy-makers the weakness of the smaller state in direct negotiations with the larger one. However, at the same time it was becoming clear that Commonwealth politics offered them considerable opportunity for manoeuvre.[1] Under the Treaty of 1921, the Irish Free State had been granted dominion status within the Commonwealth, and the aim of the Cosgrave government was to develop a legal and practical definition of dominion status which would demonstrate to other states, but especially to its opponents at home, that its acceptance of the Treaty was justified. The eventual rejection of dominion status by subsequent Irish governments indicates that, as a demonstration of political independence, this was only a beginning.

Nevertheless, the government's immediate objective — securing a definition of dominion status — was successful and resulted in the Statute of Westminster in 1931. This legislation was to be the foundation on which subsequent Irish actions were successfully based.

This may seem surprising in view of the position held by successive British governments which remained strongly opposed to a precise definition of Commonwealth relations, since in their opinion it would lead to an excessively rigid and unworkable relationship. However, in this very pragmatism lay the seeds of Ireland's opportunity, for the British emphasis on ambiguity implied an uncertain and negative diplomacy which was at the mercy of more specific demands. Furthermore, the advantages of negotiating with Britain under the aegis of the Commonwealth were realised in the Imperial Conferences of 1926 and 1930, for example, where Ireland could enlist support for her views from other dominions, such as Canada, Australia and South Africa. This was especially effective in the case of South Africa, which pursued a similar goal with equal intensity, and the combined pressure of the two relatively small powers was sufficient to achieve their immediate aim. Yet another characteristic of Commonwealth politics provided a third reason for Ireland's success in this

[1] This aspect of Irish foreign policy is the only one which has as yet received serious attention from historians.

A brief and stimulating introduction is to be found in C. Cruise O'Brien's chapter on 'Ireland in International Affairs' in O. Dudley Edwards (ed.), *Conor Cruise O'Brien Introduces Ireland*, (Deutsch, London, 1969). More detailed accounts are in W. K. Hancock, *Survey of British Commonwealth Affairs, Vol. 1. Problems of Nationality, 1918–1936* (Oxford University Press, London, 1937), especially chapters 3 and 6, and in N. Mansergh, *Survey of British Commonwealth Affairs: Problems of External Policy 1931–1939* (Oxford University Press, London, 1952), especially chapters 1, 2 and 8.

A full length study of the years from 1922 to 1932 is D. W. Harkness, *The Restless Dominion* (Macmillan, London, 1969).

field. The dominions were reluctant to formulate a united Commonwealth policy on major international issues, and there was never any
serious attempt to use the Commonwealth as an instrument for
settling the problems of European power rivalries. This, however,
suited the Irish government very well in its desire to avoid what
would have been seen at home as a humiliating submission to British
policies.

Nevertheless, the fact remains that, even if the Cosgrave government's policy towards Britain and the Commonwealth was successful,
it was the wrong policy, at least if it was to be judged by popular
support. The basic concept of dominion status, no matter how it
was defined, had little appeal for the strong nationalist element in
Irish politics. It was offered too late to eradicate the memory of the
failure of previous constitutional attempts to satisfy Irish nationalism;
it was based on the Anglo-Irish Treaty of 1921 and was thus irredeem-
ably associated with the violence and repression which led up to and
ensued from that event. Finally, of course, it offered no satisfactory
answer to the problem of partition. Indeed, the failure of bilateral
negotiations on this issue, particularly the Boundary Commission's
disputed findings in 1925, probably made more impression on the
general public than the rather abstract and legalistic successes within
the multilateral frameworks of the Commonwealth and the League
of Nations.

The government which supported the quest for dominion status
fell in 1932 and the retreat from Commonwealth membership began.
But in spite of negative reaction at home, the first phase of Anglo-
Irish relations had been one in which Irish policy-makers enjoyed a
relatively large degree of freedom from the external elements of their
environment; the Statute of Westminster ensured that further constitutional evolution could more rapidly be achieved.

Ireland's relations with states outside the Commonwealth were
generally less significant during the nineteen twenties than her
relationship with the Commonwealth states. In part this was due to
the very intensity of the people's and government's preoccupation
with Anglo-Irish affairs, but it is also a consequence of Ireland's lack
of involvement in most of the specific issues arising out of the post-war
settlement, such as the status of Germany and the questions of reparation
and of economic reconstruction.

However, in two respects, the Irish Free State was developing its overall foreign policy quite apart from its role within the Commonwealth. On the one hand, the machinery for establishing bilateral relations with other states was gradually being constructed. In 1924, a representative was appointed to the government of the USA, thereby breaking a Commonwealth precedent of collective representation through the British Embassy. By 1931, the Irish Free State was represented in France, Germany and the Holy See, in addition to the USA and the United Kingdom and, since 1923, there had been a permanent delegate to the League of Nations at Geneva.

The latter post indicates the second means by which Ireland was developing her national personality outside the Commonwealth: through membership of another international institution, the League of Nations.[2] This has now become a traditional form of Irish international activity, at least when conditions are favourable. Ireland gained several advantages by its membership of the League in the nineteen twenties. It offered a public platform for the assertion of international independence, and a symbolic demonstration of this nature was necessary as long as the concurrent policy of developing dominion status was seen as humiliating by Irish nationalists. The first Minister for External Affairs, Mr Desmond FitzGerald, subsequently explained this attitude: ". . . in the general contact with other countries which takes place in the League of Nations, I am quite willing to admit that every matter that came up we viewed rather from the aspect of narrow nationalism. . . . It was rather necessary, but personally I had a hope that if we had remained in office we should have been able to come off that."[3]

A case in point was the question of Irish participation in the working of the League itself. In 1926, the government put forward the Irish Free State as a candidate for a non-permanent seat on the Council of the League, and although this application was initially unsuccessful, in 1930, with a large measure of Commonwealth support, a seat was obtained and a firm basis for some influence in League affairs established.

---

[2] For a brief survey of Irish participation in the League of Nations, see P. Keatinge, 'Ireland and the League of Nations' in *Studies*, vol. LIX, no. 234, Summer 1970. Also see Cruise O'Brien, op. cit., Harkness, op. cit., Mansergh, op. cit.

[3] From a speech to the Dáil in 1934: Dáil Debates: 53, 207.

When the Minister for External Affairs, Mr Patrick McGilligan, claimed in 1931, ". . . we are recognised at Geneva as one of the main upholders of the complete independence of the smaller states . . ."[4], he was not exaggerating; but up to that time the contribution that Ireland could make to the League as a whole had not been fully developed.

Nevertheless, with the enactment of the Statute of Westminster in 1931, the Cosgrave government's foreign policy seemed to have resulted in "an immense increase in the international status of the Irish Free State",[5] although this position was unavoidably weakened after 1932 when there were significant changes both at home and abroad. It can be fairly said that by 1932 Ireland's existence as an independent sovereign state had been firmly demonstrated in the eyes of the world if not in those of some of her own people, and two of the traditional features of Irish foreign policy — a special relationship with Britain and participation in international institutions — had been developed.

The change of government in 1932 represented, as far as the formulation of foreign policy was concerned, a significant change in the domestic environment. The new parliamentary majority, led by Mr de Valera, was drawn from the Fianna Fáil party which had been formed in 1926 from the ranks of the opponents of the Anglo-Irish Treaty of 1921. Since they had fought a civil war because of their dissatisfaction with the implications of dominion status, it was hardly surprising that the new government and its supporters would want to develop a new relationship with Britain, which would embody a far greater measure of formal and symbolic independence and, where possible, a more marked degree of economic independence. What is perhaps surprising, bearing in mind the determination of some of these advocates of independence, is the fact that the ultimate departure from the British Commonwealth did not occur until as late as 1949. One explanation of this paradox lies in the fact that the less extreme nationalists still hoped that Northern Ireland would

[4] Dáil Debates: 39, 128.
[5] D. O'Sullivan, *The Irish Free State and its Senate* (Faber and Faber, London, 1940) p. 249.

be reunited with the Irish Free State under the aegis of the Commonwealth. But it is probable, too, that even without the change of
government, the course of Anglo-Irish relations would hardly have
continued as before.

In this respect, it was the Statute of Westminster (which became
law only six months before the Dáil was dissolved at the beginning
of 1932), rather than the change of government, which marked an
important watershed. The Statute of Westminster, indeed, represented
the achievement of the immediate aims of the Cumann na nGaedheal
government, and the next steps in constitutional evolution were
those which the new government was about to take. These involved
a gradual loosening of the bonds with Britain and the Commonwealth,
and the manner in which this was done provides some interesting
illustrations of the methods and objectives then open to the government, since in the years up to 1936 it achieved a new, if somewhat
ambiguous, relationship with the United Kingdom, and in subsequent years both consolidated it and attempted to demonstrate
its worth.[6]

During the first stage — the search for a new relationship — two
types of policy were adopted with varying success. On the one hand,
Mr de Valera reinterpreted the constitution of the Irish Free State,
until in 1937 he replaced it altogether and thus removed the constitutional humiliation whereby Ireland's sovereignty and independence were derived from the controversial Treaty of 1921. This policy
did not involve bilateral negotiations with Britain, but rather the
unilateral abolition by the Irish government of the principal symbols
of British influence — the parliamentary oath of allegiance to the
Crown, the relatively 'pro-Treaty' Senate and the office of Governor-
General — all of which were made possible by the Statute of Westminster. In 1936 an opportunity presented itself to restate the formal
relationship with Britain in a manner less mortifying to nationalist
susceptibilities. In December of that year, King Edward VIII abdicated
and, as the Statute of Westminster had made the succession to the

---

[6] For accounts of this period, see D. W. Harkness, 'Mr de Valera's Dominion: Irish
relations with Britain and the Commonwealth, 1932–1938', *Journal of Commonwealth
Political Studies*, vol. VIII, no. 3, 1970; and N. Mansergh, 'Ireland: External Relations
1926–1936' in F. MacManus (ed.), *The Years of the Great Test* 1926–39 (Mercier Press,
Cork, 1967).

throne a matter of concern to all the dominions, Mr de Valera hurriedly showed his particular concern by procuring the enactment of the Constitution (Amendment No. 27) Act and the Executive Authority (External Relations) Act, "by which the Crown [was] removed from the Irish Free State Constitution and reinstated on a simple statutory basis as an instrument which might be used by the Irish state for some purposes of external relations".[7]

Thus was revived the concept of 'external association', first mooted in the Anglo-Irish negotiations in 1921, by which Ireland would be associated with Commonwealth states as a matter of diplomatic convenience, but which did not involve any question of loyalty to the British Crown.

Along with this policy of constitutional readjustment, Mr de Valera's government introduced a policy of economic independence from Britain. Prior to this, the economic dimension of Irish foreign policy had been anything but clear. On the one hand, the need to develop an industrial sector seemed to imply a policy of protection, but on the other hand, the Irish government in the nineteen twenties subscribed to the general acceptance of free trade theories and a minimal role for governments in the control of economic behaviour. The Cosgrave government had not, therefore, been inclined to do more than tamper with the close and dependent economic relationship with the United Kingdom through the so-called policy of 'selective protection'. In effect, the essence of free trade policy prevailed even when, in the early nineteen thirties, the world-wide depression caused most other states to have hurried second thoughts about its worth. Mr de Valera, however, was no free trader and the new developments in international economics meant that, when he came into power, his economic policy coincided with the conventional wisdom of that time.

But quite apart from the widespread adoption of economic nationalism in the early nineteen thirties, Irish policy was based on a specific dispute. While in opposition, Mr de Valera had repudiated the obligation of Irish tenant-purchasers to pay the land annuities arising from British land purchase schemes effected between 1891 and 1909, but

[7] F. B. Chubb, *The Constitution of Ireland* (Institute of Public Administration, Dublin, 1963), p. 17.

the Cosgrave government had accepted this obligation as binding, both in the financial agreement of 12 February 1923 and in the ultimate financial settlement of 19 March 1926. On achieving office in 1932, Mr de Valera held to his position, and the British and Irish governments, failing to agree on a procedure for arbitration, engaged in a series of retaliations and counter-retaliations by which a high tariff barrier was erected between the two countries. This economic war, in which the Irish economy was forced to stand largely on its own, involved the reality of independence rather than its appearance, was a less effective measure than constitutional readjustment and proved considerably arduous in its effects on the Irish economy.[8]

Of course the varied success of Mr de Valera's search for a more independent relationship with Britain depended largely on the principal external factor involved — the attitude of the British government. Since Britain could find alternative sources of foodstuffs and was only marginally affected by Irish tariffs, the British response to Ireland's policy was sufficiently strong and sustained to make Ireland, rather than the United Kingdom, the principal sufferer. But the British government's reply to Mr de Valera's constitutional attack was as ineffective as her economic riposte was damaging: the British government's pragmatic attitude towards Commonwealth relationships induced it passively to accept the breaching of constitutional loopholes in the hope, and indeed belief, that these actions were not evidence of a desire to leave the Commonwealth altogether. Consequently, a blind eye was turned towards the more inflammatory and radical implications of Mr de Valera's concept of external association. This attitude was encouraged by the British government's preoccupation with its own country's serious economic condition and its tentative participation in the increasingly complicated problems of European politics.

Having achieved external association by the beginning of 1937, Mr de Valera then proceeded to demonstrate (though with appropriate ambiguity) its implications to the world in general and to his own country in particular. A new constitution, without any humiliating references to the United Kingdom or to the Treaty of 1921, was

[8] For a concise account of events leading up to the economic war, see Hancock, op. cit., pp. 339–368.

adopted in 1937 and this, in Mr de Valera's own words, put "the question of our international relations in their proper place — and that is outside the Constitution".[9] The tenuous but convenient link with the Commonwealth embodied in external association remained intact, as there was no explicit reference to the state (now called Éire in the Irish language, and Ireland in English) being a republic, which in effect it was. This significant omission proved highly unsatisfactory to the parliamentary opposition and to the violent republican extremists alike; it seemed illogical and shameful not to assert the formal claim to republicanism. But, although this was ultimately to be the Achilles heel of the concept of external association, the new relationship with Britain appeared to be reasonably acceptable to both countries in the late nineteen thirties. In practice, Ireland no longer participated fully in Commonwealth consultations as it had done under Mr Cosgrave's government in the nineteen twenties. Mr de Valera thereby demonstrated that real independence was possible under external association.

The new style of relationship conformed to the traditional mode of diplomatic contacts between sovereign states, and was typified in the negotiations leading up to the important Anglo-Irish Agreement of 1938.[10] This agreement resolved several outstanding issues. The economic war was finally brought to a close by a trade agreement which recognised a special position for Irish producers in the British economy. At the same time the British government agreed to hand over several Irish ports which it had maintained under the terms of the 1921 Treaty, a situation regarded by the Irish as yet another embarrassing violation of national sovereignty.

But the 1938 agreement cannot be seen, from the point of view of either the British or Irish governments, as just another round in the important but limited context of Anglo-Irish relations. By 1938, as the emergence of Hitler's Germany became more threatening, the wider external environment was becoming an increasingly important factor in the formulation of Irish policy. Six years previously, on his accession to office, Mr de Valera had not shown any

[9] Dáil Debates: 67, 60.
[10] These negotiations and the dispute preceding them are examined in The Earl of Longford and T. P. O'Neill, *Eamon de Valera* (Gill and Macmillan, Dublin, 1970), chapters 23–26.

great optimism about European politics, but the circumstances pertaining then had at least allowed for an initial expansion of Ireland's role in international politics. Here, the groundwork laid by the previous government through its policies in the League of Nations proved invaluable.

As it happened, it was the turn of Ireland to provide the President of the Council of the League, and in September 1932 Mr de Valera himself took that office, an indication of the importance he attached to the League's activities. That the country's role in the League mattered little to Irish public opinion (except in so far as policies towards Catholic countries such as Italy and Spain were concerned) only served to enhance the opportunities which he was given to impress his own ideas on the League.

This he did almost immediately. He lost no time in advocating the concept of a strong League which would unhesitatingly attempt to settle disputes by means of some form of international justice and not just with expedience in mind. The League, he maintained, should be radically reformed as an instrument of world government, in the face of which national sovereignty would cease to exist. This was no doubt idealistic and inconsistent in view of his government's assertion of national sovereignty, but it nevertheless formed the basis on which Ireland supported positive action against the aggressors in Manchuria and Ethiopia. Mr de Valera went to great pains to stress the importance of the smaller states playing a positive role in the League, independent of the pressures from the great powers. Later, in 1946, he maintained that "such respect as we were able to acquire in Geneva was largely due to the fact that on every question that arose we were able to express our own views independently, and that it was known that these were our own views".[11]

The anarchic nature of international society in the nineteen thirties made a strong League of Nations appear more illusory than probable, and this is reflected in the fluctuating moods of hope and despair found in Mr de Valera's pronouncements on the League. Moreover, Ireland's policy was ambiguous, and it seems that Mr de Valera's

[11] Dáil Debates: 101, 2448.

statements of intent were not acted on with notable energy.[12] This is partly understandable in view of Ireland's obsession with Anglo-Irish relations, but it may also be a consequence of the lasting disillusionment of many Irishmen after the early failure of the League to help advance the cause of Irish independence between 1919 and 1921. Thus, while the Irish government supported the League of Nations in its efforts to establish a system of collective security, its attitude towards the possibility of eventual military participation was negative, and like most other member-states, Ireland drew the line on collective security well before 'aggressor states' were inclined to take any notice.

But with the failure of the League to prevent the Italian conquest of Ethiopia in 1936, any ambiguity on Ireland's part disappeared. On the 18 June 1936, Mr de Valera stated that the League "does not command our confidence" and argued that in a world of hostile alliances there could be only one aim for the Irish Free State; "we want to be neutral", he said then.[13] In handing back the ports in 1938, the British government of Mr Chamberlain was under no illusions that this strategic loss would, at best, be counterbalanced by a neutral but sympathetic Ireland rather than by an unfriendly if not actively hostile neighbour.[14] The 1938 settlement made Irish neutrality a more realistic policy for, having relinquished its claims, a British government would be less likely to reverse this position by force and thus compromise Irish neutrality. The return of the ports was the basis of Ireland's independent foreign policy during World War II.

From 1936, Ireland's membership of the League was justified merely in terms of diplomatic convenience. But whether supporting a strong or a weak League, the government was still criticised for its role in European affairs. It was accused of being led by Britain in supporting sanctions against Italy, while its association with the atheistic Soviet

[12] Seán Lester, who throughout the nineteen thirties was either Ireland's permanent delegate in Geneva or a high-ranking League official, was persistently critical of the lack of interest of Irish policy-makers in the broader aspects of the League of Nations' political role. I am indebted for this information to Dr Stephen Barcroft, who is writing a book on Lester.

[13] Dáil Debates: 62, 2660.

[14] N. Mansergh, *Survey of British Commonwealth Affairs, Problems of Wartime Co-operation and Post-War Change, 1939–1952* (Oxford University Press, London, 1958) pp. 63–64. Where the British government *did* act under an illusion was in ignoring the possibilities of the swift defeats of Norway and France. Hence, they were faced in 1940 with a much more serious strategic situation than they had envisaged.

Union, which had joined the League in 1934, was claimed to be immoral, and its failure to intervene on behalf of General Franco in the Spanish civil war was regarded as unchristian. The government's stand on the Spanish civil war was vociferously attacked both inside and outside the Dáil; nevertheless, Mr de Valera's adherence to the non-intervention policy remained firm up to the military defeat of the Spanish republican forces.[15]

It was the pressure of external rather than domestic events which finally drove the government from a policy of well-intentioned, though hesitantly executed international cooperation to one of passive isolation and neutrality. The Irish government's last major initiative in international politics before wartime neutrality was put into practice was its somewhat ineffective support of Chamberlain's Munich adventure in 1938. Neutrality was a logical security policy, given Ireland's position in 1939. She thought she was not directly involved in Germany's provocative policies, she had little faith in the Commonwealth's ability to formulate a strong and united stand and no inclination to be part of it, and, with the failure of the League, she had no means of combining with other small states in a similar position. In short, Ireland had no commitments and, like all other small powers in Europe (and some very large powers both inside and outside Europe), she preferred to wait on the sidelines in the hope that the blow might not fall—a hope that was in her case justified by events.

However, neutrality, like most successful policies, was a stone which killed more than one bird. It was not a policy hastily conceived to meet either the collapse of the League in 1936 or the impending holocaust of 1939, for previously it had been a widely held assumption that, if possible, Ireland should remain neutral in any future European war. Given the question mark which the 1921 Treaty seemed to add to Ireland's independent status, neutrality was, as one historian has put it, "almost a psychological necessity", involving as it did" that final attribute of sovereignty which is to be found in free exercise

[15] For an account of the effect of the Spanish civil war on Ireland, see J. Bowyer Bell, 'Ireland and the Spanish Civil War 1936–1939', *Studia Hibernica*, no. 7, 1969. Also see William Tierney, 'Irish Writers and the Spanish Civil War', *Éire–Ireland*, vol. 7, no. 3, 1972, pp. 36–55.

of a choice between peace and war".[16] Ireland was the only dominion to take this course, thus emphasising her peculiar position with regard to the Commonwealth. The Irish public took the decision for granted, with two exceptions: a relatively small group sympathetic to Britain, who were allowed to enlist in the British forces alongside other Irish volunteers whose motives had little to do with Anglo-Irish relations, and some extreme nationalists who would have preferred their country to fight alongside the axis powers, as a means of ending partition.

Partition had been the one serious issue left unresolved in the 1938 Agreement. The possibility of Britain reopening the matter in exchange for Irish cooperation in defence had not been enough to initiate any breakthrough, and subsequent suggestions on the same lines came to nothing. Indeed, as the war escalated after 1941 with the entry of the USA, the persistence of partition was put forward as a further reason for the maintenance of neutrality; for in the face of pressure from American public opinion which was now hostile towards the few remaining neutrals, this was a most forceful argument.[17] In the event, the argument was accepted by the allied powers but not without serious misgivings, and Irish diplomacy was tested to its limits. The wartime period was thus characterised by "a dangerous and intractable conflict of immediate interest between a belligerent Britain fighting on alone against the might of Nazi Germany and a neutral Eire preoccupied with the maintenance of a neutrality that had come to be regarded as the final vindication of independence".[18] The well-publicised clash between Churchill and de Valera when the war ended epitomised the emotional nature of Anglo-Irish relations but did nothing to alter the fundamental relationship of external association. Ironically, in spite of the demonstration of Ireland's independence, represented by its policy of neutrality, that relationship would change only four years after the end of the war, and was to be the victim of bitter partisan parliamentary politics. Using the

[16] ibid, p. 332.
[17] See Cruise O'Brien, op. cit., pp. 121–123. Irish neutrality during World War II is also examined in Mansergh, *Problems of Wartime Cooperation*, chapter 6; in T.D. Williams, 'A Study of Neutrality', *The Leader*, January–April, 1953; in Longford and O'Neill, op. cit., chapters 28–31; and in Constance Howard, 'Eire', in A. J. Toynbee and V. M. Toynbee (eds.), *The War and the Neutrals* (Oxford University Press, London, 1956).
[18] Mansergh, *Problems of Wartime Cooperation*, p. 75.

ambiguity of the relationship as a probe, opposition members taunted de Valera into attempting a definition of Ireland's position in relation to Britain and to the Commonwealth as a whole.

As a result, Ireland's status as a republic was still left in doubt, a doubt which was to remain until after the general election of 1948 which saw the dramatic rise of a militant republican party, Clann na Poblachta, and the defeat of de Valera's government after sixteen years in office. Anglo-Irish political relations then, at last, achieved a precise definition, at least in the formal sense; the constitutional qualifications of Ireland's membership of international society, so long the major preoccupation of Irish foreign policy, were now to recede in importance. A coalition government—in which the main elements were the Fine Gael, Labour and Clann na Poblachta parties—came to office in February 1948. Within nine months there occurred a readjustment in Anglo-Irish relations which altered the temper of Irish politics.

On 7 September 1948, Mr Costello announced his intention of repealing the External Relations Act of 1936, thus replacing the ambiguous policy of external association with the Commonwealth with the establishment of a completely independent republic. On 18 April 1949, the Republic of Ireland Act came into force, and neither the British nor Irish governments made any move to revive the moribund Irish membership of the Commonwealth on a new basis, as happened in the case of India less than a year later. This act has had several important consequences for the subsequent history of Anglo-Irish relations, but before considering these it is worthwhile looking at the internal events leading up to the proclamation of the Republic, for these provide an interesting commentary on the way in which the seemingly intractable problem of Ireland's constitutional relationship with the United Kingdom was approached.

Much of the irony underlying the formulation of this legislation derived from the fragmentary nature of Mr Costello's coalition government, which contributed to the peculiar mixture of motives behind the repeal of the External Relations Act. The Fine Gael party to which the Taoiseach (Prime Minister), Mr Costello, belonged (although he was not its leader), was the direct successor of the Cumann na nGaedheal party, which had, in the nineteen twenties, sought a solution to the difficulties of Anglo-Irish relations within the context of the Commonwealth. This policy had remained a significant element in the party's electoral appeal but, whereas in 1932 it had seemed to be electorally beneficial, in 1949 its relevance appeared more doubtful. Mr Costello did not like what he regarded as the devious and illogical nature of external association which had been so clearly exposed by a former party colleague, Mr James Dillon, and he was personally determined to put an end to it.

However, Mr Costello's government relied for its survival on the active support of the new Clann na Poblachta party which had enjoyed some success at the polls. In return, that party's leader, Mr Seán MacBride, obtained the portfolio of External Affairs. Unlike Costello, he did advocate a clear alternative to external association, for he had fought a vigorous election campaign largely on the issue of breaking with the Commonwealth and proclaiming a republic. His views could not, therefore, be taken lightly and indeed found ready public support from other prominent members of the relatively loose coalition government. Under these circumstances, there could be no return to positive membership of the Commonwealth, and Mr Costello abandoned this traditional aim of his own party and declared the Republic, retaining some semblance of independence by publicly announcing the policy without prior notice and when outside the country. The British government, for its part, accepted the implications of this unilateral action by Ireland, stating that it proposed to continue regarding its relations with Ireland in a special category: Irish citizens would be treated neither as foreigners nor as Commonwealth citizens. For the sake of practical convenience, the tradition of constitutional ambiguity was thus maintained on the British side and in later years relatively little change was seen in the main lines of British policy towards Ireland.

However, the British government confirmed its sovereignty over Northern Ireland in the Ireland Act of 1949, thereby strengthening its commitment to uphold the unionist régime and frustrating the anti-partitionist claims of the new republic. Indeed, during the first coalition government's term of office from 1948 to 1951, these claims were being advocated enthusiastically. Once Mr de Valera was in opposition, he put his considerable prestige behind an attempt to raise this issue.

The political parties were therefore compelled to compete for the nationalist vote, promising to resume the outstanding dispute with Britain which had been forced into the background during the war. But the Irish government found that public opinion was a poor weapon with which to achieve tangible short-term results in the hard world of international diplomacy. Other governments were not interested and, with the exception of extreme republican sentiment, it was soon apparent that, for the public as a whole and for Irish governments, the end of partition had become a distant aspiration and one which, it seemed, would be less likely to affect the routine relationship with Britain.

The highly emotional content of Irish nationalism had thrived as much on symbolic subservience as on real subservience and, since the Republic of Ireland Act removed many of the more humiliating and frustrating symbols of the connexion with Britain, the fervour of Irish feelings subsided to a certain extent. Now that the possibility of working through the multilateral machinery of the Commonwealth had also been abandoned in the letter as well as in the spirit, it was felt that the time was ripe to make a fresh start in evolving a more balanced foreign policy.

But the broader international setting did not favour this new mood. When Mr de Valera's government fell in 1948, Ireland was, as a result of her wartime neutrality, almost wholly isolated from the mainstream of world events and without the means to influence them. In spite of the resumption of normal diplomatic relations after the war, the failure of Ireland to obtain membership of the United Nations Organization led to considerable diplomatic isolation.

In 1946 and 1947, Mr de Valera's government had applied for membership of the newly-formed successor to the League of Nations, in which Ireland, and especially Mr de Valera himself, had played a not insignificant role. Ireland was ostensibly refused admission by the Security Council veto of the Soviet Union on the grounds that she had openly sympathised with the axis powers during the war. Coming from one of the participants in the Soviet-Nazi pact of 1939, this was hardly convincing and it was soon apparent that Ireland was an unwilling pawn in the cold war tactic of procedural obstruction within the United Nations. It was not until 1955 that the deadlock was broken and Ireland at last achieved the opportunity to pursue a wider range of objectives in a multilateral setting.

As well as being outside the Commonwealth and the United Nations, Ireland remained aloof from the military alliance systems which typified the new cold war divisions. In 1939, neutrality had been based on two premises, apart from a general popular desire to stay out of war: one — the breakdown of the League of Nations' system of collective security — was external, the other — the need to assert the state's independence, particularly in view of the failure to achieve the end of partition — was largely internal. In 1949, Mr de Valera's successors were faced with a similar if somewhat less dramatic choice between military commitment and neutrality when they decided not to join the North Atlantic Treaty Organization. At that time, the second domestic factor was predominant: Ireland could not join in an alliance with that state which, by upholding partition, still compromised Ireland's sovereignty, for this, it was claimed, would be tantamount to recognising the partition of the country as permanent. Neutrality had never been simply a pragmatic reaction to a dangerous world situation, but it was now more than ever an article of faith, all the more ironic in view of the pervasive anti-communist sentiment which could be seen in most Irish political parties.

It could be argued that Ireland's isolation was in fact a blessing in disguise, for, even if she had been a member of the United Nations before this date, Ireland's policies in another international forum suggest that such an opportunity would have been wasted. This was particularly the case under Mr Costello's coalition government of 1948–1951, when Ireland's foreign policy was seen mainly in the light of her complaint against partition. Thus Mr MacBride saw the Council of Europe as a pulpit from which he could descant on Irish grievances, a policy which "in fact . . . rebounded, by creating the impression there that the Irish were suffering from persecution mania".[19] It was only in the relatively non-political institutions such as the OEEC that this intrusion of irredentism into Ireland's foreign policy did not prove embarrassing.

Nevertheless, it was Irish participation in the European recovery

---

[19] B. Inglis, *The Story of Ireland* (Faber and Faber, London, 1956), p. 248.

programme during the late nineteen forties which seemed to offer the government the most promising opportunity to develop a positive foreign policy. In the first place, the administrative burden occasioned by participation in the programme provided a further incentive to develop the state's diplomatic machinery, a move which was also a logical outcome of the final separation from the Commonwealth diplomatic network. Then there was the possibility of the technical cooperation between western European states being translated into a more radical scheme of political integration, a possibility of which Mr MacBride was fully aware. But this opportunity was lost when Britain remained aloof, and 'integrated Europe' was restricted to the six states which formed the European Coal and Steel Community in 1950. The Irish government, bearing in mind the overwhelming importance of trade with Britain, followed the British lead and membership of the Council of Europe subsequently had little effect, since that body had been outflanked by NATO on the one side and 'Europe of the Six' on the other.

Ireland's diplomatic horizons had been limited yet again by external rather than internal factors, although during the early nineteen fifties one of the principal constraints was the persistent difficulties of the Irish economy. During the term of office of Mr de Valera's government from June 1951 to June 1954 and for the first eighteen months of Mr Costello's second coalition government which succeeded it, foreign policy remained a closed book. The initiative, promise and energy of the first coalition government were replaced by withdrawal, isolation and introspection.

The early and mid-nineteen fifties were indeed a trough in Irish public life, marked by a sense of aimlessness and despair. As far as foreign policy was concerned, through a combination of international circumstances and the unforeseen effects of past policies, there seemed to be no way to turn. But later in the decade, a certain recovery became manifest. The formation of a Fianna Fáil government at the beginning of 1957 can now be seen to mark the end of a period of changing governments and the beginning of a period of just over twelve years during which one man, Mr Frank Aiken, held the portfolio of External Affairs.

But of much greater importance in the long term was the degree to which both government and administration were prepared to intervene in the economic policy of the state. While the immediate effect of this development was by no means obvious in the field of foreign policy, it may be recognised in retrospect as the basis on which current Irish foreign policy stands. Following the adoption in 1958 of a comprehensive and comparatively specific set of economic objectives, the importance of Ireland's trade performance and foreign investment was emphasised more clearly than had been the case under the European recovery programme of the late nineteen forties. Consequently, the need to move away from a position of isolation towards some form of participation in international affairs became evident.

Three years earlier, the first opportunity to develop such participation had arisen when, as a consequence of the cold war 'thaw', Ireland was at last admitted to the United Nations Organization late in 1955. In 1956 the Minister for External Affairs, Mr Liam Cosgrave, laid down the three broad principles on which Ireland's participation would depend: support of the UN's Charter, independence of 'blocs' in the UN, and a commitment to ". . . preserve the Christian civilisation of which we are a part and with that end in view to support wherever possible those powers principally responsible for the defence of the free world in their resistance to the spread of Communist power and influence".[20]

However, from 1957, the direction of Irish policy in the UN devolved on Mr Aiken and not Mr Cosgrave, and up to 1960 the principle which received most emphasis was that of independence. In her willingness to formulate plans for military disengagement and disarmament, to discuss the admission of communist China to the United Nations and to support the claims of the smaller, newer member-states, Ireland acquired a reputation as an independent state at a time when "the powers principally responsible for the defence of the free world" regarded even the slightest divergence from the rigid orthodoxies of the cold war as little short of outright opposition. The government's policies met with some opposition from the Fine Gael party, which focused its attack on the question

[20] Dáil Debates: 159, 144.

of communist China, but on the whole it seemed that Ireland was firmly established in the UN as a state with a distinctive and relatively independent foreign policy.

It was hardly surprising, therefore, that the state became more deeply involved in UN activities in the early nineteen sixties. In 1960, Dr F. H. Boland became President of the General Assembly and in 1962 Ireland served on the Security Council. Participation in the Congo peace-keeping force in 1960 marked a new step in Irish foreign policy for, as well as contributing votes and money to the UN effort, it was the first time an Irish government committed an official contingent of the Irish army to serve overseas.[21]

This precedent was followed in 1964 by the Cyprus peace-keeping operation. In the field of disarmament, the Irish delegation was among those which played a pioneering role in the formulation of the Treaty of Non-Proliferation of Nuclear Weapons, and in 1968 Mr Aiken had the privilege of being the first signatory to this Treaty. Continual efforts to reach a compromise solution to the fundamental issue of the financing of peace-keeping operations were not successful, but the expansion of the delegation's participation in the UN's 'technical' activities came to a peak when Ireland became a member of the UN Economic and Social Council (ECOSOC) from 1969 to 1970.

The greater part of this activity aroused little adverse comment; indeed there seemed to be some pride in the state's position as a power with a certain mediatory influence at the United Nations and a positive contribution to make towards the creation of a more favourable international environment. However, in the mid-nineteen sixties some aspects of the government's policy, both inside and outside the United Nations, met with criticism. The most prominent critic was Dr Conor Cruise O'Brien, a former head of the political section in the Department of External Affairs and a member of the Irish UN delegation until his secondment in 1961 to the UN Secretariat as representative in Katanga. Dr O'Brien accused the government of being subservient to American influence, both in its support for the 'two Chinas' policy on the question of Chinese representation

[21] Previously, individual Irish army officers had served with UN observer groups in the Middle East. However, the Congo operation necessitated new legislation, the Defence (Amendment No. 2) Act, 1960.

3

in the UN and in its failure to condemn American participation in the war in Vietnam. Irish foreign policy, he argued, was now based not so much on the principle of independence as on Liam Cosgrave's original third principle — the defence of the West in cold war terms. The Minister for External Affairs, Mr Aiken, denied the charge of subservience to the USA (and Britain), citing in his defence the whole of his delegation's voting record in the UN, rather than selected parts of it. The intermittent controversy on this issue did little to clarify the constraints on Ireland's freedom of action with regard to the major issues of world politics, either in the United Nations or elsewhere.[22] In 1971, when Ireland did reverse her policy on Chinese representation, although the vote was against American wishes, it was hardly the action of a maverick, for by this time the consensus was clearly opposed to the stand of the USA. The image of an independent stance was somewhat restored, but the impression of caution and discretion remained.

It could be argued, though, that the major development in Irish foreign policy in the nineteen sixties was not what Ireland was or was not doing at the UN but rather the government's decision in 1961 to apply for membership of the European Economic Community. At this point, economic rather than purely political objectives came to the fore. The government's commitment to economic reorganisation and development appeared to require following Britain into the EEC; at the same time it was hoped that this move would reduce the effects of an unbalanced economic relationship with Britain. President de Gaulle's repeated rejection of British membership from 1963 did not alter this objective, though Ireland's commitment to European integration (itself often extremely ambivalent) resulted in some ambiguity in her foreign policy. At times, the traditional policy of military neutrality seemed to be in doubt. In 1962 the Taoiseach,

---

[22] For Dr Cruise O'Brien's account of his role in Ireland's UN delegation, see Cruise O'Brien, *To Katanga and Back* (Hutchinson, London, 1965), p. 38 and his essay in O. Dudley Edwards (ed.), *Conor Cruise O'Brien Introduces Ireland*, pp. 127–132. His criticisms of the government's policy are found in the latter work, pp. 127–134, and at greater length in *Ireland, the United Nations and South Africa* (The Irish Anti-Apartheid Movement, Dublin, 1967) and in *The Irish Times*, 3 and 4 June 1968. Mr Aiken expressed his views in the Dáil: for the latest occasion see Dáil Debates, 241: 1930–1940. See also his letters to *The Irish Times*, 26, 27 May 1969 and the UN voting record issued by his department, *The Irish Times*, 3 June 1969.

Mr Lemass, argued that the existence of partition was no longer in itself a reason for refusing to join the North Atlantic Treaty Organization. But in the event, the abandonment of neutrality was not made a condition of Ireland's entry into the EEC and the government's intentions about the future of neutrality were never made very clear. It was also not clear whether there was any connexion between the application to join the EEC and what was, rightly or wrongly, seen as the government's reluctance to criticise the major policies of the western powers. The division of immediate responsibility for each of the two major aspects of foreign policy between the head of the government, who oversaw European affairs, and the Minister for External Affairs, who looked after United Nations affairs, tended to increase the apparent fragmentation of Irish foreign policy, since each minister was careful not to encroach on the other's territory.

For as long as the expansion of the EEC remained uncertain, some degree of confusion was, of course, inevitable; nevertheless, the fact that policy appeared to be unduly compartmentalised, indicated the lack of communication between a cautious and tight-lipped government and a largely indifferent public. Membership of the EEC was discussed primarily in economic terms, and the major move made by the government to prepare for the trading conditions of the Common Market was the adoption of the Anglo-Irish Free Trade Agreement in 1965.

Although this agreement also served to emphasise the fact that the preoccupation with Britain, as Ireland's largest and nearest market, was still a salient feature of Irish foreign policy, the relationship was now marked more by economic than by constitutional considerations. Although the issue of partition still rankled during the nineteen fifties, the intermittent border campaigns by armed nationalist groups were suppressed by the Irish government and the regional government of Northern Ireland alike. Cooperation over matters of common interest, such as tourism, proved possible in spite of the fact that the existence of the northern administration at Stormont was not accepted by the Irish government. When the border campaigns ceased in 1962, it became possible to work towards some degree of reconciliation between north and south.

This attempt at reconciliation was symbolised by the meeting between the two prime ministers, Mr Lemass and Captain Terence O'Neill, in January 1965. Although the meeting was readily accepted by public opinion in the south, it was perhaps instrumental in exacerbating the misgivings of some northern unionists. The consequent dissension within the Stormont government came to a head over the civil rights campaign in the autumn of 1968, after which violence set in in the six counties. The Lemass-O'Neill meeting, seen at the time as marking the beginning of an era of gradualist, pragmatic reconciliation, was swiftly overtaken by events which led in 1969 to the re-emergence of the partition issue in a more acute form than ever.

The year 1969 may, indeed, prove to have been an important turning point in the evolution of Irish foreign policy. In the summer, the crisis in Northern Ireland assumed the characteristics of a dispute between the British and Irish governments, as both intervened following violent riots in Derry and Belfast. This is not the place to trace the subsequent developments, for the outcome of the continuing crisis is by no means clear. It suffices to say that the repercussions within the Irish state have been serious, leading to a well-publicised cabinet crisis in the spring of 1970 and to the re-emergence of extra-parliamentary nationalist groups. The diplomatic relationship with Britain has also undergone much strain, although in many respects it has seldom been so close or so intensive. Anglo-Irish relations, as ever, attract a great deal of public attention.

Yet in the long term, 1969 may be seen as a turning point for a reason which has little to do with the crisis in Northern Ireland. In the spring of that year, the external environment of Ireland's foreign policy changed significantly with the resignation of President de Gaulle and the subsequent reopening of the issue of the enlargement of the European Community. Ireland's renewed negotiations were successfully concluded at the beginning of 1972 and in May of that year the negotiated terms of entry were overwhelmingly approved in a referendum. Public discussion on this undertaking centred mainly on the economic implications of membership and, although the question of the possible political consequences was raised, they were not explored in any depth.

The prospect of continual involvement with the states of western Europe, to a degree never before experienced and with regard to issues which relate to the role of the European Community in world affairs, suggests that Ireland will no longer be willing or able to remain indifferent to the international environment. The fact remains, however, that this prospect is being faced with policy-making machinery and with attitudes towards foreign policy which were developed while Ireland was still above all "the island behind the island". The examination of this machinery and of the domestic environment in which it operates indicates the extent to which the Irish political system will have to adapt to the new circumstances which surround it.

PART II

THE POLICY-MAKING MACHINERY

"The exclusive constitutional function of the Government is to formulate policy".

James Dillon, 1957
(Dáil Debates: 163, 658)

Chapter 2

THE ROLE OF THE GOVERNMENT AND ITS LEADERSHIP

"In the last resort the Government must make its own decisions."

Seán Lemass, 1957
(Dáil Debates: 163, 648)

"The real head of State should be the person really responsible for external affairs. He must be in the nature of things."

Major Bryan Cooper, 1923
(Dáil Debates: 5, 1402)

PROBABLY the most obvious feature of the development of parliamentary democracy has been the declining role played by parliaments in the making of policy. As the scope of government has extended and issues have become more complex, the formal, institutional functions of parliament have been reduced to approving or rejecting the government's policy and to influencing, in a very clumsy way, the formulation and execution of that policy. The practice of disciplined majority rule within parliament reinforces the government's ascendancy in this respect. Policy is clearly made by governments, and the people, through their representative institutions, are only a court of last appeal.

If this is true of policy in general, it is particularly true of foreign policy, in the formulation of which even these limited functions of general influence and final appeal are sometimes evaded altogether. "Even in well established democracies the idea of open politics (where appeal is open to representative assemblies and in the last resort, to the electorate) does not fully govern foreign policy";[1] the point

[1] Frankel, op. cit., p. 20.

41

finds classic illustration in the cases of the British government's decisions on the invasion of Suez in 1956 and the American administration's handling of the Cuban crisis of 1961. Admittedly these were exceptional crises, but they do demonstrate the ease with which governments ignore the representative machinery of the governmental process, as well as the general acceptance by most parliaments that governments have not merely the right, but even the obligation, to act swiftly and secretly on their own initiative. If there is a parliamentary 'revolt' — as in the case of the Suez crisis — it usually occurs *after* the decisions have been made and the action taken; moreover, even a serious rebellion within the government party will not necessarily lead to the fall of the government and a general election.

While Irish governments as a rule may not have had to react so swiftly or drastically to international events, the predominant role of the government is, nevertheless, firmly based on constitutional theory and political practice and has been jealously guarded by successive governments. The Irish Constitution of 1937 states that "the executive power of the State shall, subject to the provisions of this Constitution, be exercised by or on the authority of the Government".[2] This principle is repeated with regard to foreign policy: "The executive power of the State in or in connection with its external relations shall in accordance with Article 28 of this Constitution be exercised by or on the authority of the Government".[3]

Speaking in the debates on this Constitution, its principal author, Mr de Valera, explained that the state's international relations were "a matter of foreign policy, to be determined from time to time, according as the people's interests suggest to them that they should put this government or that government into office with powers to implement their will".[4] Bearing in mind the shortcomings of general elections as expressions of that vague concept, the people's will,[5] it can be seen that this interpretation of the Constitution gave considerable scope to the government to make its own decisions between elections. Even when the Constitution imposes some degree of

[2] Bunreacht na hÉireann, Article 28, 2.
[3] ibid, Article 29, 4 (10).
[4] Dáil Debates: 67, 60.
[5] See below, chapter 9.

constraint on the important question of declaring or participating in war (when the assent of the Dáil is needed),[6] the government remains the primary actor. If the state is actually invaded, the government is responsible for taking whatever steps it considers necessary, with the qualification that if the Dáil is not sitting it "shall be summoned to meet at the earliest practicable date".[7]

Of course, there was nothing revolutionary in Mr de Valera's view; he was not only following the practice adopted by most democratic governments in other states, but was also describing the practice employed by the first government of the Irish state. In 1923, when a deputy, Mr Figgis, argued that the executive council (i.e. the cabinet) ought to submit specific guarantees to the League of Nations for the approval of the Dáil, the president of the executive council, Mr William T. Cosgrave, took the opportunity to point out that such a persistent check on the government's powers was not practicable:

> . . . it is open to question whether . . . it is at all likely that there is a possibility of coming to an agreement if every such question and decision must be submitted to the representative Parliaments by the representatives of these Parliaments in such a body as the League of Nations . . . we know that society, in regulating its life and work, adopts simpler methods of procedure, . . . although a reactionary democrat might say it is not really the democratically expressed will of the people unless it has been subscribed to by them'.[8]

These "simpler methods of procedure" are well-established in international politics, and include the right of governments to negotiate with each other. Those who have illusions that this is not the case, protest in vain, as did Mr O. Esmonde over the question of the government's right to negotiate with the British government on the boundary issue in 1925. Mr Esmonde declared that "the Executive Council, on its own initiative, has no right to conduct those

[6] Bunreacht na hÉireann, Article 28, 3, 1°.
[7] ibid, Article 28, 3, 2°.
[8] Dáil Debates: 4, 1881.

negotiations".[9] The leader of the Labour Party, Mr Johnson, was more realistic when he said on the same occasion "I fear we are going to be faced next week with some provisional agreement which the Dáil will be told is practically an accomplished fact . . .".[10] Although the Minister for External Affairs, Mr Desmond FitzGerald, assured the Dáil that, were the negotiations to result in a revision of the Treaty of 1921, the Dáil's approval would be necessary, he made no concessions to the idea that the Dáil should somehow be included in the negotiations.[11] Thus, while the Dáil can criticise the conduct of specific negotiations, the principle is fully accepted that it is the government which negotiates.

Less enthusiastically accepted, perhaps, has been the closely related principle that the records of negotiations and correspondence between governments should not be published without the consent of these governments. This diplomatic courtesy was firmly defended in 1929 when Mr Cosgrave's government was attempting to assert the Irish Free State's international role in the British Commonwealth. The Minister for External Affairs at that time, Mr McGilligan, explained:

> It is not usual to publish the ordinary correspondence which takes place between the different members of the Commonwealth of Nations. To do so would make all constitutional progress impossible by putting a curb on the friendly interchange of views which forms the only possible basis of the special kind of relationship existing between the States members of the Commonwealth.[12]

Three years later, when Mr McGilligan (then in opposition) asked for similar information, Mr de Valera, whose views on Commonwealth relations were somewhat different, nonetheless held to the same principle and, when McGilligan protested, commented that "the Deputy set a very good headline on a previous occasion and I intend to follow it".[13]

Even in a less bitter parliamentary atmosphere than that which

[9] Dáil Debates: 13, 1177.
[10] Dáil Debates: 13, 1185.
[11] Dáil Debates: 13, 1187.
[12] Dáil Debates: 28, 7.
[13] Dáil Debates: 42, 4.

prevailed in the nineteen twenties and thirties, diplomatic confidence
has been a convenient justification for restricting discussion of government policy, thereby expanding the government's room for
manoeuvre. When the information is offered, it is often expressed
in general, vague and even ambiguous terms. An example was the
Lemass government's treatment of the political implications of joining
the European Economic Community. In June 1961 the Taoiseach
confined his comments to admitting that "there are . . . certain
political implications which, in my opinion, are not such as to make
it undesirable for this country to join the Community . . .".[14]
Even after a further eighteen months of frequent parliamentary
questions, debates and inspired leaks to the press by the government,
its obvious readiness to reconsider the traditional Irish policy of
military neutrality was rarely expressed in terms more precise than this.
Mr Lemass refused to jeopardise the government's application for
EEC membership by appearing to take sides on the political struggle
which was developing within the EEC itself, and vagueness was his
most effective weapon. In this respect he was a worthy disciple of
his former leader, Eamon de Valera, who in 1944 justified an ambiguous silence on the part of his government over the policy of external
association with the Commonwealth. Rarely can a government's
attempt to reserve to itself the powers of making foreign policy
have been more bluntly stated in a parliamentary democracy:

> We can have our own views and keep them to ourselves. When
> the time comes to express those views as public policy, when it will
> be possible for us and the people to whom we are speaking to see
> exactly what the conditions are, that will be the time at which we
> can state publicly and definitely what our policy is going to be.
> We have to wait and see what the ultimate conditions will be.[15]

In addition to expressing its policy in vague terms (or not at all),

---

[14] Dáil Debates: 190, 179.

[15] Dáil Debates: 94, 1353. In the long term, it may be argued that the opposition
parties refused to wait for the "ultimate conditions" since, on coming to power in
1948, they repealed Mr de Valera's External Relations Act of 1936, the statutory
expression of his policy of ambiguity; but this only occurred after years of parliamentary
controversy and five general elections.

the government may preserve its freedom of action by choosing the audience to which it will speak. Again, this is most effective in a situation where several alternatives are open to consideration and the government is not bound to the precise terms of a treaty or corresponding legislation. The early stages of the attempt to join the EEC provide an example of the way in which governments announce policy *outside* the legislature to the wider but much less responsive audience of the general public, and in 1962 Seán Lemass vigorously defended this practice:

> I shall make announcements anywhere and at any time I think wise. This idea that all announcements made by the government must be made in the Dáil is absurd because part of the function of the government is to inform public opinion on matters of national concern . . . to ensure that when a decision is taken and communicated to the Dáil and to the public, there will be widespread understanding of the reasons for it by the largest possible number of people.[16]

On the other hand, when it was proposed that the public be given the opportunity to deliver judgment, by way of a referendum, on whether a treaty with the EEC should be negotiated in the first place, the government's attitude was somewhat different. The Minister for Justice, Mr Charles Haughey, put it thus: "The Constitution clearly contemplates that the making of such a treaty is a matter entirely for the Government and the Oireachtas, in accordance with the procedure laid down".[17] On the whole, therefore, it is difficult for public opinion (even when expressed through the legislature) to play any positive role in policy-making between elections, and since elections are a particularly crude and often ineffective means of influencing foreign policy, the government's freedom of action is maintained.

Even such a wholehearted parliamentarian as Mr James Dillon, subsequently leader of the Fine Gael party, recognised this when,

[16] Dáil Debates: 198, 1480–1.
[17] Dáil Debates: 199, 1139–40. For further discussion of public opinion and foreign policy see below, Part III.

asking for further information about the EEC in 1957, he declared that the government has the ultimate responsibility for the formulation of policy:

> I do not see how in our system of government — and I think it is the best system of government — that ultimate responsibility can be shared. I think the Government has to come to Parliament with what it proposes and believes to be right, and if Parliament does not like these proposals, then, without any hard feelings, there must be another Government or a general election.[18]

Mr Dillon qualified his acceptance of this principle by arguing that, in time of war or national emergency, the government has the duty to consult more closely with the leaders of the opposition parties in parliament. But even if this convention is adhered to, the normal powers and functions of parliament in such circumstances are so restricted as to give the government its greatest possible freedom of action. For example, in the especially critical year of 1940, there was no discussion on the estimates for the Department of External Affairs, and in the subsequent years up to the end of World War II, the only voice to question the government's policy of neutrality in the Dáil was that of Mr Dillon, who in so doing was expelled from his party and lost the right to be consulted. Therefore, in both normal and extraordinary circumstances, it is difficult to resist the conclusion which Seán Lemass, then Minister for Industry and Commerce, drew in 1957: "all Governments must eventually stand and act upon their own judgment".[19]

If there is little mystery concerning the general role of the government with regard to foreign policy, it is not always so easy to identify those individuals *within* the cabinet who play the decisive role in specific cases. Irish cabinets are constitutionally limited to not more than fifteen members, but, in those instances where they are drawn from one disciplined party, their adherence to the theory and practice of collective responsibility makes it extremely unlikely that convincing evidence of disagreements within the cabinet will be found.

[18] Dáil Debates: 163, 660–1.
[19] Dáil Debates: 163, 649.

A striking exception to this practice of close cabinet unity was apparent during the crisis of 1970. Here the dismissal of two ministers and the resignation of two others demonstrated that there were limits to the extent to which all members of the cabinet might be expected quietly to acquiesce with the policy of their leader. There was an obvious difference of opinion over the government's policy towards the crisis in Northern Ireland, but the most remarkable point is not that this difference was made public but that it took so long for it to be made public. Throughout the autumn and winter of 1969–1970, a succession of carefully ambiguous attacks on the Taoiseach, Mr Lynch, by his Minister for Agriculture, Mr Neil Blaney, were followed by denials by both Mr Lynch and Mr Blaney that there was any serious division with the government. Only the series of events which eventually led to the arms trials of late 1970 forced Mr Lynch to take action in May of that year, and the façade of unity within both the government and the Fianna Fáil party was painfully and reluctantly removed. It was no coincidence that the issue which divided the government was the emotional one of partition, yet the fact that this dissension had such serious consequences may well have been exacerbated by the already existing rivalry between the leaders of the Fianna Fáil party.[20]

However, coalition governments have also seen the myth of unity dispelled to some extent. In the inter-party government of 1948–1951, the portfolios were shared by parties which had relatively little in common apart from the desire to prevent the largest single party, Fianna Fáil, from resuming office; in these circumstances, differences of opinion between members of the cabinet came more readily to light. For example, in 1948 the Minister for Agriculture, Mr James Dillon, publicly proposed a customs union between Britain, the USA, Canada, Australia and Ireland, but the Taoiseach, Mr J. A. Costello, made it quite clear that this was not government policy:

The Minister clearly emphasised that he was expressing his own views and not those of the Government. Since he was speaking as

[20] For an interpretation of the background to the crisis see Brian Farrell, *Chairman or Chief? The role of Taoiseach in Irish Government* (Gill and Macmillan, Dublin, 1971), pp. 74–81.

an individual, and not for the Government, the question whether his views in this matter have the approval of the Government does not arise, nor does the question of Government policy.[21]

The practice of ministers publicly unburdening their views as "individuals" was tolerated and the Minister for External Affairs, Mr Seán MacBride, took advantage of this to make personal statements on a variety of subjects, which were not always directly connected with foreign policy. There is evidence of a divergence of views between MacBride and his counterpart in the Department of Finance over policy towards international monetary procedures,[22] but on the major external policies of the period — the declaration of the Republic, the abstention from NATO and the anti-partition campaign — there is little evidence of any serious division within the cabinet; the crucial disagreements were over issues of domestic policy. The members of the second coalition government of 1954–1957 were rather more disciplined in their public pronouncements, and they appear to have kept to themselves any disagreements that they may have had on the rather limited foreign policy adopted during their term of office.

While it is not usually possible to look behind the curtain of collective responsibility, there is a certain obvious, formalised division of functions within the government which indicates the most likely source of initiative and ideas concerning foreign policy. Given a limited number of ministers, there is no possibility of avoiding departmental obligations, and the appointed foreign minister is thus very important. However, he must act in conjunction with the head of the government and, of the two, "fundamentally the head of the governments is the more important decision-maker".[23]

The head of the government's predominance in foreign policy formulation derives both from his general leadership of the government and from the special nature of foreign policy. As leader of a disciplined majority party of which he is often the principal electoral symbol (one might almost say in the case of de Valera, its *raison*

[21] Dáil Debates: 113, 309–311.
[22] See below p. 92, and Farrell, op. cit., pp. 45–46.
[23] Frankel, op. cit., p. 22.

4

d'être), the head of the government will be able to choose his own Minister for External Affairs and thus ensure a considerable measure of loyalty and cooperation. An exception to this was the inter-party government of 1948–1951 since the Taoiseach, Mr J. A. Costello, himself a compromise choice, had to yield responsibility for the Department of External Affairs to the leader of the new Clann na Poblachta party, Seán MacBride. But, in general, the only serious limitations on the Taoiseach's choice might be his own standing in the party and the ability of the potential candidates. These factors may have been important in 1959 when Seán Lemass succeeded Mr de Valera as Taoiseach. Mr Lemass had little alternative but to choose Frank Aiken as Minister for External Affairs, for Aiken's claims to that office lay not only in his previous experience of the portfolio, but also in the fact that he was one of the most senior men in the party.

Once the choice of foreign minister is made, it is primarily up to the head of the government to arrive at a satisfactory working relationship with him and with all his other ministers.[24] However the head of the government is not likely to allow his Minister for External Affairs as much freedom of action as he might see fit to allow other ministers, for foreign policy is the last line of defence of the state, and when the international position of the state is threatened, the head of the government is expected to intervene directly in the formulation and execution of policy. Thus the leaders of Irish governments have tended to reserve for themselves the role of supreme policy-maker in those areas of foreign affairs which they consider to be most vital to the interests of the state. The relationship with Britain, especially concerning the issue of Northern Ireland, is the most striking example of such a tendency. On this matter, all Irish government leaders have played the primary role, and Mr de Valera himself took charge of the portfolio of external affairs between 1932 and 1948.

The nature of international politics ensures that the head of the government is seen not only as the principal spokesman on decisive

---

[24] In practice, the relationship between the head of the government and his minister for external affairs varies from one administration to another. This is more fully discussed in chapter 3.

issues of foreign policy in his own country, but that he is also expected to act as the principal negotiator in the more important diplomatic readjustments between his and other states. Thus, the Irish delegations which have negotiated agreements with Britain (and even some of those which have only "exchanged views") have generally been led by the heads of Irish governments. Indeed, the one noticeable exception to this practice demonstrates its desirability. As head of the government of the second Dáil in 1921, Mr de Valera, whose first attempt at negotiation with Lloyd George had failed in July, refused to lead the delegation to the second and definitive negotiations. These resulted in a treaty which proved unacceptable to him and which was to be the *casus belli* for the civil war. Since then, however, Irish heads of government have intervened directly in the most important foreign policy negotiations, and de Valera himself placed great emphasis on his role as principal negotiator during the nineteen thirties. More recently, the complexity and protracted nature of the negotiations to join the EEC necessitated some delegation of authority, but the head of the government intervened at the decisive stages because national policy was involved. In 1963, as Minister for External Affairs, Mr Aiken acknowledged that "the Taoiseach is and has been, as is right and natural, in charge of major constitutional matters. . . ."[25]

The extent to which the heads of Irish governments use and have used their powers to act as supreme policy-maker is another matter. Their conduct depends in the first place on whether or not they have an opportunity to act in a positive way. Such opportunities in turn depend on both domestic and international circumstances. Where the former are unsettled, foreign policy may receive less attention, especially in Ireland, where the low military potential and geographical isolation make foreign 'adventures' an unlikely distraction from domestic troubles. On the other hand, when international circumstances are unstable, the opportunity for a small power, such as Ireland, to act positively is often negligible. All Irish heads of government have suffered to some degree from such limitations on their opportunity to pursue a positive foreign policy.

[25] Dáil Debates: 201, 1075.

The type of action taken is dependent on other factors too. One is the individual leader's will to intervene directly on any particular issue; another important factor is his ability to follow up the initiatives he takes and to win the support of his colleagues in the cabinet. Unfortunately, without cabinet records or even the published apologias of most of the individuals who have held office as head of the government in Ireland, it is impossible to examine these variables in a definitive way. Nevertheless, from the limited evidence that does exist, some tentative hypotheses may be formed.

The first head of government, Mr William T. Cosgrave, in spite of ten years in office from 1922 to 1932, encountered serious obstacles which limited his opportunities to make a mark on Irish foreign policy. This was primarily due to the extent of his government's domestic commitments. In the first place, he was faced with the task of building the political structure of a new state. Admittedly, he inherited an experienced and established public administration, but this inheritance was received in the context of a bitter civil war, the divisive effect of which was apparent throughout his term of office. The cessation of hostilities in 1923 was followed by the army mutiny of 1924 and the assassination of Cosgrave's deputy, Kevin O'Higgins, in 1927, while in the same year the entry of the new Fianna Fáil party into the Dáil ensured that the work of government had to be carried on in the teeth of a dangerously large and destructively critical parliamentary opposition.

All this gave W. T. Cosgrave little time to play the role of international statesman. In 1923, answering the charge that Mr Cosgrave had neglected his duties by not going to the Imperial Conference in London as the premiers of Canada and Australia had done, his deputy, Kevin O'Higgins, pointed out that, "while the Imperial Conference was sitting, Canada and Australia were not running a little Civil War".[26] Later, in 1928, Desmond FitzGerald, a former Minister for External Affairs, commenting on the timing of Mr Cosgrave's official visit to the USA wrote: "Six years after the signing of the treaty seems rather late for the earliest possible date, but they were six years of unceasing hard work, of crisis on top of crisis. Each day brought its

[26] Dáil Debates: 5, 1406.

new problem requiring immediate attention. Even at the end of six years circumstances here only permitted of a hurried visit".[27]

W. T. Cosgrave's opportunities to participate in international politics were less limited by external factors, and occasions to develop policies from which later governments would benefit did arise. Ireland's membership of the League of Nations, achieved in 1923, was used to establish the precedent that a member state of the British Commonwealth could play an independent role in League affairs; similarly, the general constitutional position of Ireland within the Commonwealth was developed at the periodic Imperial Conferences. However, in neither of these spheres did Mr Cosgrave play a direct role, delegating the task of personal negotiation to his government colleagues. He did act personally on the question of the Boundary Commission and made the initial approach to Stanley Baldwin in November 1925, but the delegation which continued the talks was led by Kevin O'Higgins. Even when an opportunity appeared, it seems that Mr Cosgrave was reluctant to grasp it personally. This reluctance may be explained both by his view of his office and by his limited experience of international affairs.

W. T. Cosgrave became president of the executive council at the comparatively early age of forty-two, after the more widely-known leaders of the Irish independence movement had become victims of the struggle against the British or had been alienated by the division over the Treaty of 1921. His qualifications for the post consisted of a revolutionary background — he fought in the 1916 Rising, was condemned to death, but later released — but, more importantly, of his considerable legislative experience, rare among men who owed their political position to force rather than to constitutional evolution. This experience stemmed from participation in municipal politics in Dublin and membership of the revolutionary Dáil after his first election victory in 1917; as T. de Vere White points out, he had "a knowledge of procedure which most of his colleagues did not enjoy".[28] Moreover, Mr Cosgrave held the portfolio of Minister for Local Government from April 1919. Unlike

[27] *With the President in America: The Authorised Record of President Cosgrave's Tour in the United States and Canada.* (Dublin,) 1928, p. 7.
[28] T. de Vere White, *Kevin O'Higgins* Methuen, London, 1948), p. 108.

most of the other ministries of the Dáil administration, this was no 'shadow' ministry existing in a vacuum until the departure of the British administration. Indeed, in spite of the threat of persecution by the British authorities, it succeeded in replacing the British network of local government in the greater part of the country.[29]

W. T. Cosgrave's legislative and executive experience equipped him well to become the head of the new government, and his performance in the post has perhaps been underestimated when compared with the role played by his charismatic successor.[30] But there was little in his background which had brought him into direct contact with the efforts made outside Ireland to press the case for Irish freedom, efforts which may be seen as an embryonic form of Irish foreign policy. Once in office, he did not make any seriously sustained attempt to intervene in foreign policy, preferring, where possible, to trust his colleagues, especially Desmond FitzGerald, Kevin O'Higgins and, after the death of O'Higgins, Patrick McGilligan. Mr Cosgrave maintained this position in spite of concerted pressure on him to do what Mr de Valera was to do in 1932, that is to take over personal control of the Department of External Affairs.

W. T. Cosgrave's attitude to foreign policy is seen most clearly in his remarks during the debates on the Ministers and Secretaries Bill of 1923. For a variety of reasons, opposition deputies demanded that external affairs should be the responsibility of the president of the executive council. Mr Cosgrave's reply indicates the priority he gave to foreign policy: "There are other Departments of the State just at present which would need the attention of the President very much more than the Department of External Affairs . . . ".[31] He also pointed out that office holders should have, as far as possible, special qualifications, and ". . . in asking members to take up the responsibilities of office, I had in mind always the man's own desires or capabilities for these particular posts . . . I have no particular ability whatever of any sort or kind for External Affairs . . . ".[32]

[29] ibid, p. 28.
[30] Farrell, op. cit., pp. 18–25.
[31] Dáil Debates, 5, 1410.
[32] Dáil Debates: 5, 1409. Mr Cosgrave did hold the portfolio of External Affairs from 10 July 1927 to 12 October 1927 but this was a temporary measure, following the assassination of Kevin O'Higgins.

There has been no greater contrast to W. T. Cosgrave's reluctance to become directly involved in the formulation of foreign policy than the approach of his successor, Mr Eamon de Valera, who saw fit to act as his own Minister for External Affairs from 1932 to 1948. This practice has been adopted in several parliamentary democracies.[33] Generally, it indicates the importance of foreign policy to both the domestic and external political condition of the state. It may be seen as a contingency in times of national emergency arising out of the threat or existence of war or, in the case of a new state, as an essential weapon in the government's attempt to define its position in international politics.

The practice, as Nicholas Mansergh points out, was adopted in many of the Commonwealth states which were attempting to define their status as dominions *vis-à-vis* the United Kingdom.[34] In the Dáil, several deputies had attempted to persuade Mr Cosgrave to adopt the practice in 1923, though all for very different reasons: deputies Heffernan and D. J. Gorey reasoned that foreign policy was of such negligible importance that it did not warrant a separate ministry,[35] while deputies Johnson and Figgis said that it was of such vital importance as to merit direct control.[36] Major Cooper pointed to the precedents established in other countries and to the apparent practicability of holding both offices:

The Prime Minister of Canada is able to be Prime Minister of a Dominion double our population and more, and also Minister of External Affairs. Monsieur Poincaré is able to perform the duties of Prime Minister of France and also to act as Minister of Foreign Affairs, and the foreign affairs of France are at least as involved and intricate as those concerning the Saorstát.[37]

[33] Professor Frankel (op. cit., p. 22) cites several cases, e.g. Ramsay MacDonald in 1924, Adenauer up to 1957, and Mendès France in June 1954.
[34] For example, it was not until 1947 that Canada had a separate foreign minister, and 1948 in the case of South Africa. New Zealand and Australia were less consistent, although New Zealand had a combined ministry from 1943 to 1949. On the foundation of the Republic of India, Mr Nehru became his own foreign minister. See Mansergh, *Problems of Wartime Cooperation*, pp. 406–7.
[35] Dáil Debates: 5, 1393–4 and 1403.
[36] Dáil Debates: 5, 1396 and 931.
[37] Dáil Debates: 5, 943.

Although Mr Cosgrave was reluctant to involve himself, the portfolio of External Affairs was subsequently held in conjunction with that of Justice (in 1927) and with that of Industry and Commerce (from 1927 until 1932). This was made possible because of the comparatively small scale of the operations of the Department of External Affairs and the fact that so much of its work was carried out in the well-defined areas of the League of Nations and the Imperial Conferences.

It is clear, then, that precedents were not lacking for Eamon de Valera's assumption of the portfolio of External Affairs in 1932. Nor was it surprising, given the overwhelming priority he granted to the development of Ireland's relationship with Britain, especially the important constitutional issues arising from the Treaty of 1921.[38] Even before this, as President of the first Dáil, he had spent more than a year in the USA propagating the Irish cause, an experience which confirmed in his mind the value of asserting the national presence outside the national territory. In this sense, his failure to take an equally active role in the Treaty negotiations with the British in 1921 was untypical. His subsequent policies in the nineteen thirties and nineteen forties were, therefore, a continuation of the principal aim for which he had fought in the Rising of 1916 — to establish Ireland as a sovereign republic, a status to be both achieved and represented by an independent foreign policy.

By acting as his own foreign minister, Mr de Valera was able to strengthen the authority of his government's foreign policy in three ways. Firstly, he was able to justify it with authority at home. This was particularly important in view of the unilateral nature of much of his policy, and it was just as necessary to have an authoritative government spokesman to face domestic criticism as it was to have a diplomatic spokesman to speak at international level. Mr de Valera could take personal control of the important constitutional debates in the Dáil, which culminated in the evolution of external association in 1936 and the adoption of the new Constitution in 1937. Secondly, he could play a more effective part in negotiations with other governments. In fact, although only one significant opportunity arose to do this, the success of the agreements with Britain in 1938 to return

[38] Farrell, op. cit., p. 26.

the ports and to end the economic war were due in no small measure to de Valera himself.[39] Thirdly, in a more general way, Mr de Valera could enhance Ireland's position in world politics. To help do this, he had the good fortune to be provided with the vehicle of the League of Nations, and the double good fortune to have an opportunity of making an immediate impression as President of the League's Council. From then on, de Valera's personal activities in the League contributed towards his international reputation as a statesman, although his preoccupation with Anglo-Irish affairs made it difficult to pursue his work for the League with any intensity.[40]

Because of the effective failure of the League after 1936, Ireland's difficult position with regard to the approaching war further emphasised the need for firm control of foreign policy by the head of the government rather than by any subordinate minister. During the period of the emergency, as Mr de Valera defended his policy of neutrality despite the threats of the principal belligerents overseas and the lone voice of James Dillon at home, the restriction imposed on parliamentary and public discussion served only to emphasise the measure of personal control which he exercised.

Significantly, de Valera's more lucid and forceful pronouncements on international affairs were made outside the Dáil, either in the League of Nations or on the radio, of which he made regular use.[41] In the Dáil itself he gave little away. Indeed, in 1938, admitting that he was "out of the House a good deal", de Valera confessed that it was because "I do not want to be talking too much . . . if you have to talk a lot and you do talk a lot, then you are bound sometime or other to make very serious mistakes".[42] When he did talk, usually

[39] Nicholas Mansergh claims that Mr de Valera's personal *rapport* with Mr Chamberlain was an important element in the negotiations. See Mansergh, *Problems of External Policy*, p. 315.

[40] This was the opinion of Seán Lester, who was intimately involved with the League at the same time as Mr de Valera (information supplied by S. Barcroft).

[41] Particularly to overseas audiences. Mr de Valera made twenty-two broadcasts between 4 March 1932 and 17 March 1946, three of which were on behalf of the League of Nations, while most of the others were regular Christmas or St Patrick's day broadcasts to Irish-American audiences (Dáil Debates: 103, 485). He also used the radio to much effect to answer Winston Churchill's criticisms of Irish neutrality in a broadcast on 17 May 1945; for this speech see *Ireland's Stand: a selection of the speeches of Eamon de Valera during the war* (1939–1945), (Gill, Dublin, 1946,) pp. 90–94.

[42] Dáil Debates: 71, 439.

at the end of debates when his critics had no right of reply, he would contrive at great length to avoid commiting himself; on one occasion in 1945 a frustrated deputy compared him to the man who sheared a pig, "he produced a good deal of sound, but no wool".[43]

Mr de Valera strove, during his many years in office, to maintain an impressive front of cabinet solidarity and contended that he received his colleagues' full support for his foreign policy. In 1945, when the accusation was made that a member of his cabinet had opposed his policy of neutrality, he could point to the absence of resignations and remark "that there is only one thing which particularly distinguishes their [his colleagues] views on all these matters with respect to External Affairs, and that is that they are pro-Irish".[44] This degree of unanimity was not necessarily achieved without effort. His successor, Seán Lemass, later described the conduct of Mr Valera's cabinet meetings:

> He relied upon the force of physical exhaustion to get agreement . . . he'd never let a Cabinet debate on any subject end with a vote of Ministers. He always wanted unanimity and he sought this unanimity by the simple process of keeping the debate going — often till the small hours of the morning, until those who were in the minority, out of sheer exhaustion, conceded the case made by the majority.[45]

Mr de Valera recognised the burden of administrative routine which the two offices of Taoiseach and Minister for External Affairs imposed on him. He admitted in 1941 that

> it is undoubtedly an extra task for the Head of the Government to undertake . . . it would be ridiculous to say that the details of administration could be carried out as efficiently by a person who has other duties as they could by the same person if he were free to devote the whole of his time to that particular Department.

---

[43] Dáil Debates: 97, 2652.
[44] Dáil Debates: 97, 2756.
[45] Interview in *The Irish Press,* 3 February 1969. See also Farrell, op. cit., p. 30.

However, he continued:

> if I were leaving public life tomorrow there is one piece of advice
> I would leave to those coming after me, should they care to take it,
> and it is that in this State, as in all small States, it is almost absolutely
> essential that the Head of the Government should also be the
> Minister of External Affairs. In regard to outside affairs, the nation
> ought to appear as one. In a case like that, you cannot, if there is
> any divergence of opinion, as there will be between any two
> human beings, have that showing itself . . . I believe that the
> present practice is a good practice, and that it should continue.[46]

Yet when Mr de Valera was returned to office ten years after stating
this view, he appointed a separate Minister for External Affairs.
One reason for this change of mind was, perhaps, his age — he was
sixty-eight in 1951 and had to undergo serious eye operations. Also,
he had to come to terms with the fact that the play in which he had
acted in the nineteen thirties and forties was no longer running.
The days of unilateral, constitutional manipulations *vis-à-vis* Britain
were over; their outcome, the delicate mystery of external association,
had been undermined, discredited and finally abandoned. The League
of Nations, the arena of world statesmanship which he knew most
intimately, had failed. Always aware of its weaknesses, de Valera
showed little enthusiasm over its successor which was, he believed,
repeating the mistakes of the League. Opening the debate on Ireland's
proposed membership of the United Nations on 24 July 1946, he had
said, ". . . in our circumstances, although it is impossible to be
enthusiastic, I think we have a duty as a member of the world community to do our share . . ."[47]

This note of pessimism was also reflected in the curiously detached
role he played as foreign policy spokesman when leader of the
opposition from 1948 to 1951; most of the political infighting was
left to his subordinates, especially Seán Lemass and Frank Aiken.
Ireland was still outside the UN, owing to the veto of the Soviet
Union, and the only other major opportunity for international

---

[46] Dáil Debates: 84, 1915–6.
[47] Dáil Debates: 102, 1325.

action was to be found in the Council of Europe, which by 1951 was already preoccupied with the Coal and Steel Community and other projects which primarily concerned the latter's six member states. For Eamon de Valera, as a foreign minister, this would be an empty world.

It was also a different world at home where, in general, the burdens of government had increased considerably. Even in the Department of External Affairs, in a period of comparative quiescence, the scope of administration, if not of policy formulation, had increased both in quantity and complexity, following the gradual growth in representation abroad and participation in the European recovery programme, the Council of Europe and many other technical international organisations. The responsibilities of the Taoiseach were also becoming more arduous because of the continual economic crises of the immediate post-war decade; as the pressures on governments to play a larger and more positive part in the manipulation of the economy increased, even a younger man might have thought twice before combining the two posts.

It seems, therefore, that in spite of what he had thought in 1941, Mr de Valera recognised that the practice of the head of the government being directly responsible for the administration as well as for the making of foreign policy was necessitated by the special circumstances attending the evolution of the international position of the state. In the increasingly complex and intensive diplomacy of the nineteen fifties, it was unlikely that this experiment could effectively be repeated, and when he was returned to office for a final term as Taoiseach in 1957, Mr de Valera did not try to repeat it.

By 1957, Ireland had been a member of the UN for over a year and, with Britain interested in a European free trade area, Irish participation in European politics became a reality. Nevertheless, de Valera took little positive action in an area which had formerly been one of his principal preoccupations; it was Frank Aiken, as Minister for External Affairs, who represented Ireland at the UN General Assembly, and Seán Lemass, as Minister for Industry and Commerce, who was principal spokesman on European affairs. This was hardly surprising in view of Mr de Valera's age: he was seventy-six when he resigned in 1959. In effect, this short term of office (just over two years) represented a last successful exploitation of his electoral appeal before he handed over the leadership of a strengthened party and government to a younger man; there would have been little point in trying to start a second career as an international statesman. Eamon de Valera remains the only Irish head of government to have been his own foreign minister for any length of time, for his successor after the 1948 election, Mr John A. Costello, reverted to the usual practice of appointing a separate foreign minister.

Mr Costello found varying opportunities to evolve a distinctive foreign policy in his two terms of office from 1948 to 1951 and from 1954 to 1957. In the first period, he was undoubtedly constrained by the comparative indiscipline and parliamentary vulnerability of his coalition government, and was compelled to devote much of his time to acting as mediator in several disagreements on domestic issues. Abroad, Mr Costello found that, in spite of Ireland not being in the United Nations, there was some opportunity to clarify the ambiguities of the constitutional relationship with Britain and to seek a solution to the outstanding issue of partition. The Council of Europe, of which Ireland was a founder member in 1949, was used as a forum in which to present Ireland's case.

But the extent of Ireland's isolation from the rest of the world was an overriding consideration for Mr Costello throughout his period in office. His failure to make the partition issue an important factor in world politics exemplifies this. To most other governments, partition seemed a mundane problem beside the success of the communist revolution in China and the serious extension of the cold war (especially in Korea); the Council of Europe seemed more interested in new European projects such as the Coal and Steel Community and the Defence Community.

This isolation was even more noticeable during Mr Costello's second term of office which gave him little opportunity to evolve a positive foreign policy until the last year, 1956. The government had to concern itself mainly with persistent and serious economic difficulties, especially the high level of unemployment and emigration, and few openings for international action presented themselves. The rejection of the European Defence Community Treaty in 1954 seemed to arrest progress towards European integration, and partition, though still a vital issue with Irish extremist groups, no longer evoked much general interest. Ireland's admission to the United Nations in December 1955 marked a departure from the passive stance that events had compelled Mr Costello to adopt. There was, however, little time left for him to grasp this opportunity fully, although he had his 'own man', Liam Cosgrave, as Minister for External Affairs.

There is more than a little irony in the lack of opportunities which John A. Costello suffered in the field of foreign policy, for his experience had qualified him to play a statesman's role on coming into office. When he first became Taoiseach at the age of fifty-six, he had behind him a career which reflected a broad interest in foreign policy and personal experience of its formulation and execution. A lawyer by profession, Mr Costello was appointed Attorney General in 1926 and was intimately concerned with the fundamentally 'legalistic' foreign policy of his term of office which ended in 1932. He was a member of the Irish delegation to the Imperial Conference of 1926 and participated in negotiations concerning the position of the Irish state *vis-à-vis* the Privy Council; in the following year, he accompanied the Minister for External Affairs, Kevin O'Higgins, to the Geneva naval disarmament conferences, and took over the leadership of the Irish delegation to the League of Nations after O'Higgins's death. At home, as law officer to the government, he was entrusted with the task of drawing up and advising on several treaties, such as the General Act for the Settlement of Disputes 1930, and the Commercial Treaty with France 1931, which were significant in the constitutional evolution of Ireland within the Commonwealth.[48]

In 1933, Mr Costello entered the Dáil and was a prominent opposition spokesman on foreign affairs for the next fifteen years. During this period, he displayed an interest not only in the content of Irish policy but in its formulation as well. His contributions to debates on foreign affairs were generally well-informed and perceptive and bear comparison with those of other foreign policy specialists in his party, FitzGerald and McGilligan, two former Ministers for External

---

[48] Mr Costello referred to his part in this policy in his address to the Canadian Bar Association on 1 September 1948. This speech, which reflects very clearly the importance of international law to the foreign policy of the Cosgrave government, was published under the title of *Ireland in International Affairs*, Dublin, 1949. See especially pp. 15–26.

Affairs, and the irrepressible James Dillon.[49] By 1948, he had many of the qualities to become Mr de Valera's successor as Minister for External Affairs, should his party gain power.

Ironically, when Costello became de Valera's successor in 1948, it was as Taoiseach and not as Minister for External Affairs. The price for his party's partial success at the polls was that the external affairs portfolio went to another party in the coalition. That the post was regarded as an attribute of party rather than of personality is indicated by the fact that the foreign minister's 'stand-in' as parliamentary spokesman was his only, and very junior, party colleague.[50] Though not leader of his party, Mr Costello was reluctantly persuaded to assume overall leadership of the coalition government. Even in these difficult circumstances, he attempted to assert his position as the principal source of foreign policy in the government.

Just how far he succeeded is a matter for conjecture. Like his Minister for External Affairs, Seán MacBride, he was in favour of repealing the External Relations Act of 1936, though he lacked MacBride's radical republican motives; rather, he wished to remove the constitutional issue from Irish politics, particularly in view of the violence it had engendered. At first, the two ministers differed on the question of whether the abandonment of external association should be followed by secession from the Commonwealth; their respective parties, Fine Gael and Clann na Poblachta, had been opposed on this point in the general election at the beginning of 1948. Nevertheless, on 7 September of that year, Mr Costello, in reply to a journalist's question, announced that it was government policy to secede from the Commonwealth. This announcement was made while he was on a visit to Canada, and its timing, as well as its content, caused some surprise.

Nicholas Mansergh suggests (as have many lesser authorities) that Mr Costello's decision was affected by a personal slight received at the hands of the Governor-General of Canada.[51] However, Costello,

[49] A good example of Mr Costello's constructive criticism of the government is his speech during the debate on the League of Nations estimate in 1936, in which he discusses the weakness of the Dáil and the apathy of public opinion towards the formulation of foreign policy. (Dáil Debates: 62, 2774–81).
[50] Farrell, op. cit., p. 45.
[51] Mansergh, *Problems of Wartime Cooperation*, pp. 282–3.

speaking during the debate on the Republic of Ireland Bill in November 1948, made no reference to any alleged insults. Indeed, he claimed that he had been forced to face the Commonwealth issue when answering questions in the Dáil during the previous July and August. He went on: "The result of all these questions and the discussion which took place between the questions . . . was that both the Minister [Seán MacBride] and myself, having to come down one way or the other, finally came down on the line that we were not a member of the Commonwealth . . . ".[52] Interviewed in 1967, Mr Costello reiterated his claim that the decision to repeal the External Relations Act was his own, that it was not in any way influenced by his foreign minister and that the cabinet was in agreement that it ". . . should be done in the Autumn".[53] It would appear that the decision concerning the timing of the announcement was prompted by a desire to forestall further press leaks.[54] In this subsidiary aspect of the affair, Costello acted on his own, thus underlining the fact that the ultimate responsibility lay in his hands.

He also took the lead in the subsequent propaganda campaign against partition, which was sparked off by the British parliament passing the Ireland Bill in 1949. In a long speech on 10 May 1949, he proclaimed what was later to be known as the policy of 'raising the sore thumb', but the nature of this policy, with its emphasis on mobilising international opinion, did not leave a great deal of scope for the head of the government. In his second ministry, from 1954 to 1957, his opportunities to participate in foreign affairs were again limited, but when they did arise, Mr Costello played an important role. In October 1954, he was the government's spokesman on a private member's motion on partition and, shortly after Ireland was admitted to the UN in December 1955, an official visit to the USA gave him the opportunity to speak on Irish foreign policy to American audiences. In the following July, the part he played in the debate on the External Affairs estimates was revealing. He made an unusually long speech for a head of government, and stressed with considerable enthusiasm

[52] Dáil Debates: 113, 374.
[53] The Citizen, vol. 3, no. 1, May 1967, p. 4. Mr Costello gave a much fuller version of the incident in The Irish Times, 8 September 1967.
[54] Farrell, op. cit., pp. 47–50.

the opportunities which UN membership offered to Ireland. A vote on estimates prepared by the Minister for External Affairs became to a large extent the Taoiseach's debate.[55] Even in opposition after 1957, John A. Costello contributed to discussions on foreign policy, although he tended to stand down in favour of the younger men of his party.

The fourth Irish head of government was Mr Seán Lemass, who succeeded Eamon de Valera as leader of the Fianna Fáil party and Taoiseach in 1959. The domestic circumstances of the seven years of Mr Lemass's term of office were, on the whole, favourable to the pursuit of a positive foreign policy. Although the encouraging recovery of the economy was checked by the direct effects of Britain's financial crisis in the autumn of 1964, there was no return to the high levels of unemployment and emigration of the early nineteen fifties which had jeopardised the stability of successive governments. In spite of small parliamentary majorities, Mr Lemass was not tempted to ignore important foreign policy issues. International developments were more conducive to the development of positive policies than ever before in the history of the state. Membership of the UN offered several alternative policies to a small state such as Ireland, depending on the government's attitude towards the cold war, the new states of Africa and Asia, racial discrimination, disarmament and the peace-keeping role of the UN itself. For the first time since the heyday of the League of Nations, an Irish government had an opportunity of formulating policy on a broad range of important and complicated issues of world politics.

In addition to these opportunities offered by membership of the UN, Britain's change of heart towards European unity in 1961 offered new opportunities for an Irish initiative on this vital question. Although President de Gaulle's veto in 1963 on British entry to the EEC (and, by implication, on Irish entry) demonstrated yet again that Irish foreign policy evolved largely as a consequence of external factors, the uncertainty of the outcome allowed Mr Lemass rather more room to manoeuvre on foreign policy matters than most of his predecessors had enjoyed.

[55] Dáil Debates: 159, 609–618 and 620–627.

5

Seán Lemass had a great deal of ministerial and parliamentary experience by the time he became head of the government at the age of sixty. In this respect, he was better qualified than both W. T. Cosgrave and Eamon de Valera had been on their appointments as Taoiseach and had more first-hand experience of government than Mr Costello had when he took office in 1948. Although he had never been Minister for External Affairs, Seán Lemass had been directly concerned with the economic aspects of Irish foreign policy in his capacity of Minister for Industry and Commerce, a post which he held for most of the twenty-one years up to 1959 during which Fianna Fáil was in power.[56] This important ministry's responsibility for foreign trade gave Lemass more opportunity than most of his colleagues to recognise the close connexion between foreign policy and trade, and the awareness of this liaison marked his attitude towards foreign policy when he became head of the government.

During the nineteen thirties, Mr Lemass witnessed at close quarters the harmful effects of the economic war with Britain — an instance of a rigid, constitutional approach to foreign policy prevailing over one based on the material needs of the state. His own approach to foreign policy when Taoiseach was something of a contrast. Even on the one issue — that of partition — where 'political' and 'nationalist' factors remained at a premium, Mr Lemass eschewed the righteous indignation of his predecessors and placed his hopes in an economic solution to the problem. Although he had been directly involved in the independence struggle and the civil war, these experiences did not colour an essentially pragmatic approach to public policy. Practical cooperation was stressed more than protest and Mr Lemass's personal diplomacy with the Premier of Northern Ireland, Captain O'Neill, was a hallmark of this policy.

But Seán Lemass's interest in foreign policy did not stop at the obligatory involvement in the question of partition. It has been claimed that his decision to allow the Irish army to operate on behalf

[56] From 1932–1939, 1941–1948, 1951–1954, 1957–1959. The only time he was *no t* the Fianna Fáil minister for industry and commerce was from 1939 to 1941. This was because he was in charge of the new, and more important, Department of Supplie : which was established during World War II. He was in charge of *both* Industry and Commerce and Supplies from 1941 to July 1945, when the latter department was disestablished.

of the UN outside the state was given despite objections on ideological and financial grounds from members of his government, including his foreign minister.[57] However, it was above all towards economic foreign policy that Mr Lemass's energies were applied. Although his political inheritance included a senior Minister for External Affairs who advocated an independent political role for Ireland in UN politics, by 1961 it had become clear that the government's foreign policy was characterised by its commitment to a wider economic association — in the first instance with the EEC and, after that failed in 1963, in the context of an Anglo-Irish free trade area. In pursuit of this objective, the political implications of his predecessors' and of his Minister for External Affairs' policies were largely discounted; he seemed to be ready to sacrifice the traditional policy of neutrality, to which previous governments of both main parties had subscribed in order, *inter alia*, not to recognise the separate existence of Northern Ireland.

Mr Lemass's position on this issue illustrates not only his predominance in the cabinet but his personal part in presenting an important foreign policy decision. Early in 1962, when it seemed that Ireland's exclusion from the North Atlantic Treaty Organization might prove to be an embarrassment in applying for membership of the EEC, Lemass made it his own business to demonstrate cautiously that neutrality had outlived its usefulness. His replies to questions in the Dáil on this subject were generally ambiguous and, even when pressed to an adjournment debate on 8 March 1962, he avoided admitting outright that neutrality was no longer a central pillar of Irish foreign policy. He satisfied himself (if not his opponents) by reinterpreting the North Atlantic Treaty — which he admitted to having read for the first time "recently" — as having nothing to do with partition, and then shrugged off the whole problem as "academic".[58]

However, he was considerably more active outside the Dáil, where he used his authority as head of the government and principal international spokesman of the state to make his position clear to those to whom it mattered, the governments of the EEC. This was achieved by a series of speeches and interviews with foreign journalists. As

[57] Farrell, op. cit., p. 72.
[58] Dáil Debates: 193, 1321–1324.

early as December 1960, in a speech to the Solicitors' Apprentices' Debating Society in Dublin, Mr Lemass declared that Ireland was not "indifferent to the outcome of an East-West conflict",[59] although she still wished to remain outside any military alliance system. This hint of the Taoiseach's attitude had, by the middle of 1962, developed to such an extent that the opposition leader, James Dillon, could reproach him for admitting to an American journalist that "we are prepared to go into an integrated union without any reservations at all as to how far this will take us in the field of foreign policy or defence commitments".[60] Mr Dillon protested in vain in the Dáil that "if the Taoiseach has to make categorical statements of that kind, this is the place in which they should be made, not to columnists, however influential, from New York".[61] But if James Dillon spoke for the spirit of parliamentary government, Seán Lemass represented its reality.

In 1966 Mr Lemass retired, having led his country towards EEC membership and the beginning of a *de facto* reconciliation with the Stormont government. His successor, Mr Jack Lynch, accepted this legacy, and in 1967 had the opportunity to engage in personal diplomacy with several European leaders in connexion with the unsuccessful EEC application of that year. Continuity was the essential feature of Irish foreign policy during the late nineteen sixties. This was hardly surprising, for Mr Lynch inherited his predecessor's policies (and his Minister for External Affairs), and had to consolidate his position as leader of the party and government after a relatively open contest for that position. Furthermore, although he had acquired a wide range of ministerial experience during his political career,[62] there was little evidence of a particular interest in foreign affairs.

But in 1969 the pressure of events obliged Mr Lynch to become intensively concerned with two major issues of foreign policy: the dispute with Britain over Northern Ireland and Ireland's entry to the EEC. It is too early to identify, let alone to unravel, many of

[59] *The Irish Times*, 2 December 1960.
[60] Dáil Debates: 196, 3375.
[61] Dáil Debates: 196, 3375-6.
[62] Mr Lynch entered the Dáil in 1948, was a parliamentary secretary from 1951 to 1954, and between 1957 and 1966 held the portfolios of the Gaeltacht, Education, Industry and Commerce and Finance.

the threads in the subsequent developments. But behind the sometimes ambiguous reactions to successive stages in the Northern Ireland crisis, there could be discerned a willingness to rely on a close if occasionally strained diplomatic relationship with the British government and to avoid moves which could be costly either in terms of resources or lives.[63] This willingness must be seen against a domestic background in which Jack Lynch's leadership, both of his government and of his party, came under persistent attack,[64] a combination of circumstances with which no previous Irish premier had had to contend to the same degree.

Nevertheless, under Mr Lynch, the tradition of personal intervention by the Taoiseach in policy concerning Northern Ireland was clearly consolidated. He increasingly played the leading role in the Dáil, and a succession of summit meetings with his British counterpart, Mr Edward Heath, underlined his predominant position in both the formulation and execution of policy. Nor did Mr Lynch stand aloof from the EEC negotiations which continuously involved the Minister for Foreign Affairs, Dr P. J. Hillery, for these negotiations demanded intervention by the head of government as did the subsequent referendum campaign on the terms of entry.

When Fianna Fáil was defeated in the general election of February 1973, Jack Lynch was succeeded by Mr Liam Cosgrave, at the head of a national coalition government, composed of Fine Gael and the Labour Party. Son of the Irish Free State's first head of government, Mr Cosgrave became the first Taoiseach to have previously served as Minister for External Affairs, a post he held under John A. Costello from 1954 to 1957. In that post, he had been primarily associated with Ireland's entry into the United Nations, but as Taoiseach he was confronted with a broad range of foreign policy issues of considerable complexity which will remain a high priority for Irish governments in the foreseeable future.

There are, then, some dissimilarities in the extent to which Irish heads of government have exercised their right to participate in the formulation of foreign policy. Mr de Valera's practice between 1932

[63] For Mr Lynch's own view of his Northern Ireland policy, after three years of crisis, see J. M. Lynch, 'The Anglo-Irish Problem', Foreign Affairs, vol. 50, no. 4, July 1972.
[64] Farrell, op. cit., pp. 74–81.

and 1948, of being his own foreign minister, has proved to be the exception rather than the rule. W. T. Cosgrave had little inclination to play a direct role and preferred to leave as much as he could to his subordinates. Costello was interested in foreign policy, but domestic and international circumstances limited his opportunities to pursue this interest. Mr de Valera in his second term of office was content to rely on younger men; while Seán Lemass, who had a special interest in the economic aspects of foreign policy, became considerably involved in the evolution of policies. Mr Lynch, whatever his views about the Taoiseach's role in foreign policy, was thrown into the maelstrom and could hardly avoid being closely involved in policy-making. Neither can his successor. But no matter what role the government heads played or wished to play, they have usually worked in partnership with a specialist foreign minister. The problems associated with this relationship and the role of the foreign minister are examined in the following chapter.

Chapter 3

THE MINISTER FOR EXTERNAL AFFAIRS
AND THE GOVERNMENT

*"We have the Minister for External Affairs. What does he do
when external affairs are in question?"*
Professor W. Magennis, 1926
(Dáil Debates: 14, 1235)

A LTHOUGH, as we have seen, the head of the government
may reserve to himself the final decision on matters of foreign
policy, and on vital issues will usually do so, the fact remains
that his other governmental obligations generally prevent him from
taking direct responsibility for the day-to-day administration of
external affairs. When the head of the government acts as his own
foreign minister, as in the case of Mr de Valera who himself filled
both posts for sixteen years, the advantages gained must be weighed
against the burden which this arrangement imposes. Thus, during
his later terms of office, de Valera appointed a separate foreign minister.[1]
Other states have, on the whole, employed a similar practice. The head
of government may act in specific instances without (or against)
the advice of his foreign minister, but in the long run he finds it
convenient to appoint one.

It is probably more accurate to say that the head of government
would find it inconvenient not to appoint a subordinate minister,
for, as in most aspects of government, the post requires a specialist
who must be able to supervise a government department, act as
public spokesman for that department, and in addition bear the

[1] In 1971 the minister's — and his department's — title was changed in its English
version from external affairs, a terminology largely associated with the dominions
in the British Commonwealth, to foreign affairs. However, since we are concerned
mainly with individuals operating under the former title, it is maintained here, except
where inappropriate.

burden of acting as the state's principal full-time diplomat. This latter duty consumes a great part of the time and energies of the foreign minister. On the one hand, there is the supervision of *ad hoc* negotiations with other governments on a wide range of political and technical issues which often call for the personal participation of the foreign minister; while, on the other hand, there are more orthodox obligations imposed on the minister by his state's member-ship of international organisations. For a small state, these latter commitments may be of much importance, in so far as international institutions offer the principal means of pursuing national objectives on a multilateral scale, and effective participation may require the personal intervention of the foreign minister. Notwithstanding the view that "the job of the Minister for External Affairs is to be at home at the head of his Department",[2] these commitments require the frequent and prolonged absence of ministers from their own states. This in itself is a compelling reason for the appointment of a subordinate minister with special responsibility for foreign policy.

Such an appointment has been the rule in the Irish state, and the role played by the successive foreign ministers is an important con-sideration in an analysis of the formulation of Irish policy. Although the role of each individual minister can only be assessed in a general way, some tentative conclusions may be drawn both about the general powers and functions of the minister and about the varying ways in which these have been exercised by specific ministers.

★   ★   ★   ★

While we are not concerned here with those foreign ministers acting under the abnormal or short-term conditions of the unrecognised or provisional governments of the first and second Dáil, a brief survey of their activities will show that they had little chance of acting as foreign ministers in the accepted sense of that term.

The first Minister for Foreign Affairs (as the office was then described) was Count Plunkett, who held the post in the first Dáil from 22 January 1919 and, in the second Dáil, until his resignation on 26 August 1921. Plunkett did not even have a skeleton department under him

---

[2] This view was expressed in the Dáil in 1961 by a Fine Gael deputy, Mr O. J. Flanagan. Dáil Debates: 186, 900.

until February 1921; prior to that date, the representatives abroad, who were not legally recognised by any other government, had been directly responsible to the Dáil and were often members of it. Since parliamentary activities were necessarily limited and diplomatic activities were non-governmental, Count Plunkett had little scope as a foreign minister.

However, his successor, Arthur Griffith, did perform one important task as foreign minister: he led the Irish delegation to London and was the principal Irish signatory of the Treaty of 1921. This action was repudiated not only by some members of his delegation but also by some members of his government, including its leader, Mr de Valera. Mr Griffith was forced to leave foreign affairs to George Gavan Duffy on becoming leader of the pro-Treaty group of the second Dáil on 10 January 1922.

During 1922, a series of frequent changes and short-lived occupancies bedevilled the office of foreign minister. Gavan Duffy resigned on 25 July. Griffith took over the portfolio, in addition to leading the government, but died on 12 August, whereupon the Minister for Education in the provisional government, Michael Hayes, took responsibility until 9 September 1922. On that date, Desmond FitzGerald was appointed minister and was confirmed in this appointment when the provisional government became the recognised government on 6 December 1922. He was the first man to hold the post for any length of time under comparatively normal conditions, and was the first man to be called 'Minister for External Affairs'.

Since 1922, nine men have held this post as an office distinct from that of head of the government: Desmond FitzGerald, Kevin O'Higgins, Patrick McGilligan, Seán MacBride, Frank Aiken, Liam Cosgrave, Patrick Hillery, Brian Lenihan and Garret FitzGerald (see Table 1).† O'Higgins was assassinated less than three weeks after taking office, although he exerted considerable influence on foreign policy in his capacity as an ordinary member of the cabinet, before his appointment as Minister for External Affairs.[3]

[3] See below pp. 91-2. There remains one other holder of the portfolio of external affairs: the first president of the executive council, William T. Cosgrave, who took it over on O'Higgins's death on 10 July 1927 until the appointment of Patrick McGilligan on 12 October 1927. But Mr Cosgrave was not greatly interested in foreign affairs, and this was a temporary measure during the parliamentary recess.

† See p. 74.

Table 1

Irish Foreign Ministers since 6 December 1922

Name	Date of appointment	Resignation
Desmond FitzGerald	6.12.1922	23.6.1927
Kevin O'Higgins (also Minister for Justice)	23.6.1927 (From 10.7.1927 to 12.10.1927, the portfolio was held by W. T. Cosgrave, President of the Executive Council.)	10.7.1927
Patrick McGilligan (also Minister for Industry and Commerce)	12.10.1927 (From 9.3.1932 to 18.2.1948, the portfolio was held by Eamon de Valera, President of the Executive Council and Taoiseach.)	9.3.1932
Seán MacBride	18.2.1948	14.6.1951
Frank Aiken	14.6.1951	2.6.1954
Liam Cosgrave	2.6.1954	20.3.1957
Frank Aiken	20.3.1957	2.7.1969
Patrick Hillery	2.7.1969	29.12.1972
Brian Lenihan	29.12.1972	14.3.1973
Garret FitzGerald	14.3.1973	

At the outset, the point must be made that no obvious pattern can be discerned in the background of these men. To some extent, their varied paths to power reflect the special conditions prevailing in a new state, delayed in its development by a civil war and the consequent political divisions. Yet even within these divisions, which gave rise to the formation of political parties, none of these ministers seem to have been groomed for this role. None of them was, for any length of time prior to his appointment, an opposition spokesman on foreign policy; and since Ireland lacks a developed system of junior governmental posts, there has never existed a clear system of preferment for a parliamentary deputy. Liam Cosgrave remains the only one to have been a parliamentary secretary before his appointment as minister. These men held positions of importance within their parties or within inter-party coalitions, but the office of foreign minister itself, although enjoying a certain distinction, is not the most prominent in the governmental hierarchy. No foreign minister has as yet proceeded directly from that position to become head of the government,[4] and foreign policy has perhaps been too near the periphery of the Irish political consciousness to make the portfolio of external affairs a likely means to the ultimate office.

Desmond FitzGerald, the first Minister for External Affairs, like all his colleagues in Mr W. T. Cosgrave's government, did not have what are regarded in established political systems as the orthodox qualifications for governmental office: parliamentary experience and some junior ministerial experience under an ordinary government. But although he was thirty when he took office and Ireland's youngest foreign minister, he had considerable knowledge of the practical problems of several extraordinary governments. A journalist by profession, FitzGerald participated in the 1916 Rising and was elected as a Sinn Féin candidate in 1918. More important than this revolutionary and quasi parliamentary background was his service as director for publicity of the first Dáil: this was a branch of the unrecognised government and, like the Ministries of Home Affairs and Local Government, had very real duties to perform. Indeed, in some respects, the publicity department may be seen as the domestic counterpart of the propaganda activities of the Irish representatives abroad, for the conduct of foreign policy before the Treaty, and for some time after, was largely a question of propaganda. So, Mr FitzGerald, on becoming minister, with the merging of the publicity department with the Department of External Affairs, was as well-equipped for the job as circumstances allowed.

Desmond FitzGerald was Minister for External Affairs for just under five years, from 30 August 1922 to 23 June 1927.[5] During this period he played an important pioneering role which did not then

---

[4] Farrell, op. cit., pp. 11–12. In 1973 Liam Cosgrave became the first Taoiseach to have previously held the external affairs portfolio, after a period in opposition of no less than sixteen years.

[5] This includes over three months under the provisional government.

(or even now) receive the recognition it deserved. To a large extent this is due to the striking part which Kevin O'Higgins played in the negotiations concerning the Boundary issue and in the Irish delegation to the Imperial Conference of 1926. FitzGerald's achievements were of a more routine and less publicised nature but have been of some significance in the long term. Principally, they lie in his administrative work and in his attempt to establish guidelines for the public discussion of foreign policy. He had the unenviable task of building up the Department of External Affairs out of an administrative vacuum; this in itself might have represented a welcome challenge had it not been for the continual parliamentary criticism of the department's very existence, and the meagre funds at its disposal. In 1926, a deputy, commenting on a French journalist's report that Desmond FitzGerald had been condemned to death nine times, said, "I really think the journalist must have confused the Minister with his Department, in which case it was a gross understatement".[6] In spite of the accusations in the Dáil that the department was ". . . an advisory committee on etiquette . . ."[7] which was ". . . playing with theatricals . . .",[8] FitzGerald managed to establish a headquarters, the first delegations to the League of Nations and the first mission to Washington of any Commonwealth state outside the United Kingdom. In the Dáil, he continually stressed the need to have a coherent foreign policy and an efficient diplomatic organisation to carry it out. His own assessment of his achievement, after he had left the Ministry of External Affairs and become Minister for Defence, is convincing: "We took over a situation very indefinitely and an office naturally varying in experience, and within the very minimum of time the State became one of the foremost of the Dominions in the understanding of its position, and in the bettering of that position".[9]

After the election of 9 June 1927, Desmond FitzGerald left the Department of External Affairs and was replaced by Kevin O'Higgins. The president of the executive council pointed out that the reason for the change was not ". . . that the Minister who had charge of

[6] Dáil Debates: 14, 1858–59.
[7] Dáil Debates: 16, 330.
[8] Dáil Debates: 5, 940.
[9] Dáil Debates: 27, 447.

the Department was incompetent", but because he was at the time "very ill".[10] Mr FitzGerald was subsequently given the portfolio of defence, a critical task in view of the army mutiny of 1924. The new Minister, Mr O'Higgins, already vice-president of the executive council and Minister for Justice, was described by W. T. Cosgrave as ". . . one of the most hardworked of all the Ministers, who told me within the last week that as his work had lessened in his Department he thought he would be able to take on the work of the Ministry of External Affairs".[11] In the few weeks before his murder on 10 July, Mr O'Higgins justified his appointment by creating attention at the Geneva conference on the limitation of naval armaments. A Japanese jurist remarked: "The Conference has been a failure for all except the Irish. They have used it to assert their international status, in which they have fully succeeded".[12] With the reputation he had built up during the Imperial Conference of 1926 and his influential position within the cabinet, O'Higgins had the potential to become a most effective foreign minister.

When Kevin O'Higgins became Minister for External Affairs, he retained the posts of Minister for Justice and vice-president of the executive council. After his death and the interregnum of Mr Cosgrave, a similar practice was adopted when Mr Patrick McGilligan, who had already been since April 1924 the Minister for Industry and Commerce, was appointed Minister for External Affairs as well. To some extent this reflects the comparatively small scale of foreign activity; the administrative machine at home, established under Mr FitzGerald, was still small, and representation abroad had developed as far as finances would allow and diplomatic considerations would merit, which was not very far. On the other hand, it indicates the success which McGilligan and, to a greater extent, O'Higgins had made of their ministerial posts, for even if its routine burdens were lighter than those of other portfolios, external affairs still remained a vital position and not one to be given to an unproven man.

Patrick McGilligan, a barrister, was far from unproven. By the time he became Minister for External Affairs at the age of thirty-eight,

[10] Dáil Debates: 20, 59.
[11] Dáil Debates: 20, 59–60.
[12] Quoted in T. de Vere White, op. cit., p. 237.

he had won his ministerial spurs by his vigorous and successful promotion of the Shannon electrification scheme, and by his parliamentary
ability during the Dáil debates on this matter. He was appointed
Minister for External Affairs on 12 October 1927 and held office
until the defeat of the government in March 1932. Diplomatically,
he pursued with some success the policies of his predecessors. In
1930, he led the Irish delegation to the Imperial Conference where
he helped consolidate the previous Conference's moves towards
full and equal dominion status, recognised a year later by the British
government in the Statute of Westminster; McGilligan was "by
general consent one of the three or four outstanding personalities
at the Conference . . .".[13] Outside Commonwealth politics, too,
Mr McGilligan built on the foundations secured by his predecessors:
in 1928, the Briand-Kellogg Pact was signed, the first multilateral
treaty *negotiated* by an Irish government, and in 1929, by adhering
to Article 36 of the Statute of the Permanent Court of International
Justice, the Irish government again demonstrated that members of
the Commonwealth could act independently. Then, in September
1930, Ireland was elected a non-permanent member of the Council
of the League of Nations, not in her capacity as a member of the
Commonwealth, but rather as an independent sovereign state, a
precedent established by Mr FitzGerald in 1926.

As a diplomat, Mr McGilligan successfully continued and developed
earlier policies. His responsibility for another important government
department did not prevent him from carrying out a thorough
reorganisation of the Department of External Affairs, increasing its
staff at home and abroad and standardising the grades and salaries
of civil servants under his ministration. The proportion of total
government expenditure assigned to external affairs rose significantly
during his term of office.[14] As was to be expected, McGilligan laid
considerable stress on the responsibility of the Department of External
Affairs to promote Irish trade, but took care to point out that trade
was not the sole, or even the most important, justification for the
existence of a foreign ministry. For example, in 1929 he criticised
"a disposition . . . to say that the office [External Affairs] is successful

[13] O'Sullivan, op. cit., p. 252.
[14] See Figure 1. p. 309.

or unsuccessful according as the volume of trade has increased or decreased".[15]

On his renomination for both posts (after the government had resigned and been chosen again by the Dáil on 3 April 1930), Mr McGilligan was attacked not for his activities as Minister for External Affairs but rather for his alleged negligence as Minister for Industry and Commerce: his opposite number, Seán Lemass, was ". . . convinced that the work of the Department of Industry and Commerce has been seriously prejudiced by the fact that the Minister has been gadding around international conferences in Europe . . ."[16] Mr Lemass succeeded Mr McGilligan as Minister for Industry and Commerce and, on his retirement from politics in 1969, had not altered his view that McGilligan had tended to neglect that department in favour of the Department of External Affairs.[17] However, some of the diplomatic gadding around had been done by Mr McGilligan's predecessor, Mr FitzGerald. It was he, for example, who accompanied Mr Cosgrave on his American visit in 1928. McGilligan's double task may also have been somewhat eased by his predecessor's active support in the Dáil.[18]

It was in the Dáil that Patrick McGilligan — ". . . whether he be the Tweedledum of Industry and Commerce or the Tweedledee of External Affairs . . ."[19] — found his advocacy of Irish foreign policy constrained in a manner not experienced by his predecessors. The Dáil had become an arena of emotionally partisan conflict where rational debate was often irrelevant, for McGilligan's appointment to External Affairs coincided with the entry into the Dáil of the anti-Treaty Fianna Fáil party. However, if he was denied the opportunity to discuss and explain his policies as fully as he might have wished, he was nonetheless well suited to counter the criticism he received;[20]

[15] Dáil Debates: 30, 800.
[16] Dáil Debates: 34, 520.
[17] See interview in *The Irish Press*, 24 January 1969.
[18] See, for example, FitzGerald's part in the External Affairs Estimate debate in 1928. Dáil Debates: 27, 442–449.
[19] Dáil Debates: 28, 346.
[20] Mr McGilligan ". . . as a parliamentarian ranks as one of the great vitriolics" (T. P. Coogan, *Ireland since the Rising*, Pall Mall, London, 1966), p. 55. A good example of his style may be found in the debate on the ratification of the Kellogg Pact in 1929— see Dáil Debates: 28, 357–372.

his subsequent career as Minister for Finance from 1948–1951 and Attorney General from 1954–1957, up to his defeat, at the age of seventy-six, in the general election of 1965, is evidence of his political stamina.

After the sixteen years during which the head of the government, Mr de Valera, was his own Minister for External Affairs, the next man to occupy the post was Seán MacBride. It might have been expected that after twenty-six years of parliamentary government the qualifications for ministerial office would have included a notable parliamentary career with ministerial or front bench responsibilities. Mr MacBride was to demonstrate that such normality could not be taken for granted. The reason for this is to be found in MacBride's political career, which, up to the end of World War II, had run along extra-constitutional lines. Born into an intensely republican family, he had from his youth been associated with extremist republican organisations which accepted the constitutional policies of neither of the two major parties;[21] as a barrister, he was known for his successful defence of republican extremists charged with acts of violence.

However, in 1946 Mr MacBride entered parliamentary politics as co-founder and leader of the Clann na Poblachta party, which had as one of its principal objectives the early abolition of partition. He was elected to the Dáil in 1947, so that by the time he became Minister for External Affairs at the age of forty-four, he had had much less than a year's parliamentary experience — which was more than could be said for his cabinet colleague, Dr Noel Browne. On the face of it, it might seem to have been something of a gamble to appoint to an important post a man whose conversion to parliamentary democracy was so recent; but without his support there would have been no coalition government in the first place.

In a short but eventful period of office of just over three years, Mr MacBride's activities left their mark on most aspects of foreign policy. Previously known for his pronounced views on relations between Britain and Ireland, he also showed an interest in the politics

[21] In 1929, for example, he was a member of the executive committee of Saor Éire, subsequently declared illegal in 1931: see Coogan, op. cit., p. 257. MacBride's parents had been closely associated with the nationalist movement. His father, John MacBride, was executed after the 1916 Rising and his mother, Maud Gonne, was one of the principal figures in the nationalist literary revival.

of European cooperation and integration. In 1948, he led Ireland into the OEEC and became closely associated with the administration of the European recovery programme; in 1949 he was an enthusiastic advocate of the new Council of Europe, which he used to a greater extent than any succeeding Minister for External Affairs. Although this approval of the Council of Europe coincided with the policy of raising the 'sore thumb' of partition abroad, it also reflected Mr MacBride's broader interests.

Born and partially educated in France, he was a consistent advocate of European unity and, since holding ministerial office, served on the economic committee of the Council of Europe from 1954 to 1957 and was a member of the executive of the Pan-European Union; subsequently, he developed a serious interest in questions of international law and more especially in the treatment of political prisoners. While in office from 1948 to 1951, he was vice-president of the OEEC and 1950 was president of the Council of Foreign Ministers of the Council of Europe. He can be said to have grasped firmly the few opportunities open to Ireland in those years for pursuing an active foreign policy.

Seán MacBride was also responsible for important administrative changes and made a vigorous attempt to bring the Department of External Affairs up-to-date with the new and increased demands of the post-war world; indeed, expenditure in the department in relation to total government expenditure had never been so great as in 1950.[22] The headquarters staff was increased and reorganised, press attachés and information officers were introduced, training courses established and cultural activities were encouraged. Mr MacBride's insistence on the importance of publicity for Irish foreign policy was evident in his establishment of the Irish News Agency in 1949, which he fought for against stiff parliamentary opposition.

Mr MacBride was one of the most outspoken foreign ministers in the history of the Irish state. His speeches in the Dáil were generally long, comprehensive and detailed. In part, his success may be attributed to the gradual erosion of the bitter party antagonisms which accounted for some of the reticence of previous ministers; but these antagonisms

[22] See Figure 1. Mr MacBride was perhaps fortunate in having as Minister for Finance a former foreign minister, Mr McGilligan.

had by no means vanished completely in the late forties, and MacBride was a pioneer in the sense that he articulated long-term national objectives in a Dáil which all too frequently succumbed to the temptations of short-term partisan advantages.[23] There can be no doubt that Seán MacBride made a considerable impact on parliamentarians of all parties; even an opposition deputy admitted in 1949 that ". . . if he had a case to make he is more capable of making one than any other member of the House".[24] No matter how we may judge his policies, he was a notable foreign minister with a keen appreciation of his democratic responsibilities, a fact all the more ironical in view of his extremist background. Possibly he was too outspoken for his own political good and his vision of world politics may have seemed irrelevant to a largely insular public. He was himself anything but insular and remains an unusual personality in Irish politics.

If Seán MacBride's qualifications for office were unorthodox, the reverse must be said of those of Liam Cosgrave, Minister for External Affairs in the second coalition government. In an established parliamentary democracy his progress to a place in the cabinet would have been considered the norm. Eldest son of William T. Cosgrave, he came from a well-established political family, and one which, since 1922, had been committed to parliamentary government. Like MacBride (and McGilligan) he was a barrister, but, unlike the former, he had been first elected to the Dáil in 1943 at the age of twenty-three. When his party, Fine Gael, came into power in 1948, he was appointed parliamentary secretary to both the Taoiseach, Mr John A. Costello, and the Minister for Industry and Commerce, Mr D. Morrissey. Thus he had over three years' junior ministerial experience before he was appointed Minister for External Affairs in 1954 at the age of thirty-four, and as Parliamentary Secretary to the Taoiseach he had attended cabinet meetings. To a large extent, then, Mr Cosgrave's political career follows a conventional pattern of training for ministerial office: a political background, eleven years

---

[23] He set the tone in his first speech on the department's estimates in 1948 (see Dáil Debates: 112, especially 900–902). Subsequently, in opposition, he spoke constructively on foreign affairs and on the conduct of foreign policy, e.g. in 1953, (see Dáil Debates: 136, 1171–77).

[24] Dáil Debates: 117, 817.

in parliament, a gradual initiation into the business of administering a government department and answering for it in the legislature, and finally, a cabinet appointment at an age when political ambitions and energies may be tempered by experience, yet remain unsoured by frustration.

However, his term of office lasted under three years and severe economic crises made it difficult for him to continue the expansion of his department. Mr Cosgrave had few opportunities for diplomatic initiatives until his last year in office. His principal distinction was to be elected chairman of the Committee of Ministers of the Council of Europe in 1955; but this was a Council of Europe which had manifestly failed to play the leading role in European integration which had been its original *raison d'être*. In December 1955, Ireland was admitted to the United Nations, and Liam Cosgrave was able to lead the Irish delegation to its first UN Assembly session in the autumn of 1956; here he was able to lay the broad foundations for the UN policies of succeeding Irish governments, and he made it clear that the issue of partition was not to be raised at the expense of the common peace-keeping aims of the UN.[25]

However, Mr Cosgrave had little chance to apply his general principles to difficult cases and it is hard to assess his performance on the results of this single year before the coalition government was defeated at the polls. The important issues of 1956 — the invasion of Suez, the Hungarian rebellion and British policy towards Cyprus — did not cause the Irish government much heart-searching, since they were all questions where outright condemnation was comparatively easy for an uncommitted small state; there was no difficulty in interpreting Mr Cosgrave's three principles of UN policy on these issues.[26] However, these principles were sufficiently broad to allow of very different interpretations, and Mr Cosgrave's party, Fine Gael, was subsequently to oppose the succeeding government's policy in the UN on the interpretation of the second and third points — independence from blocs and defence of the 'free world'.

[25] See B. J. O'Connor, *Ireland and the United Nations* (Tuairim Pamphlet, no. 7, Dublin, 1961) p. 4.
[26] Expounded in the External Affairs Estimate debate of 1956. See Dáil Debates: 159, 139–145; and above chapter 1, p. 32.

As an administrator, Liam Cosgrave was limited by the financial difficulties experienced by the coalition government and consequently had little chance to display the sort of initiative taken by Mr MacBride in this quarter. It was as a parliamentarian that he showed his greatest promise. Paradoxically, these parliamentary abilities were most apparent when he had very little specific about which to speak. Nevertheless, he was prepared to comment on world events and to try to relate them to what was, of necessity, an isolated Ireland.[27] This was a marked contrast to the parliamentary style of his predecessor and successor, Mr Aiken, and demonstrated his appreciation of the government's obligation to give a lead in educating public opinion.

Mr Frank Aiken was Minister for External Affairs on two separate occasions: for three years from 1951 to 1954 and for twelve years from 1957 to 1969. Had we only his first term of office to consider, we might be excused for dismissing him as a nominal foreign minister; but the difficult economic circumstances between 1951 and 1954 were a hindrance to his task and were subsequently to inhibit Mr Cosgrave, and world events thwarted the pursuit of an active foreign policy. Unlike Mr Cosgrave, Frank Aiken, unable to express himself in deeds, was unwilling to express himself in words. His predecessor, Mr MacBride, not inappropriately described him in 1953 as ". . . the only Minister of Foreign Affairs or of External Affairs in the world who can get up here and introduce his Estimate without even mentioning that there is an international situation in the world, or mentioning that we have any policy".[28]

Frank Aiken was, however, a man with much political experience who had been intimately concerned with the struggle for independence and with the violent division which followed the Treaty of 1921. He was the last chief-of-staff of the anti-Treaty forces and had followed Mr de Valera into the Dáil in 1927 to start a parliamentary career which lasted over forty years. The greater part of his career included important and varied ministerial experience. From 1932 to the outbreak of World War II, Mr Aiken was Minister for Defence. In 1932 this ministry was of critical importance, since the loyalty

---

[27] See, for example, his speech on the External Affairs Estimate in 1955. Dáil Debates: 152, especially 538–546.
[28] Dáil Debates: 138, 779.

of the pro-Treaty army was the main guarantee of the maintenance of democratic government. When Mr de Valera's anti-Treaty administration came into power in 1932, conceivably there might have been serious mutinies or political purges within the army. That this did not occur and that the army accepted its recent enemies as the new government was in no small measure due to Mr Aiken's handling of the Ministry of Defence.[29] During World War II, he was appointed to the special Ministry for the Coordination of Defensive Measures and, when this department was dissolved in July 1945, he became Minister for Finance until the fall of Mr de Valera's government at the beginning of 1948.[30]

Thus, when he came to External Affairs in 1951 at the age of fifty-three, he had a wealth of governmental experience. His offices had involved him in quasi diplomatic duties such as his visit to the USA in 1941 to negotiate (albeit with little success) for arms with the US government. Also, in his wartime capacity as defence 'overlord', he was responsible for the strict censorship of the Irish press (one of the more disagreeable by-products of the neutrality policy). This censorship entailed a strict impartiality towards both sides in World War II, an impartiality which did not often accord with the feelings of the Irish public. Mr Aiken's stand was criticised as being in effect anti-British; however, the only parliamentary advocate of this view was Mr James Dillon, whose own attitude towards neutrality was plainly not impartial.[31]

During his brief period out of office, Frank Aiken was Mr de Valera's companion on his celebrated world trip in 1948 to whip up support for the anti-partitionist cause; he was, therefore, as near to the sources of Irish foreign policy from 1932 to 1948 as it was possible for any member of Mr de Valera's cabinet to be. A long and rather unusual political career had made Mr Aiken a man with some considerable qualifications for the portfolio of external affairs.

The twelve years of Mr Aiken's second term of office — the longest

---

[29] M. J. MacManus, *Eamon de Valera* (Talbot Press, Dublin, 1944), pp. 282–3.
[30] Mr Aiken also temporarily held the portfolios of lands (for five months in 1936) and of agriculture (for two months in 1957). In April 1965, he was appointed Tánaiste (Deputy Prime Minister) and at the time of his retirement in 1969 was the longest serving minister in Irish history.
[31] See Dáil Debates: 97, 2605 and 2756.

held by any individual Minister for External Affairs — reveal his distinctive contribution to Irish foreign policy. Most importantly, he established a reputation as a statesman in UN politics. Under his leadership, the Irish delegation took initiatives (rather than merely reacted to those of other states) and sponsored assembly resolutions as well as voted on them. Since some of these policies, particularly during the late nineteen fifties, were at variance with the rigid positions taken up by the principal participants of the cold war, Mr Aiken was seen, both at home and abroad, as either a fearlessly independent statesman or a fellow-travelling stooge. In particular, his early military disengagement plan for central Europe and his willingness to discuss the admission of communist China to the UN were viewed with distaste by the US government and with horror by his Fine Gael critics who regarded this policy as a stab in the back for Christian civilisation.[32]

Although after 1961 Mr Aiken's policy appeared to be a good deal less distinctive, the fact remains that he made his mark and showed an active interest in his role as foreign minister in the United Nations. This is confirmed by the emphasis he placed on Ireland's UN role in most of his speeches on foreign policy in the Dáil, and by the publication of his principal speeches in the UN General Assembly for each year since 1957.[33] He developed a particular interest in the problems of disarmament and peace-keeping, which, with the pursuit of functional cooperation through the UN specialised agencies, constituted the bulk of the work for his delegation in New York; his personal contribution to negotiations on these issues went beyond those of most foreign ministers representing the smaller states. Towards the end of his term of office, he was accused of adopting an unnecessarily cautious, if not subservient, attitude towards American foreign policy but it is difficult to establish the validity of such criticism.[34]

From 1958 on, Mr Aiken was strongly criticised for his lack of interest in other aspects of Irish foreign policy, especially the question

[32] See, for example, the debate on 28 November 1957 on a motion of disapproval of the government's foreign policy (Dáil Debates: 164, 1168 ff.)
[33] Published annually under the title of 'Ireland at the United Nations' (Browne and Nolan, Dublin).
[34] See above, chapter 1, pp. 33-34.

of Europe. During the debate on the External Affairs estimates in 1959, Mr Declan Costello pointed to ". . . the undoubted lack of interest which the Minister has shown in the affairs of the Council of Europe".[35] At that time the Council of Europe was the principal means by which the government could keep in touch with European developments, but even when Ireland applied to join the EEC, Mr Aiken's interest was hardly more convincing. In 1961, he attempted to demonstrate his enthusiasm by citing his support for the Coal and Steel Community at its inception more than ten years previously,[36] but in 1966 in a debate in the Seanad, Senator Garret FitzGerald claimed that during the previous three years' debates on the External Affairs estimate, Mr Aiken had spoken only 58 words about Europe out of a total of 20,000.[37] However, even if Mr Aiken can be accused of a lack of interest, it is by no means fair to ascribe the vagaries of policy-making with regard to Europe to him alone, for Europe appears to have been treated as an 'economic' rather than as a 'political' problem, and consequently reserved for the 'economic' ministers and above all for the Taoiseach.[38] Indeed, it seems as if Mr Aiken made a tacit agreement with his colleagues not to intervene on the question of Ireland's entry into the EEC.

Mr Aiken's achievements as an administrator were his consolidation of the position of the headquarters office and the gradual expansion of the network of missions abroad. It is significant that representation was extended to Nigeria and India, thus establishing governmental contact with states, and indeed continents, where previously the Irish presence had been mainly religious. The publicity and cultural work of the department also continued under his leadership, although in 1964 an information booklet, *Facts about Ireland*, published by the Department of Foreign Affairs, received an exaggerated notoriety because of its alleged political bias. The subsequent controversy revealed much about the persistence of divisive civil war attitudes. As far as foreign policy was concerned, it revealed only the general indifference of Irish parliamentarians.[39]

[35] Dáil Debates: 176, 685.
[36] Dáil Debates: 191, 662.
[37] Seanad Debates: 61, 1851-3.
[38] See below, pp. 93-94.
[39] See especially Dáil Debates: 208, 989-1002. The effect of the civil war on parliamentary discussion is further discussed in chapter 10, pp. 228-230.

The most obvious characteristic of Frank Aiken's parliamentary style was a certain reticence which was particularly noticeable in the way he conducted the debates on foreign policy during his first term of office. On the principal occasion on which foreign policy was discussed in the Dáil—the debate on the External Affairs estimate— he usually made only a brief introductory statement in Irish.[40] Since he was one of Mr de Valera's closest followers, this practice seemed to be a rather exaggerated aping of his leader's example. But it would be unjust to suggest that it was only imitation. Mr Aiken was never the most forthcoming of ministers; his public reticence seems to have been a manifestation of a natural taciturnity that he believed befitted his role as foreign minister. In 1960 he remarked:

> I do not think that it is any sort of valuable exercise to debate general principles stated in general terms. It is much better to test the general policy of the Minister by examining in details the actions he took. I am prepared to be judged and the Government are prepared to be judged by our acts or lack of action in any international matters in which we should appropriately have acted. We are not bound to comment on every incident in international affairs. We have the freedom to remain silent as well as the freedom to speak and sometimes it is valuable to keep silent just as on other occasions one must be prepared to speak one's mind and to represent clearly and definitely where one's country stands.[41]

Mr Aiken's political style had its merits and paid dividends, but it was often an obstacle to the effective discussion of foreign policy in the Dáil. If parliamentary representatives are "to test the general policy of the Minister by examining in detail the actions he took", they must first be presented with a continuous supply of detailed information; they should also be able to look to the minister for a full explanation of his choice of objectives and the policies he is pursuing in order to achieve them. Mr Aiken's reticence made these conditions hard to fulfil. As a consequence, the deputies' and general public's understanding of international affairs remained undeveloped

[40] For criticisms of this practice, see Dáil Debates: 167, 261.
[41] Dáil Debates: 182, 800.

at a time when the complexity of their government's foreign policy was increasing. In the short term, the effects of this may not have been noticeable, but in the long run it could only encourage the latent insularity of Irish public life. Where the need for consensus on foreign policy is emphasised (by implication) to the extent that public discussion is discouraged, there is a danger that alternative policies will not be considered and that policy will become excessively rigid.

Mr Aiken's successor, Dr Patrick Hillery, was, like Mr Liam Cosgrave, a member of a different political generation. A Dáil deputy since 1951, he was Minister for Education (1959–1965), for Industry and Commerce (1965–1966) and for Labour (1966–1969). In the course of this ministerial career, he represented Ireland abroad, particularly at the International Labour Organisation; his term in the Department of Industry and Commerce, at a time when this department was preoccupied with preparations for EEC membership, made it unlikely that he would confine his attentions to the United Nations, as Mr Aiken was inclined to do. As it happened, changes in international affairs when Dr Hillery became foreign minister made it impossible for him to adopt such a limited role, even had he so desired. His term of office was not long — a little over three years — but it was eventful to say the least. Less than two months after taking up his new position, he was appearing before the UN Security Council to speak on the Northern Ireland issue and was also obliged to prepare for the impending negotiations to enter the EEC. In the succeeding years, both these issues demanded his continuous attention.

While it is too early to make anything but the most tentative assessment of his role, certain judgments can be put forward. Although the Taoiseach was clearly the central figure in the Northern Ireland crisis, Dr Hillery was closely involved in the important diplomatic link with the British government and with representations made to other governments; he also played a significant part in parliamentary debates on the issue. He became even more closely associated with the question of EEC membership and bore the burden of continuous negotiations during 1970 and 1971 and the subsequent campaign to ratify membership in the spring of 1972. His attitude to other issues was understandably less fully developed, although his reversal of Ireland's position on the representation of communist China in the UN may in the long term prove to be one of his more significant decisions. On the whole, he developed a more open and candid parliamentary style than his predecessor and on occasion attempted to encourage a broader understanding of Irish foreign policy in the Dáil.[42]

Patrick Hillery's departure to Brussels in January 1973, as Ireland's first EEC Commissioner, was not altogether surprising. He was succeeded by Mr Brian Lenihan who, although he was only forty-two at the time of his appointment to the portfolio of foreign affairs, had been a member of the cabinet for nearly nine years, with responsibility for the Departments of Justice (1964–1968), of Education (1968–1969) and of Transport and Power (1969–1972). However, Mr Lenihan had barely time to acquaint himself with his new post before the Fianna Fáil government was defeated in February 1973, and Mr Lenihan himself lost his seat in the Dáil. Although this defeat was largely a consequence of local circumstances and the difficulties of strengthening his party's position in a multi-member constituency, it also served as a reminder that the portfolio of foreign affairs provides its holder with few opportunities to consolidate his electoral base.

Under the new coalition government of the Fine Gael and Labour parties, Dr Garret FitzGerald of Fine Gael was appointed Minister for Foreign Affairs, at the age of forty-six. This was his first cabinet appointment, but in many respects he was well-equipped for this particular post. Son of the state's first Minister for External Affairs, Desmond FitzGerald, he had been closely concerned with the development of Irish attitudes towards the EEC, initially as an economist and journalist and later as a senator from 1965 to 1969, and as a member of the Dáil since 1969. As a deputy, he quickly acquired the reputation of being an indefatigable source of information and comment on most issues of foreign policy, even though his major preoccupation was the development of the Irish economy. Indeed, he is one of the few Irish politicians, whether inside or outside government, who have attempted to develop their ideas about Irish foreign policy at any length.[43]

[42] Notably in his speech to the Dáil on 18 April 1972. See Dáil Debates: 260, 384–406.

[43] His speech during the 1969 External Affairs Estimate debate is a characteristic example of Dr FitzGerald's approach; see Dáil Debates: 241, 1983 ff. His views on the possible evolution of the Northern Ireland crisis and on Irish membership of the European Community are found in G. FitzGerald, *Towards a New Ireland* (Charles Knight, London, 1972).

It must be stressed at this point that, by attempting to examine each foreign minister in isolation, we are doing less than justice both to them and to the complexity of the policy-making process. The foreign minister is but one member of the cabinet, and his policies are subject to the criticism and influence of his colleagues; indeed, his responsibility for conducting a wide range of governmental business with other states makes him especially vulnerable to the interference of other ministers. As the first Minister for External Affairs pointed out in 1923, "the External Affairs Department has to serve as a co-ordinating factor . . . and has to consider the point of view of the various Departments that may be contradictory and present the national or political view".[44] Two years later, Desmond FitzGerald illustrated this point: "When a question of trade arises, I automatically turn and consult the Minister for Industry and Commerce",[45] and the latter must take the foreign minister's guidance in "diplomatic, political or national points". However, Mr FitzGerald was stating the ideal point of view, for in spite of the secrecy of cabinet discussions and the orthodoxy of collective responsibility, it is evident that, in practice, such a tidy allocation of powers and functions does not always exist.

In the first place, the normal activities of other ministers are inextricably bound up with those of the foreign minister: the latter depends on the Minister for Finance for his diplomatic machinery, on the Minister for Defence for policies which involve military participation, as in the Congo and Cyprus, and on the Ministers for Industry and Commerce and for Agriculture for trade policies. These are the most obvious examples. Occasionally, what seems to be a "diplomatic, political or national point" is dealt with mainly, if not exclusively, by a minister other than the Minister for External Affairs. The first — and perhaps the most notable — example of this came during the term of office of Desmond FitzGerald himself. Owing to poor health, he was unable to lead the Irish delegation to the Imperial Conference in 1926 and the delegation was led by the Minister for Justice, Kevin O'Higgins, who firmly established a reputation as a diplomat as a result. O'Higgins was ultimately

---

[44] Dáil Debates: 5, 1400.
[45] Dáil Debates: 11, 1450–1.

given credit for being the architect of Irish Commonwealth policy,[46] and Terence de Vere White, writing in 1948, claimed that Desmond FitzGerald ". . . did not possess the dynamic qualities which were required in the position that he held and once O'Higgins began to take an interest in foreign affairs, FitzGerald had to play second fiddle to him."[47] Some six months after the Imperial Conference of 1926, Mr FitzGerald became Minister for Defence and Mr O'Higgins was appointed his successor.

No such direct intervention has occurred since, and, given the extent of cabinet secrecy, it is usually impossible to discern what power individual ministers have enjoyed. But from time to time the struggles of foreign ministers with their cabinet colleagues have been partially revealed. Not surprisingly, the coalition government of 1948 to 1951 provides some examples. The Minister for Agriculture, Mr Dillon, advocated a Commonwealth–American–Irish free trade area, but was repudiated by the Taoiseach, Mr Costello.[48] Then in 1949, when the Taoiseach, Mr Costello, and the Minister for Finance, Mr McGilligan, supported the concept of bilateral trade arrangements in order to protect sterling, the Minister for External Affairs, Seán MacBride, was criticised for publicly advocating in Paris that multi-lateral arrangements within the framework of the OEEC should be adopted. Seán Lemass was prompted to speculate that "there is perhaps a suspicion in some quarters that the Minister for External Affairs acts in these matters independently of his colleagues or even in conflict with them."[49] Both Mr MacBride and Mr Costello spent a good deal of time in a not altogether convincing attempt to deny that there was any such dissension within the cabinet.[50]

It is, however, inevitable that the indistinct boundaries between the areas of competence of different departments are transgressed to some extent, particularly in foreign affairs, which can be held to encompass the external aspects of all areas of public policy. Attempts

[46] This was Mr McGilligan's assessment in 1931. See Dáil Debates: 39, 2307.
[47] T. de Vere White, op. cit., p. 218. To be fair, Desmond FitzGerald's career in government has unfortunately not yet received attention comparable to that of O'Higgins.
[48] See above, chapter 2.
[49] Dáil Debates: 117, 926.
[50] Dáil Debates: 117, 1055 ff.

to establish a clearer division of responsibilities may be necessary for satisfactory day-to-day working relationships, but a consequence of this may be an over-simplification of issues and a neglect of important aspects which do not fall readily into a preconceived pattern. This seems to have occurred in the case of the Fianna Fáil government's European policy from 1957 onwards. In this case, the foreign minister, Mr Aiken, had very little to do with the formulation of policies towards European cooperation. Partly this may have been due to a lack of interest on his part, but the fact that Ireland's position in Europe was stressed in economic rather than in political terms suggests that the foreign minister's traditional specialism was being eroded to some extent. From 1957 to 1959, the question of Ireland's relationship with the proposed free trade area in Europe and with the EEC was plainly in the hands of the Minister for Industry and Commerce, Seán Lemass; for example, when a motion to establish a committee to discuss Ireland's position *vis-à-vis* Europe was made in July 1957, the government spokesman was Mr Lemass, not Mr Aiken.

The opposition, too, was inclined to think of Europe in economic rather than in political terms.[51] Although this was understandable in view of the wide-reaching economic adjustments which entry into Europe would give rise to, even when the government applied for membership (with its implications of political change), there was little evident attempt to entrust the foreign minister with the overall political question. The political implications of membership of the EEC were decisive to the future course of Irish foreign policy; indeed, it could be argued that the application to join the EEC in 1961 represented the end of an independent foreign policy. But the political significance of entry was not discussed publicly until *after* the government had committed Ireland to membership, and even then it was not discussed effectively. Mr Aiken took the attitude that the whole thing was the Taoiseach's affair, while Mr Lemass dismissed it as a "hypothetical question". The original negotiations for EEC membership were to be carried out by the Minister for Industry and Commerce under the general supervision of the Taoiseach.[52] This exclusion of the foreign minister also occurred during the United Kingdom's

[51] Dáil Debates: 163, 629 ff.
[52] Dáil Debates: 192, 125.

negotiations for entry to the Community, though here it could be argued that the British foreign secretary could not possibly have taken on the extra burden of work. This argument was not so convincing in the case of Ireland, however, where by 1961 the Minister for External Affairs seemed to be not a foreign minister but rather a minister for United Nations affairs.

However, when negotiations with the EEC finally did take place, from July 1970 to January 1972, it was the foreign minister who was most closely concerned, and the restricted view of his duties which had prevailed throughout most of the nineteen sixties no longer applied. That it survived for so long was partly a consequence of the stalemate over the enlargement of the EEC, but may also be attributed to the personalities of the ministers concerned. The combination of Mr Aiken's apparent indifference towards Europe and (more importantly) Mr Lemass's enthusiasm for and commitment to the policy of entry accounted for this arbitrary and transitory division of responsibilities. The incident underlines the fact that the relationship between the head of the government and his foreign minister represents one of the more important variables in decision-making.[53]

This relationship is one where "the ideal combination is that of persons holding closely related views which permit full cooperation without the subservience of the minister".[54] One of the factors which prompted Mr de Valera to be his own foreign minister from 1932 to 1948 was the difficulty of attaining or even approaching such an ideal. He confessed in 1941 that he was

> at pains to see how the system of having a Secretary for Foreign Affairs different from the Head of the Government works in other States. It is, however, only done in this way: that in that particular Department of work, the Secretary for Foreign Affairs is really not as complete and as absolute a master of his Department as the Ministers in other Departments generally are . . . the ideal would be if the Head of the Government could be a sort of senior partner in every Department, but . . . that is not possible under modern conditions. In regard to External Affairs . . . the practice in other

[53] See Frankel, op. cit., p. 21.
[54] ibid, p. 22.

countries has been: that where there was a Secretary for Foreign Affairs, other than the Head of the Government, he was so constantly in touch with the Head of the Government in regard to various matters, that the Head of the Government was really the senior partner.[55]

Mr de Valera saw the relationship of the foreign minister and the head of the government as essentially one of unequal partnership where "closely related views" (originating with the head of the government) could be taken for granted. But, whereas he was correct in emphasising that the relationship was likely to be a close one, Mr de Valera did not (in 1941 at any rate) appreciate the variety of ways in which it could be modified, depending on the personalities of the two men and the issues which they faced.

Of the two periods of Mr de Valera's own experience of partnership with a separate Minister for External Affairs, the relationship between 1951 and 1954 might be interpreted as that described above, although the isolation of the state during this time prohibits extensive evidence of this. During the second de Valera administration, though, Mr Aiken was given much more scope in the United Nations, and although he may well have followed the broad approach long since established by Mr de Valera in the League of Nations, the specific policies were his to develop and defend.

In contrast, the relationship between Mr Costello and Mr MacBride was clearly not one between senior and junior partners, for in spite of Mr Costello's active interest in foreign policy, the exigencies of the coalition government, in which the two men represented different parties, made it difficult for him to assert the normal authority of a head of government. Therefore, although MacBride was not the ultimate policy-maker, he was in a position to exert more influence than might otherwise have been the case. The fact that the two men had been colleagues at the bar prior to their term in power and that Costello had been instrumental in bringing MacBride into parliamentary politics may well have facilitated the relationship.[56]

The foreign ministers in W. T. Cosgrave's government were in

[55] Dáil Debates: 84, 1916.
[56] Farrell, op. cit., p. 44.

a favourable position to advance their policies, but for a different reason — the comparative lack of interest in a foreign policy of the head of the government. Kevin O'Higgins, had he lived, might have been an unusually powerful foreign minister. Even his successor, Patrick McGilligan, in spite of other departmental obligations — or, perhaps, because of their relevance to external trade policy — was able to take a leading role in policy-making. The exception to this was Desmond FitzGerald, but his authority was restricted by his colleagues (especially O'Higgins) rather than by Cosgrave himself.

In these cases, the foreign minister was in a position to resist the intervention of his superior. However, the relationship between Mr Costello and Mr Liam Cosgrave in the 1954 to 1957 government was the more conventional one in which the foreign minister works together with a superior who is both conscious of his position as ultimate policy-maker and exerts his authority unequivocally. This particular combination approximates Frankel's ideal. The two men had worked closely together during Mr Costello's previous government, so presumably their views were "closely related", and there is no evidence to suggest that Liam Cosgrave felt in any way subservient. However, the two men did not remain in office long enough to enable us to assess the extent of their cooperation, nor did they have sufficient opportunity to formulate positive policies.

If we can characterise the relationship between Costello and Cosgrave as one in which a superior retained the final decisions on questions of policy, it is difficult to place the liaison between Seán Lemass and Frank Aiken in quite the same category. Mr Aiken's idea of the partnership involved considerable autonomy for the foreign minister, but, as we have seen, only in the rather restricted field of United Nations policy.

It was also notable that Seán Lemass, in common with previous premiers, regarded the question of partition as the preserve of the head of the government: this was illustrated quite clearly in the case of his meeting in January 1965 with the Prime Minister of Northern Ireland, Captain O'Neill, in which Mr Lemass's foreign minister had no particular role to play.[57] Earlier, the question of partition,

[57] ibid. p. 12.

along with other issues connected with Anglo-Irish relations, had prompted Mr de Valera to be his own Minister for External Affairs. But from 1969, the issue of partition became so complex that the Department of Foreign Affairs was once more involved in negotiations about the future of Northern Ireland; day-to-day diplomatic contact with the British government and with other governments inside and outside the UN became much more significant. This inevitably led Mr Aiken's successor, Dr Hillery, to a close working relationship with his head of government, Mr Lynch, particularly following the departure from the cabinet of so many senior ministers in 1970. Nevertheless, the principal spokesman on Northern Ireland was, and is, the Taoiseach.

On issues where the Taoiseach intervenes to the extent that Mr Lynch did over the Northern Ireland problem, it is he, rather than the foreign minister, who must bear the brunt of criticism, because the position of the government, and not merely that of an individual minister, is at stake. This is the situation which confronted Mr Lynch from the autumn of 1969 to the spring of 1970 when a group of ministers, notably the Minister for Agriculture, Mr Neil Blaney, opposed his policy on Northern Ireland. It is difficult to see how Mr Lynch could have avoided such close involvement with the North, for the irredentist claim to a united Ireland has always been regarded as more than an 'external affair'. It may be fair for any minister, whatever his departmental obligations, to promote his own interpretation of this national objective within the cabinet; but when differences persist and are aired outside this caucus, the head of the government cannot stand aloof.

★   ★   ★   ★

The locus of the formulation of foreign policy within the cabinet is not necessarily established in any particular ministerial office; it may be concentrated in the person of the head of the government, it may be diffused among the cabinet as a whole, or it may be found in individual ministers or among a group of ministers. In spite of his formal responsibility for foreign policy, the foreign minister does not necessarily play the predominant role, for, as we have seen, his room for manoeuvre is limited by a variety of considerations.

As foreign policy increases in complexity, the concept of a foreign minister with precisely defined overall responsibilities — an unreal notion at the best of times — demands continual reassessment, even in the comparatively simple structure of Irish government. In 1961, Mr Lemass hinted at the creation of a new portfolio to deal specifically with relations with EEC affairs,[58] though in the event the issues which had important diplomatic aspects were looked after by the Department of the Taoiseach, the 'economic' departments (especially the Department of Finance), and (coming a poor third) the Department of External Affairs. The disadvantage of this diffusion of responsibility was that it led to an arbitrary and misleading separation of 'economic' and 'political' viewpoints. It was criticised in 1966 by Dr Garret FitzGerald, then a senator. He argued that the foreign minister had an important political role as a coordinator of foreign policy, and that if the job was too much for one man, a parliamentary secretary should be appointed to be responsible for a specific area, such as the United Nations.[59]

When Dr FitzGerald became Minister for Foreign Affairs in 1973, there was speculation that a 'minister of state', a new post without full cabinet status, would be appointed to the Department of Foreign Affairs, perhaps with responsibility for European Community matters.[60] While such an appointment might share more evenly the increasing burden of administrative and parliamentary work, it must be remembered that in the diplomatic aspects of his work where prestige and rank tend to count for more than they do in domestic circumstances, a junior minister attached to a foreign ministry starts at a disadvantage. The foreign minister would still be obliged to intervene in the crucial stages of European negotiations and would probably remain the more important figure where the key decisions on policy were concerned. There is no reason to suppose that such a role is necessarily beyond the capabilities of one individual. His duties are perhaps more wide-ranging than those of most ministers, since he must concern himself with a microcosm of national policy, but this in itself should not prove an insuperable obstacle to an energetic politician.

[58] Dáil Debates: 192, 125.
[59] Seanad Debates: 61, 1866.
[60] *Irish Independent*, 19 March 1973.

A limiting factor is probably more likely to be the support that the minister receives from his department, rather than the nature of the task he is called upon to perform. It is, after all, unrealistic to suppose that the members of the cabinet are the only individuals who influence the formulation of policy, for they are themselves influenced by their permanent advisers in the civil service. The civil service 'specialists', in the foreign ministry and elsewhere, play an important role, and one too easily masked by the more obvious one played by their politically responsible superiors.

Chapter 4

FOREIGN POLICY
AND THE DEPARTMENT OF EXTERNAL AFFAIRS

*"A good deal of talk has gone on about the Ministry of
External Affairs being a luxury, and so on . . . you cannot get
away from it . . . this is now a Sovereign Nation, and it has to
do with other countries."*

Desmond FitzGerald, 1923
(Dáil Debates: 5, 1397).

THE government makes foreign policy and its members take
the responsibility for the success or failure of that policy:
such is the constitutional theory underlying the Irish system
of government. This theory, however, tends to overlook the role
played by the permanent bureaucracy which advises ministers and
executes their policies. In theory, civil servants are the impartial
servants of the minister and the government, but in reality the nature
of their task allows them opportunities to influence policy to a
considerable degree.

As far as foreign policy is concerned, these opportunities occur
mainly within the foreign ministry but, although the activities of
this particular government department are of primary importance,
it cannot be stressed too often that its control of matters of foreign
policy is by no means exclusive. A great many recommendations
which have important implications for the country's foreign policy,
originate in other government departments and are discussed not only
inside the cabinet but, perhaps to an even greater extent, within the civil
service. Nevertheless, despite this broad participation in policy-making,
the Department of External Affairs[1] has been able to bring to bear
its own point of view. As Ireland's first recognised Minister for External

---

[1] Since 1971, it has become the Department of Foreign Affairs. See above (chapter 3
note 1).

Affairs, Desmond FitzGerald, pointed out when defending the existence of his department in 1923, one of its principal functions was to act as a coordinating agent which, notwithstanding other departments' special interests, would present the "national or political view".[2]

Thus, while other departments contribute to the formulation of policy by presenting information, ideas and proposals, the members of the Department of Foreign Affairs, as professional experts in this field, must relate these contributions both to the realities of inter-state politics and to domestic political demands. Under certain political conditions, their contribution to the policy-making process is very important. When a new minister assumes office, he will have to accept his department's advice at its face value, for it will be some time before he can gain the experience to provide a more independent assessment of policy. This is particularly true when the minister has had comparatively little acquaintance with foreign affairs before his appointment, a situation that has been the rule rather than the exception in Ireland. Apart from Desmond FitzGerald, who was a pioneer like his advisers, few Irish ministers have been sufficiently experienced in the field of foreign policy to readily disregard the advice of the top officials in their department.

Even a minister who is clear about what he wants and the ways in which he can get it, must depend on his department for the information with which to justify his case both to his colleagues in the cabinet and, through parliament, to the country as a whole. Furthermore, he depends on his department to execute his policies efficiently; its staff are responsible for explaining policy to foreign governments and international institutions, and their interpretation of detailed aspects of a policy can go far to ensure its success or failure. Due to the decentralisation of much of the department's staff in the overseas missions, it is difficult for the Minister for Foreign Affairs—or, indeed, for the permanent officials at home—to be sure of the ways in which policies are being executed; unlike those ministers in charge of domestic business, he cannot easily establish his own informal sources of information as a yardstick against which to measure the performance of his officials.

[2] See above, p. 91.

The permanent officials' expertise in foreign policy is, therefore, authoritative; they are the eyes and ears of the government in matters which often seem outside the immediate scope of government and which make little immediate impact on public opinion. In Ireland, the lack of parliamentary interest in foreign policy[3] may serve to further emphasise the independence of these officials. However, this independence must be seen in the light of their relationships with not only the minister, whom they might be tempted to tell what he wants to hear, but with each other. When there is a divergence of opinion amongst the officials, the minister is called upon to act as the final arbiter in reaching a decision. The minister may be forced to choose, for example, between two opposing policy options put forward by the officials in his economic and political sections. This is perhaps the normal situation in a healthy department, and it is in the minister's own interests to stimulate a wide range of opinion among senior officials rather than be faced with a general consensus formed at a lower level. One of the advantages of a comparatively small department, such as the Department of Foreign Affairs, is that it is easier to formulate policy in this way because of the shorter and less formal lines of communication.

The dialogue between officials and the minister does not, of course, take place in public, and consequently there is a danger that, "owing to the highly technical nature of their work, foreign ministry officials tend to become isolated from the atmosphere of domestic politics to the point of becoming annoyed when the latter intrude".[4] Officials see the public as indifferent, uninformed, and a threat to the conduct of delicate negotiations, while the public tend to see the foreign ministry as an ivory tower in a diplomatic dreamworld. This mutual resentment should be countered by a willingness on the part of the minister to explain his officials' work to the public, to show that they are not only—or even predominantly—foreign policy experts, but have other functions to perform as well, such as coordinating the external activities of other government departments and promoting the commercial, cultural and political interests of their country.

This multiplicity of duties is common to most foreign ministries

[3] See below, chapters 7 and 8.
[4] Frankel, op. cit., p. 31.

and it is important to distinguish between the making of foreign policy and the maintenance of foreign relations. The former activity implies an element of long-term planning, of identifying objectives and deciding what initiatives the government might take in the future and what adjustments might be made to present policies; the latter is concerned with maintaining political, economic and cultural links with other states. This is not so much a matter of planning ahead but of routine administration and friendly diplomacy, encouraging trade between one's state and those with which it does business, accounting for the activities of one's nationals abroad, protecting their interests, and so on. Although the distinction between such day-to-day administration and the more abstract planning of general policy is not always clear, it is clear enough to be reflected to a certain extent in the specialisation of the larger foreign ministries— a specialisation which may well bring in its train considerable difficulties in coordinating the many aspects of the department's work.

The limited staffs and budgets of smaller foreign ministries do not allow such a high degree of specialisation, and so the dangers of over-specialisation are usually avoided. But such ministries also lack many of the advantages which specialisation may bring, especially that which allows the official concerned with policy-making to concentrate on policy and so become an expert in his field. In the case of the Irish Department of Foreign Affairs, this consideration is of some importance, for if it is true that the policies formulated by its officials are not subjected to intensive and continuous parliamentary scrutiny, it is only fair to point out that comparatively few officials within the department will have the time to devote to policy rather than to administration. On the whole, these officials are 'jacks-of-all-trades' who may, in the course of their careers, find little or no opportunity to act exclusively as policy-planners. More often than not, such work has to be fitted into a demanding administrative routine.

The difficulties facing diplomatic officials might best be illustrated by the case of an ambassador in one of the smaller overseas missions, who, with the help of one or two subordinates and a small secretarial staff, must cope with a wide range of diplomatic, consular, commercial and cultural work: these duties may leave him with relatively little time or energy to devote to his function of policy adviser.

Admittedly, press coverage of international politics has often made political reporting by officials seem superfluous, although for a small state whose interests will probably not be reflected in the reporting or editing of the independent press agencies, it is still important. However, the Irish official, fully occupied with the varied routine of his office, may be tempted to neglect political reporting altogether and, even if he does not overlook it, may be unable to find the time to develop his own sources of information in order to make it effective. This problem is aggravated by the very thin diplomatic representation which a small state can provide, for embassies may be the listening posts for whole continents rather than for one state.

The extremely varied nature of the work undertaken by the Department of Foreign Affairs not only makes it difficult for the official to act as a policy adviser, but has also made the part played by the department in the formulation of foreign policy somewhat ambiguous in the eyes of critics outside the department. Although they are varied, the services which the department provides are generally of a somewhat intangible nature, and the frequency with which ministers for external affairs have felt it necessary to point this out is an indication of the fact that it is rarely appreciated. In 1956, for example, Mr MacBride, no longer minister, but a supporter of the government, said ". . . it is always easy to criticise the expenditure of a department, such as the Department of External Affairs, on a popular basis because, as far as the public are concerned, they see little or no tangible results from the work of such a service . . .".[5] During the same debate, another former Minister for External Affairs, Mr de Valera, pursued the same theme: ". . . no other Estimate presents such an easy target for uninformed or for perverse criticism as this does . . . while the expenditure was clear and definite, the advantages were far from being so definite . . .".[6] Earlier, in 1951, while still in opposition, Mr de Valera had pointed out that "it is easy enough for the Department of Industry and Commerce to produce statistics here in proof of what is being done. It is not so easy for the Department of External Affairs to do that . . . it is peculiarly vulnerable to criticism here . . .".[7]

[5] Dáil Debates: 159, 590–1.
[6] Dáil Debates: 159, 432.
[7] Dáil Debates: 124, 1412–1413.

Nor has "uninformed" and "perverse" criticism been lacking in a Dáil which has largely been indifferent to foreign affairs.[8] Indeed, there has been a noticeable tendency to justify or condemn the expenditure of the Department of External Affairs on the basis of the only one of its activities which is readily quantifiable — the promotion of trade. As John A. Costello pointed out in 1934, the department "was regarded in the House, by Deputies of various Parties, either with complete unconcern or merely as being something in the nature of a trade concern which ought to send out commercial travellers all over the world . . .".[9] While the promotion of trade is one of the most important functions of the department and one that should probably be expanded, it is not the only function, nor has the Department of External Affairs exclusive responsibility for it. Nevertheless, it remains a convenient scapegoat for the failure of other government departments and for the inadequate performance of individual exporters, for trade figures are the one piece of concrete evidence available to the public.

As a result of this narrow and somewhat distorted view of the functions of the Department of External Affairs, its development as a foreign ministry has been hesitant. It has been difficult at times for ministers to justify increases in expenditure both to the Dáil and to the Department of Finance, which with meagre resources at its disposal not surprisingly has looked for a clear justification of expenditure and, again not surprisingly, has not always found it. Consequently, the department has generally been under-staffed both at home and abroad, and specialisation has been hindered. Thus, while the lack of strong parliamentary control might appear to give the permanent official considerable scope to become an influential government adviser on foreign policy, the complex nature of his job and the restrictions under which he works will tend to make him a part-time adviser, subject to many distractions. The calibre of the official must be high for well-informed and carefully analysed advice to be obtained under such conditions.

The part played by the civil servant in making foreign policy depends, therefore, on the limitations to which he is subject in the

[8] See below, chapters 7 and 8.
[9] Dáil Debates: 53, 259.

organisational framework within which he operates and on his personal abilities and the opportunities which he has to develop them. These factors are discussed in this and the following chapter; firstly by examining the development and organisation of the Department of Foreign Affairs and its relationship with other government institutions, and secondly by examining the background, recruitment, training and work of the personnel of the department. Unfortunately, unlike their British counterparts, the permanent heads and ambassadors of the Irish Department of External Affairs have so far been reluctant to divulge their experiences. Nevertheless, it is possible to describe the work of the civil servant in the department by taking into account its institutional structure and the careers of certain individuals.

The development of the Irish Department of External Affairs was beset by difficulties from its inception. Its origins substantiate Mr J. A. Costello's contention that it was "the Cinderella of Government Departments".[10] Unlike nearly all other government departments, the Department of External Affairs was a completely new institution, arising from the formal creation of the Irish state, and it did not enjoy the administrative tradition of the former British administrative offices in Ireland, which had been transformed with comparatively little difficulty into full government departments. To the greater part of the civil service, which consisted of officials who had agreed to transfer their allegiance and remain in their posts, External Affairs appeared decidedly amateurish, if not dangerously political.

With no real experience of diplomacy, the new department could hardly fail to look unprofessional. The only precedent for its organisation and procedures was the perfunctory and unrecognised foreign ministry of the first and second Dáil. This had consisted mainly of members of the Dáil who endeavoured to promote the cause of Irish independence wherever they could, often in somewhat unorthodox ways. Their methods are described in Mr Gavan Duffy's report from Spain in 1921 that "Irish nuns in Madrid who are very influential in high circles are all with us . . . if we made ourselves strong in Madrid, the result would be of the utmost importance in Rome,

[10] Dáil Debates: 53, 259.

where Spain stands very high indeed".[11] By August 1921 there were 'official' missions abroad in France, Italy, the USA, the United Kingdom, Germany, the USSR, the Argentine and Chile;[12] these were run by small, often part-time, office staffs which were recruited from a variety of sources. In June 1919, for example, the Paris office consisted of "Victor Collins, who was Paris Correspondent of an American paper", Mrs Gavan Duffy (whose services were unpaid), a Mr Caulfield whose payments were "very small", and Madame Vivanti ". . . an Italian lady well known as a leading novelist in Italy . . . notified by an Italian lawyer to leave Italy for the good of her health . . .".[13] The head of this mission, Seán T. O'Kelly, failed to achieve recognition for Ireland at the Paris Peace Conference.

In more ordinary circumstances, the diplomatic arm of the first and second Dáil might have proved a satisfactory foundation on which to build a foreign service. But since a high proportion of the people involved in offices abroad were politically active, the position of overseas missions was seriously affected when the civil war broke out in 1922. There were some wholesale desertions from the Free State government service: on 30 January 1923, for example, the Minister for External Affairs, Desmond FitzGerald, announced that "the former Irish Trade Agent in Paris has now passed into the care of the Irregulars. This is due solely to treachery on the part of the late Trade Agent".[14] Moreover, the missions' geographical distance from the jurisdiction of the Irish government made them vulnerable to the activities of anti-government forces, even when the loyalty of the officials was unquestioned. In this way, the consular office in New York was occupied by force and only regained with the aid of the New York police.[15]

The headquarters of the ministry was also uncomfortably associated with the political dissension of the civil war period. This was largely because it incorporated the former publicity department of the Dáil governments whose main function during the civil war was to promote the case for the acceptance of the Treaty of 1921; inevitably the

---

[11] Official Report of Dáil Éireann 16–26 August 1921, 28 February–8 June 1922, p. 19.
[12] ibid., p. 16.
[13] First Dáil Report, p. 124.
[14] Dáil Debates: 2, 1079–80.
[15] See R. Briscoe, *For the Life of Me* (Longmans, London, 1959) pp. 194–203.

department was seen as an arm of the Treaty party, Cumann na nGaedheal, rather than of the government. This state of affairs provoked the opposition of Captain Redmond, who in 1923 took objection to the department on ". . . strictly constitutional grounds . . . no Government should have at its back a publicly paid Department, which they can use, and which . . . has been used in this case for nothing but purely party propaganda".[16]

The origin of the Department of External Affairs was, therefore, hardly auspicious and the poor impression it made on large sections of public opinion is reflected in the debate on the Ministers and Secretaries Bill of 1923 which formally established the ministry.[17] Mr Darrell Figgis claimed that there was "really no need for this Ministry . . . not only is it unnecessary now, but . . . it will always be unnecessary, because the people of this country and the Dáil, will naturally look . . . to the President of the Executive Council".[18] Mr D. J. Gorey maintained that "to the mind of the average man in the country, the Ministry of Foreign Affairs or External Affairs, or whatever you like to call it, will be known as a Ministry for finding a job for somebody".[19] At the committee stage of the debate, Mr Heffernan introduced an amendment ". . . aiming at eliminating the ministry of the least importance in the affairs of this country";[20] this was, he said, in the interests of efficiency and economy.[21] Mr Heffernan was, perhaps, typical of the large number of Irish parliamentary representatives who regard foreign policy as an irrelevant extravagance.[22] For him, any effort spent on foreign affairs was an impediment to the good conduct of internal policy and his words exemplified a puritanical horror at the prospect of the state exceeding its humble and passive place in international politics: "like the frog in the fable, we are apt to blow ourselves out and regard our own opinion as of such importance in the affairs of the world that we may be in danger of bursting just with the sense of our own importance

---

[16] Dáil Debates: 5, 951–2.
[17] See especially Dáil Debates: 5, 931 ff., and 1392–1414.
[18] Dáil Debates: 5, 931–2.
[19] Dáil Debates: 5, 940.
[20] Dáil Debates: 5, 1412.
[21] Dáil Debates: 5, 1393.
[22] See below, chapter 8.

as the frog did".[23] Mr Heffernan's amendment was defeated, but against the government's forty-nine votes he had raised the significantly large number of twenty-seven. The Department of External Affairs was born, but it was not a popular addition to the central administration.

It is not surprising that, after this difficult start, the growth of the department was slow. This tardy development is reflected in the expenditure on foreign affairs and the extent of diplomatic representation overseas. Expenditure on the diplomatic service and that incurred by membership of the League of Nations rose very gradually from around £40,000 per year during the early nineteen twenties to little over £90,000 per year in 1938. Expressed as a proportion of total government expenditure, it can be seen in Figure 1 that External Affairs' share of the government's resources (including expenditure on the League of Nations vote) rose to a peak in 1932 and subsequently levelled off until 1948. One pound in every three hundred for external representation hardly represents an extravagance.

During the first years, overseas missions were kept to a minimum. The essential High Commissioner's office in London was established in January 1923, but the fact that, during the next fifteen years, only five other diplomatic offices were opened and that these were legations rather than full embassies, reflects the priorities of the foreign policy of the period. In October 1924, the establishment of the legation in Washington marked not only a gesture of independence for Ireland (no other Commonwealth state apart from the United Kingdom was independently represented in the USA), but also emphasised the close links between Ireland and the important Irish-American community in the USA. This relationship was further extended by the establishment of four consular offices in the USA (New York, Boston, Chicago and San Francisco) between 1930 and 1933, which were necessary in order to deal with trade and with legacies due to Irish nationals. Apart from this foothold in the USA, which was essentially an administrative network, the only other important legations were in the Holy See, France, Germany (1929), Belgium (1932) and Spain (1935). The principal motive for establishing relations with these states, except the Holy See, was to encourage trade, and

[23] Dáil Debates: 5, 1412–13.

it is no coincidence that the most important legations, in France and in Germany, were instituted under the aegis of Mr McGilligan who was, in 1929, both Minister for External Affairs and Minister for Industry and Commerce.

However, up to 1938, the political activities of the Department of External Affairs outside the state were pursued mainly in the League of Nations and by delegations to Imperial Conferences. The department was also instrumental in framing the constitutional legislation leading up to external association with Britain in 1936. By the time external association was consolidated in the Anglo-Irish agreements of 1938, which ended the economic war and settled the question of the ports, collective security through the League of Nations had manifestly failed. Consequently, it was clear that in order to speak independently, the Irish government should extend its diplomatic scope. This Mr de Valera did, and during his remaining ten years of office seven new missions were set up—in Italy, Canada, Switzerland, Portugal, Sweden, Australia and the Argentine. This did not demand a significantly increased share of the government's financial resources, as can be seen in Figure 1.

The new missions were established for a variety of reasons. The legations in Italy, Switzerland, Portugal and Sweden assisted the establishment of friendly relations with most of the remaining west European states; Canada had been an important partner in the evolution of the Commonwealth and was also a potential market for exports; Australia had a large expatriate Irish population; and the Argentine represented a foothold on the South American continent. Some of these missions, particularly those in the neutral states, were useful in protecting Irish interests throughout World War II, while Ireland's diplomatic relations with the principal belligerents in the war were the lifeline without which Mr de Valera would have been unable to explain or defend his policy of neutrality. The missions were modest establishments but, until the war had proved their worth, they were often criticised in the Dáil.

It is worth noting that, in reply to this criticism, Mr de Valera insisted that representation was not to be justified by any tangible benefits, such as trade, which might accrue. He said in 1937:

We have never taken up the attitude that trade is a fundamental thing in regard to the appointment of diplomatic representatives. In a variety of ways, it is important for a State like ours, one claiming recognition as a State amongst the States of the world, that we should be represented in all the principal States of the world.[24]

Although some of his critics were shortsighted in making trade the sole criterion for diplomatic representation, it can be argued that Mr de Valera was equally shortsighted in dismissing this important function in such an offhand manner, for the lack of permanent trade offices abroad was to prove to be yet one more reason for the failure of the highly protected Irish economy to adapt itself to the freer trade conditions of the post World War II era. Mr de Valera's insistence on a purely 'diplomatic' Department of External Affairs, though largely justified in the nineteen thirties, did perhaps establish a tradition within the department which made it reluctant to seize the opportunities offered by mid-twentieth century diplomacy, in which it is often difficult to distinguish between the pursuit of political and economic objectives.

By 1948, the basis of Ireland's diplomatic network had been established, and from then until 1973 only five completely new offices were opened (see Table 2).† These were the missions to the Netherlands (1950), Nigeria (1960), Denmark (1962), India (1964) and the EEC (1966). Although other states have diplomatic relations with Ireland, no change in the basic organisational framework is necessary since the Irish representatives are non-resident. Representation in the United Nations, though more complex since there are permanent missions in both New York and Geneva, replaced that in the League of Nations, and establishment of relations with the Federal Republic of Germany in 1951 replaced the mission that maintained diplomatic representation with the whole of Germany up to 1945. A consulate was established in Hamburg in 1962.

The Department of External Affairs expanded rapidly in the period after 1948 and flesh and muscle was put on the skeletal organisation both at home and abroad. The constitutional issue (with the exception

[24] Dáil Debates: 69, 2260–1.
† See p. 307.

of partition) had been resolved and, with the machinery of Common-wealth consultation being no longer available (not that it had been used to any great extent since 1932), the geographical horizons of Irish diplomatic activity broadened. As Figure 1 shows, the depart-ment's share of total government expenditure increased at a significantly higher rate, particularly between 1948 and 1950. Indeed in 1950, expenditure on the Department of External Affairs itself (i.e. not including expenditure incurred by membership of international organisations) reached a proportion of total government expenditure which had never previously been achieved. The increase was due to the new functions undertaken by the department and to the fact that Mr MacBride was extending its traditional duties. The most immediate new function which had to be taken into account was the administration of Ireland's part in the European recovery programme; this involved an extension of the Washington office and the setting up of a new section within the Dublin headquarters. This reorganisation at home salso included the establishment of a separate trade section and the addition of a second assistant secretary in 1948, and in the following year, provision was made for a third assistant secretary, two new sections dealing with political affairs and information, and the establish-ment of an advisory committee on cultural relations. Mr MacBride, committed to his anti-partition propaganda campaign, emphasised the need for press attachés and information officers overseas.[25]

Naturally, the Department of External Affairs had to increase its staff to cope with these new duties. During the debate on the External Affairs Estimate in 1949, Mr MacBride claimed that when he took up office the previous year,

> some of our most important missions abroad were so understaffed that their members were unable to get away from their desks to maintain essential contacts with the outside world. The head-quarters of the Department itself was in the same position. The staff were overwhelmed with the mass of work arising in the ordinary course of departmental duties, and there was little or no provision for the steady systematic work which must be done if our major objectives in the political field are to be achieved.[26]

[25] See Dáil Debates: 117, 857–8.
[26] Dáil Debates: 117, 857–8.

8

Since Seán MacBride's tenure of office, the total staff of the department, both at home and abroad, has increased from about 200[27] to well over 400 in 1973, but the scope of its work has more than doubled in the same period. In 1956, the UN delegation was established and Ireland's application to join the EEC had by 1972 placed very considerable demands on the mission to Brussels and on the central organisation. Expenditure on both external affairs and international cooperation rose from just under £200,000 in 1948 to over £1,280,000 in 1968; much of this rise was due to monetary fluctuations, but in relative terms, as Figure 1 shows, it did not keep pace with total government expenditure but rather constituted a stable percentage of it. The department's own share of government resources dropped somewhat between the mid-nineteen fifties and the late nineteen sixties. Nevertheless, the level of expenditure on external affairs since 1948 has, on the whole, been significantly higher than during the first twenty-six years of the state's existence, and this probably indicates the increased opportunities for the establishment of diplomatic, economic and social relations with other countries, which have arisen since the end of World War II. It is noticeable, too, that external affairs received priority under the government of Mr W. T. Cosgrave (from 1922 to 1932) and the first coalition government of Mr J. A. Costello. It may be no coincidence that one man, Patrick McGilligan, was closely concerned with external affairs in both these governments, as Minister for External Affairs (and for Industry and Commerce) in the first, and as Minister for Finance in the second. However, in addition to the particular attention to external affairs paid by these governments, other factors were probably more important. There was an obvious need for expansion during the nineteen twenties because the department was being built up from scratch, while, in the later period, the revival of international cooperation following World War II provided the incentive.

The present Department of Foreign Affairs is based, therefore, on a system of diplomatic representation which was gradually developed before 1948 and on a central organisation which acquired

[27] The earlier figure is from an unpublished lecture by L. T. McCauley, an assistant secretary in the Department of External Affairs, to the Civics Institute of Ireland on 15 March 1949. Both figures include 'service personnel', such as clerical staff and messengers.

many of its most salient characteristics since then. The department underwent further expansion as participation in the European Community, and the continuing Northern Ireland crisis made new demands. Between 1967 and 1972, the number of officials at the department's headquarters increased by some 50 per cent. and the number of officials overseas also rose, though to a lesser degree.[28] There is no reason to suppose that this expansion is yet complete, for, until experience is gained of the demands of EEC membership, it is difficult to forecast the extent of the department's growth. What is clear, however, is that the organisation of the department, especially at home, has reached a degree of complexity and specialisation which distinguishes it from the nineteenth-century simplicity which characterised its first twenty-five years.

We shall now examine the institutional environment in which the civil servant plays his two main roles of foreign relations administrator and foreign policy adviser in the present Department of Foreign Affairs. As we have seen, the organisation of the department has been responsive to changing circumstances, and in recent years has had to be particularly adaptable to special contingencies. What follows is a picture of the department at a particular time—the summer of 1972, when Ireland was on the threshold of the European Community —although a comparison with the organisation at an earlier date indicates those administrative units which are comparatively settled and those which are the obvious growth areas.[29]

The headquarters in Dublin—located mainly in Iveagh House (though recently it has been found necessary to expand into neighbouring buildings)—includes seventy-four officials of foreign service or equivalent rank, backed up by 165 service staff.[30] Like many small

[28] See Figures 2 and 3, pp. 310 and 311.
[29] See Figure 2, relating to 1972, and Figure 3, relating to 1967.
[30] See Figure 2. The nomenclature of ranks within the administrative grade follows diplomatic practice and not that employed in the domestic civil service. The main corresponding ranks are: Head of department, Secretary= Secretary, ambassador (Grade 1). Assistant secretary=assistant secretary (at home), ambassador (Grade II). Principal officer—counsellor. Assistant principal=1st secretary. Administrative officer=3rd secretary (and in some missions overseas, secretary or 2nd secretary). Many of the variations between diplomatic titles (e.g. 2nd secretary and 3rd secretary) reflect subtle distinctions in diplomatic status in specific conditions, rather than the career status of the men who are appointed to such posts.

foreign ministries, it is organised on a functional rather than a geo-graphical basis, and the sections are grouped together in four principal divisions, each of which is supervised by an assistant secretary. One of the largest of these is the administration division, which might be described as a 'service group', maintaining the routine organisation of the department both at home and abroad. The important sections in this division are those which supervise the financial aspects of the department's work and oversee its personnel. Its duties include the preparation of accounts for the Comptroller and Auditor General and the supervision of the finances of overseas missions, a task made more complex by the different currencies and rates of exchange and the need to adjust overseas allowances and expenditure accordingly.

The 'establishment' or personnel work is also more complex than that of the average domestic government department. In the first place, over half the staff is abroad and can only be supervised by a cumbersome system of regular reports submitted by the heads of overseas missions. Also, owing to the variety of duties which they will eventually have to undertake in the small overseas offices, officials are moved frequently from section to section in order to gain the widest possible experience. As in most diplomatic services, mobility between overseas offices and headquarters is considered desirable in order to prevent officials from 'going native' overseas; they must be kept in touch with their national environment and this necessitates regular service at home. Thus the work of the personnel and accounts sections, although of a routine administrative nature, is considerable and important; in order to maintain continuity, it is carried out by home-based officials who have normal civil service status.

Another important unit in the administration division is the consular section. Although there is no distinction between the consular and diplomatic status of the department's personnel, the routine consular duties of protecting the specific rights and interests of Irish citizens (as opposed to the diplomatic responsibility of protecting the general interests of the Irish state) are administered by a separate section which deals with the work of the consulates, honorary consulates and also with the consular work of the diplomatic missions. The routine administration, which constitutes the bulk of this section's work, is carried out by a staff of three foreign service officials and one higher executive officer; it comprises advice to Irish nationals, financial aid or repatriation in cases of hardship, supporting legitimate claims to property overseas, and issuing passports. The consular section administers the Passport Office in Dublin to look after the latter task. One important function which in the nineteenth century was generally regarded as consular—the promotion of trade—is now, of course, sufficiently important to be dealt with by a separate section.

Two further sections fall within the broad category of the administration division. One is the protocol section, which is responsible for maintaining the correct diplomatic procedures in all formal communications with other governments, organising the considerable number of formal diplomatic occasions such as state receptions, and entertaining distinguished foreign visitors. This is a small section, consisting of two foreign service officials of lower ranks; however, it comes under the direct control of the chief of protocol who holds the rank of counsellor. The legal section, which has expanded in recent years, consists of the legal adviser himself, three assistants holding the rank of first secretary, and one third secretary. This section advises not only all other sections of the Department of Foreign Affairs on their legal problems, but may also be called in to help other government departments and the legal system of the state, particularly where conflicts between national laws or the interpretation of international law are concerned. Since Ireland joined the EEC, this section has assumed greater significance than at any time since most of the constitutional ambiguities of Anglo-Irish relations were in effect resolved in 1948.

The largest single division in the department is the economic division which contains a particularly large number of more senior staff members. This division deals with conventional economic foreign policy, including participation in international economic organisations such as OECD and GATT, and is concerned with the important question of foreign trade policy. Each of these aspects of economic activity is administered by a small separate section. At first sight, the weakness of the foreign trade section is surprising. In 1969, the Devlin Report commented on "the urgent need to strengthen the economic role" of the department, and was above all concerned that a "total trade policy" be formulated at home and executed by heads of the overseas missions. It recommended that the responsibility for trade which was shared by the Departments of Finance, Agriculture, Industry and Commerce, and External Affairs ought to be coordinated by and, indeed, concentrated in the Department of External Affairs.[31]

These recommendations have not yet been implemented and a former Secretary of the Department of External Affairs, Dr F. H. Boland, questioned the assumptions on which they are based.[32] He maintained that the existing system of interdepartmental coordination, though loosely structured, worked well and that the necessary contacts with industrial, agricultural and business interests were best made through their respective departments. It is certainly difficult to see these departments readily abandoning their former responsibility for foreign trade, and as Dr Boland feared, the end result could well be an unnecessary accretion of competing centres, all attempting to coordinate trade policy. Nevertheless, with EEC membership leading to an increasingly diversified trade policy, there may well be a need for some coordinating centre, not merely for trade policy as such, but for all external aspects of economic policy.

Perhaps the other part of the economic division, which is concerned with the European Community, will become such a coordinating centre. This is clearly the more important part of the division, and although it was a small section up to the winter of 1969/1970, it has now become the fastest developing unit in the whole department. With no less than seventeen officials and a translator directly employed on EEC matters, a further division into more specialised sections is probable.[33] The European Community unit of the economic division is also unique in being the direct responsibility of a chargé d'affaires, who is equivalent in rank to a deputy assistant secretary. The unit is likely to play an important role as a centre coordinating all matters pertaining to the EEC for all government departments, and while it

[31] It was also recommended that the Irish Export Board, Córas Tráchtála, should report to the Department of External Affairs rather than to the Department of Industry and Commerce. *Report of Public Service Organisation Review Group*, 1966–1969. Prl, 792 (Stationery Office, Dublin, 1969), Paras. 24.31 to 24.42, pp. 259–260.

[32] See F. H. Boland 'Diplomatic Devlin' in *Public Affairs/Léargas* vol. 2, no. 7., March 1970, pp. 4–7.

[33] In the summer of 1972, it seemed likely that there would be three separate sections, though the precise functions of each was not yet determined.

will not be the immediate source of policy proposals (which will come from the individual departments), in so far as it must reconcile inconsistencies and attempt to establish priorities, it could well become an influential part of the policy-making process.

It is not yet clear, however, how far the European Community unit of the economic division will be concerned with the political aspects of European politics, for, in 1972, questions on European political affairs were dealt with by a separate division, the political and cultural division, which has its own assistant secretary. This division consists firstly of the general political and United Nations section, a small group of four officials, who are responsible for keeping in touch with all international political developments which could affect Irish interests and for preparing reports on which specific policy decisions will be based. As the section's title suggests, much of this work is preparing briefs on policies to be presented at the United Nations, and the counsellor in charge (and perhaps other members of his staff) often reinforce Ireland's permanent delegation to meetings of the UN General Assembly in New York.

Another section of similar size deals with other international organisations, except those with a specifically economic or cultural bias. This section is concerned with technical bodies such as the World Health Organization, the Food and Agriculture Organization, and with the regional organisations of which Ireland is a member, especially the Council of Europe. As the section acts as a channel through which information from these organisations can pass to other government departments, much of its work is routine, but some of its duties are closely related to policy formulation, especially on European affairs; the counsellor in charge of the section is also the non-resident permanent representative to the Council of Europe.

Grouped with these political sections is a small unit dealing with cultural affairs and international exchange scholarships. It is supplemented by the voluntary Advisory Committee on Cultural Relations which is divided into three subcommittees on the visual, musical, and literary arts and which meets about once a month. It sponsors documentary films, publications on various aspects of Irish culture and Irish contributions to international cultural festivals. Apart from helping to promote the arts in Ireland, this sponsorship contributes in the long run to the promotion abroad of a sympathetic image of Ireland. The Advisory Committee on Cultural Relations is the only such body under the responsibility of the Minister for External Affairs and, while he can reject its proposals, he cannot spend any of the funds allocated to cultural relations without its approval.

The fourth division in the Department of Foreign Affairs also has the composite characteristics of the third. It includes the Anglo-Irish political section with a staff of eight officials. The section was established as a direct consequence of the crisis in Northern Ireland in 1969 and has increased in size and importance since that time. Because of the importance of maintaining close diplomatic contact with the British government and with non-governmental groups in Northern Ireland, this section has played an important role, even if the irredentist issue is (as it always has been) primarily a matter for the Taoiseach rather than for the foreign minister.

The other section in the fourth division is the information section. This was previously grouped with the cultural section, for they both in their different ways were responsible for propagating an attractive national image abroad. Originally, before it became independent, the information section performed a service by supplying the overseas offices with up-to-date information about Irish affairs which enabled the overseas official both to keep in touch with national events and to interpret more effectively the whole range of government policy abroad. This service is still an important function of the information section, but the section was expanded and has become a public relations office for the state. It is now responsible for providing material for foreign newspapers and visiting journalists, an important function in a state which does not usually attract world-wide interest. Although the information section, with two first secretaries and two third secretaries, has by no means the smallest staff in the department, a case can be made for increasing the size of its personnel and financial resources. In an age of lively competitive journalism, the coverage and impact of the regular bulletin it produces is disappointing, particularly abroad, where it is not supplemented by a comprehensive network of full-time press attachés. This deficiency was particularly noticeable in the summer and autumn of 1969 when a hasty campaign was set up to inform the world of the Irish government's view of the

Northern Ireland situation; the use of public relations officers from outside the department resulted in more confusion than clarification. This tendency to adopt an *ad hoc* approach to the propagation of information was further exemplified by the employment by the government of the private public relations agency, Markpress, in 1971. Consequently, the projection of Irish policy was the responsibility of no less than three agencies, for the Government Information Bureau, attached to the Department of the Taoiseach, also briefs journalists and arranges conferences on behalf of government departments. In the long term, such a triplication of effort made for an unduly expensive as well as for a potentially inconsistent interpretation of policy.

The organisation of the overseas missions is noticeably less specialised than that of the headquarters in Dublin. The geographical representation achieved by 1972 can be seen in Figure 4.† The USA ,Canada and all the west European states have Irish diplomatic representation, and there are further diplomatic outposts in the Argentine, Nigeria, India and Australia.

Most of these missions can be justified simply because they facilitate relations between Ireland and the countries in which they are situated, though these relations, and particularly the amount of trade that might accrue from them, are often not fully exploited, as in the cases of Bonn and Canberra where the diplomatic and commercial centres are independent. Australia, Nigeria, the Argentine and India are in effect 'continental' rather than single-state outposts. The Argentinian and Indian missions appear to have been established because of historical associations, rather than for reasons of commercial development. By the early nineteen seventies it became clear that two important omissions in Ireland's diplomatic network were permanent representation in Japan and communist Europe.[34]

† See p. 312.
[34] In July 1973, ambassadors were designated for resident posts in Japan and Luxembourg (which had previously been the only member of the European Community without a permanent mission). Mr Liam Cosgrave's government also agreed in principle to establish an embassy in the USSR, although this decision had not been finalised by July 1973. Looking further ahead, the Minister for Foreign Affairs, Dr Garret FitzGerald, envisaged an expansion of the Irish diplomatic network in east Europe, Africa, Latin America, and China. (See Dáil Debates: 265, 745-6; 748; 752.)

The details of the staff of these missions (Table 2) make it clear that this diplomatic system has been developed on slender resources; as a consequence, there has been little scope in overseas legations for the specialisation of duties found in the department's head-quarters in Ireland. There is an almost even balance between the number of staff at headquarters—seventy-four officials—and overseas, where there are eighty-five full-time staff. This contrasts with the practice of many countries, where a proportion of two officials abroad to one at home is usual; problems frequently arise when the numbers abroad exceed this ratio.[35] If problems do arise in the Irish diplomatic service, they do not occur so much because of bottlenecks at headquarters, but because of the paucity of officials abroad.

Of the twenty-one diplomatic establishments,[36] only four have a foreign service staff of five or more people, and not all of these can boast of a staff extensive enough to allow them a measure of specialisation. London—traditionally the largest overseas mission—has room for full-time trade officers, who may be on secondment from other departments. The British mission also includes a local advisory officer whose duty it is to coordinate the welfare work of voluntary charitable organisations which help the large Irish population in England. One of the other big offices, in Washington, includes an official with full-time responsibility for trade, and many of this mission's routine duties are undertaken by the four consular offices in New York, Boston, Chicago and San Francisco, which between them employ nine foreign service staff.

But it is the Brussels office accredited to the European Community which has shown the most spectacular development since negotiations to join the EEC opened in 1970, and it has now overtaken the London office as the largest single overseas mission. It not only has a large overall staff but, even before membership officially started in January

---

[35] See *Diplomatic Service: Formation and Operation* (Longman, London, 1971) pp. 91–92, and the table on p. 131. This is an anonymous report of a seminar of representatives of Commonwealth diplomatic services which met in Singapore in 1970. Among those countries represented, New Zealand is the country whose foreign service most closely approximates that of Ireland in its size and the balance between the number of its personnel at home and abroad.

[36] Offices in the *physical* sense, not including non-resident missions. This figure does not include the four American consulates and the one in Hamburg.

1973, employed by far the greatest number of senior officials, including no less than seven counsellors and seven first secretaries in addition to the head of mission. The most striking feature of this concentration of senior staff, which paralleled that of the European Community unit at headquarters, was the large number of officials on secondment from other departments. Four of the seven counsellors came into this category, one each being seconded from the Departments of Finance, Industry and Commerce, Agriculture and Fisheries, and the Office of the Revenue Commissioners; of the seven first secretaries, two were from the Department of Industry and Commerce and one each from the Departments of Finance and of Labour.

There are three medium-sized offices with a foreign service staff of three members. Two of these are ordinary embassies—in Rome and Bonn—and the Ambassador to Italy is also accredited to Turkey. The third medium-sized office is the permanent mission to the United Nations in New York. This consists of three members of the foreign service, which is probably the minimum number capable of coping with the complex work of the UN General Assembly and its specialised committees. During the General Assembly sessions, this permanent mission is supplemented by the Minister for Foreign Affairs and by officials from Iveagh House, from other embassies or from the American consulates.

Even so, the Irish delegation remains a small one in comparison with other small European states. In 1965, for example, the Irish delegation comprised ten officials—nine diplomats and the minister. In contrast, Australia had a delegation of twenty-four (two ministers, nineteen diplomats and three parliamentarians), Denmark sent twenty-three (one minister, fifteen diplomats, three parliamentarians and four non-governmental individuals) and Norway sent twenty (one minister, twelve diplomats, six parliamentarians and one individual). Only Portugal with twelve (one minister, nine diplomats and two individuals) had a delegation of a comparable size to Ireland's.[37]

As far as the formulation of policy is concerned, the permanent mission to the UN has been of special importance since it has had to deal with a wider range of international issues than the other

[37] These figures are from *Delegations to the United Nations*, October 1965 (UN Publication).

embassies. The mission is continually in touch with other delegations about these issues and, since the Minister for Foreign Affairs is able to intervene personally in UN politics for only three or four weeks in the year, it is clear that the expert knowledge and informal diplomatic contacts of the members of the permanent delegation make them among the more authoritative policy advisers in the department.

The remaining fourteen overseas missions are small by international standards. The one in Portugal has only one diplomat and the rest have two each. Of these, the office in Switzerland also has ambassadorial responsibility for Austria, that in Sweden has ambassadorial responsibility for Finland, and the office in Denmark has responsibility for Norway and Iceland. This circumstance necessitates at least two visits per year by the ambassadors concerned and a certain amount of paperwork. The embassies in Nigeria, India and Australia are Ireland's diplomatic listening posts for vast areas outside the states to which they are accredited. Here, specialisation is impossible and the small staff must take ceremonial, trade, cultural, consular and political responsibilities into their own hands.[38] The opportunities available to these missions to provide political information and advice are comparatively infrequent and, because of administrative duties, it may be difficult for them to find the time or energy to develop to any significant extent their political and commercial functions. A wider use of full-time trade attachés, who are at present restricted to London, Washington and Paris, seems to be the only answer to the problems of the smaller offices. Admittedly, the overseas offices of the Irish Export Board (Córas Tráchtála Teoranta) assist the development of export trade and indeed operate in countries where there is no diplomatic representation, but this body is answerable to the Department of Industry and Commerce and the coordination of activities is therefore sometimes difficult.

It is clear that a wide range of duties is carried out in the Department of Foreign Affairs as a whole, although these are mostly concerned with administration rather than with policy-making. As we have seen, advice on policy is formulated by certain sections and must be readily available to the Minister for Foreign Affairs. The responsibility for advising the minister devolves mainly on the staff at headquarters

[38] An instructive account of the varied activities of the Nigerian and Australian missions is given by Bernard Share in *The Irish Times,* 16 and 17 August 1966.

and the efficiency with which this advice is made available depends
on the ability of senior officials to properly coordinate the department's
activities. The recall of heads of missions for a conference at the
headquarters has generally been regarded as an excessively costly
procedure, and has been reserved for unusual circumstances, such as
existed in 1945 after World War II and in 1961 when the government
applied for membership of the EEC. In April 1973, a similar conference
was held, with a special emphasis on clarifying policy objectives,
required by increased participation in European politics and the
possibilities of a settlement in Northern Ireland. It is possible that
this type of consultation will be more frequently used in the future.
However, the normal practice is for heads of missions to communicate
individually with the head office or with the minister, on the occasion
of ministerial visits to their country.

At the head office, the officers who are chiefly responsible for
coordinating the department's activities are the assistant secretaries,
who are directly responsible to the Secretary, the permanent head
of the department. A lesser degree of coordination is effected by the
counsellors, two of whom are responsible for two sections each.
This is a reasonable arrangement since the Secretary need only deal
directly with four subordinates, and no assistant secretary has to deal
directly with more than five officials ranking above first secretary.
As far as the formulation of policy is concerned, in spite of the
nomenclature of the divisions within the department, important
political issues are the preserve of at least three divisions: the economic
division impinges on European policy, the political and cultural
division on policy in general and in the UN, and the Anglo-Irish and
information division is concerned with Anglo-Irish relations, particularly relating to Northern Ireland. Even the administration division
—especially its legal section—may have a part in making political
decisions. Consequently, decisions will be made on most issues only
after several sections have given their views and differences have been
arbitrated and reconciled by the assistant secretaries, supported by
their respective counsellors.

Ultimately, coordination of policy proposals and views is the
responsibility of the Secretary of the department who is concerned
not only with the overall administration of the department's activities
but is the principal policy adviser to the Minister for Foreign Affairs.

Sometimes, these duties have to compete for the Secretary's attention. In the much simpler organisation of the pre-1948 Department of External Affairs, when there was only one assistant secretary, this official would, as Mr de Valera put it in 1948 ". . . in fact be the day-to-day manager of the office, doing the work of a general routine character and any other work which might come his way". The Secretary, on the other hand, ". . . should be free and should not be tied to daily tasks at a desk . . .".[39] Obviously, with the increased duties and size of the department, Mr de Valera's precepts are no longer viable. Nevertheless, the principle that he was trying to maintain—that the head of the department should not be overburdened with routine work—is if anything more important in the nineteen seventies, both on account if the increased complexity of the department's work at home and overseas and because of the more intensive diplomacy demanded by membership of the EEC.

The principle of distinguishing between policy-making and routine administrative or executive functions was one of the outstanding concerns of the Devlin Report of 1969. This report recommended that the formulation of policy proposals should be performed by a comparatively small top-level group within the department called the *aireacht* (minister's cabinet) and composed of the Secretary of the department, the heads of four staff units (finance, planning, organisation, personnel) and the assistant secretaries in charge of the broad functional areas. The latter would be backed by small staffs, while the routine work within their areas would be carried out by a quite distinct executive office, with its own director.[40]

This fairly radical suggestion has yet to be implemented by the Irish civil service as a whole, but in the meantime the Department of Foreign Affairs might introduce what has hitherto been lacking, a unit with specific responsibility for policy planning.[41] In some

---

[39] Dáil Debates: 112, 921.

[40] *Report of Public Services Organisation Review Group* 1966–1969, chapter 13 and its application to the Department of External Affairs, chapter 24.

[41] To some extent, the general political and United Nations section has acted as a policy-planning group and, given the regular consultation on political cooperation among the member states of the European Community, it could further evolve along these lines in the future. But the specific responsibility for United Nations affairs suggests a narrow view of the content of foreign policy, as well as more administrative work than is usually found in a policy-planning unit. The Devlin Report's proposed reorganisation is found on p. 265 of *Report of Public Services Organisation Review Group* 1966–1969. To date the *aireacht* idea is only being applied to the Departments of Health, Industry and Commerce, and Transport and Power.

other countries, policy planning may be partially undertaken by a "historical and research division",[42] for speculation about the future requires extensive knowledge of past and present policies; alternatively, a special policy-planning unit is used. The increasing pressure of daily business for all staff, up to and including the Secretary of the department, and the need to maintain a certain degree of detachment from such pressures if the general policies of the department are to be considered rationally and calmly, make a policy-planning unit a necessary element in a foreign ministry. Otherwise policy tends to be no more than "a series of reactions to events beyond the control of the government in question".[43] Such a structure has the added advantage that junior staff can participate in evolving views on important issues at a stage in their career when they are most receptive to new ideas. It is extremely important to encourage and provide for some means of 'thinking ahead', the more so since Ireland lacks a developed intellectual tradition in international affairs.[44]

Of course, to separate policy formulation and routine administration in the overseas offices would be difficult. Dr F. H. Boland argues that "in practice, the manner in which a policy objective is pursued usually calls for as much political judgment as the adoption of the objective itself", and that consequently it is impossible and dangerous to treat policy-making and its execution separately.[45] This argument has some weight in so far as the overseas official's most mundane act is seen as a reflection of his government's diplomatic policy, but the heart of the problem is really that even the biggest missions overseas are too small to make separation between policy-makers and executives workable. What can be done, however, and what should be done is to provide overseas missions with more specialist staff to deal with the bulk of the routine work in trade promotion or public relations. This would allow the head of the mission and his principal aides more scope for their most beneficial contribution to policy formulation—establishing and maintaining sources of

[42] See *Diplomatic Service: Formation and Operation* p. 8.
[43] ibid. p. 12. See also pp. 11–13 for the emphasis placed on this component in a foreign ministry's structure. This represents the consensus—though not the unanimous opinion—of the participants of the seminar in Singapore in 1970.
[44] See below p. 176.
[45] F. H. Boland, op. cit.

information and reporting on political developments in their respective countries.

★　　　★　　　★　　　★

The formulation of foreign policy is undertaken by no one part of the Department of Foreign Affairs in isolation, but rather, according to the particular circumstances, by a varying combination of the different sections and overseas missions, and a similar pattern is found throughout the Irish public service. The Department of Foreign Affairs, in spite of its formal responsibility for external relations, is not the only department concerned with the formulation of policy. The offices of the Minister for Justice and of the Attorney General participated in the development of Anglo-Irish constitutional relations because of their specialist knowledge, and since membership of the EEC, these departments are again obliged to examine the small print of Ireland's obligations under the Rome Treaties. The Department of Defence was closely associated with the formulation of the neutrality policy during World War II and plays a significant part in decisions about the military support which the state can offer to United Nations peace-keeping missions. Despite this, there is no formal attempt by the two departments to maintain consistency of policy, unlike most states where defence and foreign policy are closely integrated. But recently, it has been the 'economic' departments—Industry and Commerce, Agriculture and Fisheries and, especially, Finance—which have become more actively engaged in the making of foreign policy, particularly that pertaining to Europe. Thus, the extent and nature of interdepartmental coordination have become important factors in the overall policy-making process.

For the most part, interdepartmental cooperation is informal and personal, since the compact size and centralised character of the Irish civil service lends itself to the exchange of views and information by telephone and *ad hoc* meetings both inside and outside office hours. Thus, it is difficult to say where the predominant influence for a particular policy is to be found. One danger of this form of cooperation is its tendency to be too casual and to depend overmuch on the success of specific personal relationships. In 1948, for example, Major

Vivion de Valera claimed that before World War II there was insufficient day-to-day contact between the Departments of Defence and External Affairs:

> Information available to the Minister himself, when he considers it of sufficient importance, will undoubtedly be exchanged at meetings of the Cabinet but there were . . . a lot of details which might be overlooked by him but which, taken in conjunction with other facts, might be rather significant.[46]

Thus, because of increasing scope of governmental action and the corresponding increase in the number of officials engaged in decision-making (even in a relatively small administration), interdepartmental committees were established. One of the first of these was the foreign trade committee. In addition to the representative from External Affairs, this committee included representatives from the Departments of the Taoiseach, Agriculture and Fisheries, Finance, Industry and Commerce, and Lands. In 1951, when the Minister for External Affairs, Mr MacBride, was asked by Mr de Valera which was "the driving Department . . . charged with looking after the thing as a whole, to push it definitely",[47] he answered that ". . . by and large, it is all centred in the Department of External Affairs, but you always have conflicting interests . . . between the Department of Agriculture, the Department of Industry and Commerce, and very often the Department of Finance. By maintaining a position of neutrality and by trying to provide a good service, the Department of External Affairs exercises a good deal of influence".[48]

Mr MacBride was probably justified in suggesting that the Department of External Affairs played a positive role in formulating Irish economic foreign policy in 1951, for his department had the principal responsibility for administering the European recovery programme (for which a separate section was established at headquarters), and Mr MacBride himself had been closely associated with the foundation of the Organisation for European Economic Cooperation. But with

[46] Dáil Debates: 112, 979.
[47] Dáil Debates: 124, 1425.
[48] Dáil Debates: 124, 1425.

the first programme for economic expansion, introduced in 1958, which committed the government to a programme of national development and economic planning, the initiative for the more important aspects of foreign policy came from the 'economic' departments rather than from the Department of External Affairs. Although the foreign trade committee became an important coordinating body in the formulation of economic foreign policy, the role of the Department of External Affairs tended to decline, particularly when a second interdepartmental committee, informally called the "committee of secretaries", was established to deal with Irish policy towards the EEC.

This EEC committee, consisting of representatives (either secretaries or assistant secretaries) from the Departments of Finance, Foreign Affairs, Agriculture and Fisheries, and Industry and Commerce, meets frequently (though not regularly) and has assumed many of the more general functions of the foreign trade committee which is now a less significant policy-making body. It is worth noting that neither of these committees is now sponsored by the Department of Foreign Affairs: the foreign trade committee is sponsored by the Department of Industry and Commerce and the committee of secretaries by the Department of Finance. The sponsoring departments provide the chairman and secretary to each of these committees and organise the working parties at principal and assistant principal level; in each instance, they possess important divisions responsible for long-term policy formulation. The economic policy division in the Department of Finance is responsible for long-term economic forecasting and for revising the programme of economic expansion. In the Department of Industry and Commerce, the foreign trade and exports division is responsible, *inter alia*, for considering "the implications for this country of world trading developments, particularly those arising from the establishment of the European Economic Community (EEC) . . . ."[49] The committee on foreign trade is one of these committees which have been ". . . characterised by people associated with them, as being very effective in obtaining Government and Ministerial acceptance of their advice and recommendations . . . ."[50] The committee on the EEC was probably even

[49] *The Department of Industry and Commerce* (Institute of Public Administration, Dublin, 1961), p. 7.
[50] D. P. Leon, *Advisory Bodies in Irish Government* (Institute of Administration, Dublin, 1963), p. 106.

more influential, particularly during the years leading up to the accession of Ireland to the European Community; but it remains to be seen whether an *ad hoc* body of this type is able to cope with the increased burden imposed by membership.

It was, perhaps, significant that the delegations prior to formal negotiations for entry to the EEC were generally led by the Secretary of the Department of Finance—diplomacy was far from being the preserve of the diplomatic service. This was hardly surprising, so long as the Department of External Affairs itself was used merely as a channel of communication between the EEC and the economic departments. However, it was argued at this time that if the economic departments were, in Senator Garret FitzGerald's words, ". . . bringing in the Department of External Affairs merely for protocol reasons, it must inevitably mean that the Department of External Affairs will not be as interested, enthusiastic or energetic"[51] and that, consequently, the department would neither effectively fulfil its 'post-office' function nor would be equipped to play a more positive role when the important political aspects of EEC membership arose. Indeed, the more enthusiastic supporters of EEC membership felt that the Department of External Affairs was not as effective as it might have been in promoting Ireland's first EEC application of 31 July 1961, which the EEC Council of Ministers did not accept as a basis for negotiations until October 1962. At that time, Ireland did not have a separate mission to the EEC and was thus poorly equipped to assuage the doubts of EEC officials, who were probably less well-informed about Ireland than about any other applicant country. (Of the latter, only Norway remained without a separate mission; however, their case was put by a strong delegation especially selected for this purpose). Because of the French veto in 1963, Ireland's weakness was not tested, and the accreditation of a separate mission in 1966 and reinforcement of the headquarters office to deal with EEC questions ameliorated the situation. The renewed applications of 1967 and 1970 appear to have been more energetically promoted.

In the early nineteen seventies, membership of the EEC was not the only issue of foreign policy to impinge on the administration as a whole. The Northern Ireland crisis resulted in the establishment

[51] From a speech in the Seanad, 19 July 1966: Seanad Debates: 61, 1963.

of two more interdepartmental committees, and in these the Department of Foreign Affairs played a central role. An interdepartmental unit for Northern Ireland was created, consisting of representatives from the Departments of Foreign Affairs, Finance, and the Taoiseach and reporting to the Taoiseach through the Minister for Foreign Affairs, or directly, depending on the circumstances. With the parallel establishment of the strong Anglo-Irish political section in the Department of Foreign Affairs, that department was obviously in a position to exert considerable influence on policy towards Northern Ireland, even if this particular issue was regarded as the preserve of the Taoiseach rather than of his foreign minister. The Department of Foreign Affairs was also the sponsoring department of the interdepartmental advisory committee on publicity abroad which also represented the Departments of Finance, Industry and Commerce, Agriculture and Fisheries, Transport and Power and the Government Information Bureau. However, the information section of the Department of Foreign Affairs was poorly equipped to provide strong support, and the use of Markpress, the private public relations agency, further complicated the situation.[52]

One further means of ensuring coordination between departments exists: the practice of seconding officials from other departments to serve as members of the foreign service overseas. In the past, this secondment has occurred on a rather limited scale. Nevertheless, it was not unusual to find several officials—often of comparatively high rank, such as principal officers from the Departments of Industry and Commerce and Agriculture and Fisheries—acting as trade officers in the larger embassies, particularly that in London. In 1970, for example, no less than five counsellors, including two in London and one in Washington, and one higher executive officer were seconded in this way.

But it is membership of the EEC, which requires officials to maintain a high degree of expertise on a considerable range of government policy, that makes secondment a practice which is now more widespread and is likely to remain so; thus, in the summer of 1972 eight of the fifteen members of the EEC mission were on secondment.

---

[52] The rationalisation of governmental information services was treated as an important priority by the coalition government when it came into power in March 1973.

This practice not only brings a measure of special expertise into the Department of Foreign Affairs but also enables the officials and those with whom they work to gain an insight into the problems and opinions of other departments. In the long run this may encourage a more informed and, possibly, a more sympathetic cooperation between departments on matters of foreign affairs.

Although the seconded officials in Brussels will report directly to their own departments and will no doubt suppose that their careers will continue to be with these departments, the fact that they will be expected to act as spokesmen for a consistent national policy further emphasises the important coordinating duties of the Department of Foreign Affairs. Indeed, the experience to date of the European Community system suggests that foreign ministries play a more important role than is generally recognised. The system is still primarily intergovernmental; the greatest benefits have been gained by those governments which have appreciated the political implications of the whole range of their activities and which have taken care to co-ordinate their efforts in some detail. Even when the content of policy is 'economic' or 'social', negotiations have been most effectively pursued by diplomats.[53]

Thus, it is possible that the Department of Foreign Affairs, which under Mr de Valera was in many respects "the centre of administrative effort"[54], might become once again a central rather than a peripheral element in the administration. Certainly the quality of the department's advice on policy decisions will be tested more severely than at any time since the first twenty-five years of the state. Its capability will depend on a continual willingness to adapt its organisation to more complex circumstances; its effectiveness will depend on a readiness on the part of the government to define clearly the procedures for interdepartmental consultation and coordination. But in addition to these structural aspects of the policy-making system, an important consideration is the calibre of the officials who serve it in the diplomatic service.

[53] The experience of the original six members of the EEC and some of the problems associated with expansion are examined by Helen Wallace in *National Governments and the European Communities* (Chatham House / P.E.P., London, 1973).
[54] Farrell, op. cit., p. 12.

Chapter 5

THE IRISH DIPLOMATIC SERVICE

"In the Department of External Affairs the nation is magnificently served."

Eamon de Valera, 1948
(Dáil Debates: 112, 922).

"It is no good depending on office boys."

Jack McQuillan, 1962
(Dáil Debates: 196, 2932).

ALTHOUGH the civil servants of the Department of Foreign Affairs are by no means the government's only professional advisers on foreign policy (particularly in cases where it has important economic implications), they are, nevertheless, the principal foreign policy advisers by virtue of their coordinating role at home and abroad and are thus able to exert considerable influence on the formulation of foreign policy. However, as the previous chapter indicated, the officials in the Department of Foreign Affairs do not act solely as advisers, but are also administrators concerned with a wide range of activities; moreover, the small scale of the department's human and financial resources, both at home and abroad, hinders the division of work into specialised duties. In the offices overseas, it is possible to differentiate between commercial work and diplomatic work in only a few cases, and for the most part the individual civil servant personally undertakes the whole range of activities for which his department is responsible. The size of the central organisation allows for a greater degree of specialisation, but even here the consideration of long-term policy objectives is but one of the many functions to be performed.

It is clear that, in order to overcome these limitations, the civil servant in the Department of Foreign Affairs must be able to avail himself of a wide range of skills, some of them different from those required in the administration of domestic affairs. These skills must be applied under a variety of conditions which may severely test the officials. On the whole, it appears that the Irish foreign service has met this challenge with some degree of success and despite difficult circumstances has generally produced reasonably high standards of diplomacy. Therefore, in order to fully understand the role the civil servant can play in the formulation of foreign policy, it is necessary to look first at the development of the Irish foreign service and then to examine in more detail its present characteristics. In this way, it is possible to make a general assessment of the personal qualities of its members and the extent to which their capabilities may help to offset the handicap of the department's limited financial resources.

*   *   *   *

The essential point about the origins of the Irish foreign service is that, unlike the greater part of the civil service, it was not founded on the basis of a solid tradition of administrative experience acquired throughout the nineteenth century. As we have seen,[1] the early quasi diplomatic service of the Dáil had, of necessity, to rely on certain members of the Dáil itself and on a limited number of its supporters to act as overseas representatives; they had some (but rarely all) of the necessary qualifications to serve in an embryonic foreign service.

The conditions under which these representatives attempted to pursue their diplomatic tasks were anything but normal. They often had to cover several states. Mr Gavan Duffy, theoretically assigned to Italy, dealt also with Spain and Germany, and Mr Seán T. O'Kelly, the Dáil's representative in Paris, was also active in Spain, Switzerland, Germany, Denmark and Belgium. Moreover, the diplomatic titles which these Dáil representatives assumed could not hide the fact that, as far as the normal world of intergovernmental intercourse was concerned, they were the unaccredited agents of a rebellious minority group in one state—the United Kingdom. Although they often met with sympathy, their activities were formally ignored by governments more often than not. Their operations in states belonging to the

[1] See above pp. 107-110.

British empire were particularly difficult. On 17 August 1921, the Minister for Foreign Affairs, Count Plunkett, had to report to the Dáil that Mr O. Esmonde had been deported from Canada, and that in London Mr Art O'Brien was ". . . considerably hampered in his work owing to raids, arrests and deportations . . . [which] have made such a terrible mess of things that it will be a long time before he can get things straight".[2]

The qualities required for these activities were not necessarily the same as those demanded in a recognised foreign service using long-established and rigid methods of diplomatic procedure; nor were the strong and overt political commitments of many of these early diplomats a factor which facilitated the formation of an impartial service. In April 1921, Mr de Valera—then President of the Dáil—found it necessary to write to a diplomat warning him against trying to propagate his personal views: "Our representatives abroad, whether they be members of the Dáil or not, must regard themselves unequivocally the direct agents of the Department of Foreign Affairs, and must carry out the instructions of the Department, whether they personally agree with the policy of not".[3] De Valera also deplored the practice of writing unofficial letters to friends at home, and stressed that ". . . were our circumstances not what they are, there would be no thought of having a member of the Dáil appointed as an ambassador abroad".[4] Indeed, even if the civil war had not taken place, it is probable that the more prominent Dáil representatives, such as Mr Seán T. O'Kelly, would have pursued a political rather than a diplomatic career once the independence of the state was recognised, and this in itself would have deprived the new Department of External Affairs of experienced personnel. That being the case, the nucleus of the foreign service would have consisted of those representatives who were not attracted into party politics.

However, the civil war depleted this nucleus, and some members of the Dáil service, who might otherwise have become career diplomats (and who did in fact rejoin the Department of External Affairs in 1932), were alienated by the acceptance of the Treaty and refused

[2] Dáil Éireann Official Report for periods 16–26 August 1921 and 28 February–8 June 1922, p. 21.
[3] Quoted in ibid., p. 135.
[4] ibid., p. 136.

to serve in the new foreign service. As a result of this dissension during its establishment, the Department of External Affairs lost men of experience and talent, and its personnel inevitably became uncomfortably associated with the political views of the government which they served. When, in 1923, Mr D. J. Gorey called the department ". . . a Ministry for finding a job for somebody",[5] he was making a general attack on the department's very existence, but after the Fianna Fáil party entered the Dáil in 1927, this kind of accusation became a prominent feature of the new party's attitude towards individual members of the Department of External Affairs.

Fianna Fáil saw the value of a diplomatic service: in 1929, their spokesman, Mr Seán T. O'Kelly, approved of the appointment of a representative to the Holy See and maintained that the official ". . . would have to be up early and up late . . . fighting for the rights of Ireland against the English interests and influence there".[6] However, the party was critical of the background of certain representatives and of their activities abroad, particularly those men with allegedly pro-British sympathies. During the estimate debates in 1929, Mr O'Kelly berated the Irish High Commissioner in London, Professor Timothy Smiddy, for joining the British Empire League,[7] and in 1930 Mr Lemass also picked on Professor Smiddy, when he referred to a press report that "the only Oxford accent heard at the London Naval Conference was that of the Irish delegate".[8] Similarly, in 1930, Dr Binchy, the representative in Berlin, was censured for publicly supporting Irish membership of the Commonwealth.[9]

It was fortunate that Fianna Fáil's parliamentary criticism of the Irish diplomats did not go beyond these personal jibes, for when Mr de Valera came to power in 1932, he had to rely, both as head of the government and as Minister for External Affairs, on the civil servants whom his party had maligned. The decisive test of the political impartiality of the staff of the Department of External Affairs, and indeed of the civil service as a whole, came with the election of the de Valera government in 1932. In the event, the loyalty of the civil

[5] Dáil Debates: 5, 940.
[6] Dáil Debates: 30, 818.
[7] Dáil Debates: 30, 815–6.
[8] Dáil Debates: 34, 139.
[9] Dáil Debates: 33, 2092.

service was assured and, later, when referring to the Department of External Affairs in 1937, Mr de Valera admitted that he ". . . was very fortunate to have officials in the Department who have been working there and who have been acquainted with the work of the State since the State was founded. It was an old Republican Department which was carried on . . . ".[10]

Mr de Valera's claim that the Department of External Affairs could trace its ancestry to the "old Republican" days of the first and second Dáil must be acknowledged, but so too must the changes that took place within the department while he was in opposition. Continuity was not achieved without some political difficulty. The principal bone of contention was the reinstatement of former civil servants who had relinquished their posts to support the republican cause in the civil war. The fact that these reinstatements had been started under Mr W. T. Cosgrave's administration averted a *furor*. By the time Mr de Valera's government took office on the 9 March 1932, twenty-five officials had been taken back into the civil service as a whole without being obliged to appear before selection boards.[11]

Similar reinstatements by the new government were generally accepted without it suffering the charge of political bias, although the reappointment of the former commercial attaché in Paris raised the parliamentary temperature more than a little in 1933. Mr Desmond FitzGerald, a former Minister for External Affairs, went to great lengths to build up a case against the appointment, accusing the government of political patronage and the official of a lack of integrity;[12] and in spite of Mr de Valera's defence of the appointment, FitzGerald repeated the attack the following year.[13] The charge of political bias was somewhat confused by suggestions of communist influence and romantic allegations of intrigue on the French Riviera and, in retrospect, the whole affair seems to have received a great deal more attention than it deserved.

However, this case was not the only instance of reinstatement to the Department of External Affairs to be disputed in the Dáil, for objection was also made to 'outsiders' being employed, because of the

[10] Dáil Debates: 67, 793.
[11] Dáil Debates: 50, 535.
[12] Dáil Debates: 48, 2132–2146.
[13] Dáil Debates: 53, 218–226.

effect this would have on morale in the department. Again it was Desmond FitzGerald who pointed out in 1934 that it was

> . . . unfair to the staff of the Department of External Affairs . . . it is quite right that the Department recruit men, but obviously the Department at some time had cadetships in which young men with special qualifications were brought in and trained for the special work of this Department. . . . This year . . . an outsider, not a young man, was brought in . . . arbitrarily from a certain newspaper associated with the President . . . and sent over to America without any training for the position.[14]

In 1935 he claimed that ". . . as far as my knowledge goes, the men who have been brought into this Department were brought in to the detriment of the ordinary progress of promotion, and consequently of good order, the contentment of the staff and of ordinary justice to men who have given good service".[15]

It would have been surprising if the policy of reinstatement had not produced feelings of resentment within the civil service, but this was a risk which had to be taken, because the alternative was to have a civil service which did not represent an important and active political group and whose administration on that account would fail to be respected. Moreover, the reinstated men did possess some qualifications for their appointments. For example, Mr de Valera claimed that Robert Brennan, the 'outsider' in 1934, had been ". . . in the service of Ireland in Republican days . . . he was Under-Secretary of the Department of External Affairs . . . actually head of that Department".[16] On the whole, it appears that reinstatement occurred on only a small scale,[17] for Mr de Valera very soon became aware of the considerable expertise which had been built up in the Department

[14] Dáil Debates: 53, 226–7.
[15] Dáil Debates: 56, 2205.
[16] Dáil Debates: 53, 271.
[17] Between 9 March 1932, when Mr de Valera's government came to office, and the end of that year, there were twenty-two cases of reinstatement of former members of the British, Dáil or Saorstát civil services (Dáil Debates: 50, 535). Of the twenty-seven people appointed "in the public interest", i.e. without competitive examination, to the established civil service (all grades) during 1932, only three were appointed to External Affairs and only two of these were reinstated members (Dáil Debates: 50, 536–40). Subsequent reinstatements appear to have been on a similar scale.

of External Affairs during the ten years of W. T. Cosgrave's government and realised that a large measure of continuity was essential.
Indeed, in 1934, he said that

> one of the things that we set ourselves to do when we came to
> office was, as far as it was at all possible—even if we were to make
> big sacrifices in order to achieve it, big as the difference in general
> outlook between the two administrations was—to take advantage
> of all the knowledge that was possessed in this Department on
> things that had gone on before. I doubt if there was any Department
> of State to which that knowledge was more valuable. . . .[18]

For Mr de Valera at least, the staff of the Department of External
Affairs had proved their worth and they were not subsequently
seriously threatened by political interference. By the mid-nineteen
thirties, it was becoming clear that career prospects for officials
depended on ability rather than political affiliations; the future of
the career foreign service was assured. It has since been the exception
rather than the rule for the activities of individual civil servants to
incur parliamentary criticism and, when they have been censured,
the responsibility, even in controversial cases, has been placed on the
Minister for External Affairs. Yet again, the victim of Desmond
FitzGerald's earlier criticism seems to have been the principal exception,
and he was the object of unfavourable comment when he was accredited
to the Spanish republican government during the Spanish civil war
in 1936[19] and when he was alleged to have made an anti-British
speech in the Argentine in 1947.[20]

   The civil servant in the Department of External Affairs has, of course,
the normal political rights enjoyed by the civil service as a whole,
and in 1955 on the one occasion when it was alleged in the Dáil
that a civil servant—the private secretary to the Minister for External
Affairs—had exceeded these rights by engaging in active canvassing
during an election, the minister, Liam Cosgrave, denied the charges.[21]
Of course, by this time, the difficult conditions of World War II

[18] Dáil Debates: 53, 278.
[19] Dáil Debates: 65, 775.
[20] Dáil Debates: 106, 2307–8.
[21] Dáil Debates: 152, 784–7.

had given the staff of the Department of External Affairs many
opportunities to demonstrate to the general public that they could
effectively protect the interests of Irish citizens in those countries
directly affected by the war. The work of helping Irish citizens
stranded in belligerent states altered the public's view of the diplomat,
particularly since these services were often rendered under conditions
of hardship and physical danger which the Irish public did not share.
The diplomat was now seen as a hard-working public servant rather
than as a pawn in the party struggle. Whereas, before the war,
references in foreign affairs debates in the Dáil to the staff of the
department were more likely to be critical than not, during and after
the war, it was rare to hear a debate on the Department of External
Affairs in which the dedication of its staff did not receive praise from
all sides of the House.

This is not to say that the work of the civil servants in the Department
of External Affairs has been free from criticism, but that their integrity
and political impartiality are now accepted. Criticism of the civil
servant has been concerned not with his political inclinations but
with his administrative duties. The problems that these duties gave
rise to were not new to the foreign service, but when the government's
foreign policy became less exclusively preoccupied with the constitutional relationship with Britain, and the Department of External
Affairs was compelled to take on additional functions in an increased
number of overseas missions, the questions of organisation and
training for specialised functions came to the fore. By 1948, it had
become clear that the existing staffing arrangements and the organisation of the department's headquarters would have to be overhauled;
a period of expansion was under way during which the total number
of staff was to increase by 50 per cent.[22]

This experience posed—and membership of the EEC again poses—
the dilemma which confronts any rapidly expanding organisation:
how to simultaneously maintain standards of recruitment and training
and meet the urgent demand for new officials. In 1949, the Minister
for External Affairs, Seán MacBride, referring to the position of
recruits to the department, admitted that ". . . unfortunately, because
of pressing staffing needs, many of them will have to be assigned to

[22] See above, p. 115.

duties without having gained the experience which I would have liked them to have gained in different divisions of the Department".[23] The leader of the opposition, Mr de Valera, was equally disturbed:

> . . . when there is a very rapid expansion, I think we ought to see a certain danger in it . . . you have a situation in which you have to take in a number of young people who are inexperienced and put them at work for which they should have years of preparation. You have to improvise by means of lectures and so on to give them an acquaintance with the nature of their work. I think it would be far better if they gained that by actual experience in the ordinary way.[24]

But while the commitments of the foreign service have been increasing, it has not always proved easy to train its members "in the ordinary way", that is to say, on the job. The main difficulty is, of course, that while the very different aspects of the job ideally should be comprehensively mastered by experience in all the specialised branches of the home office, this may not be possible when new posts must be filled overseas. Perhaps one way to remedy such deficiencies in training would be to arrange for officials to take intensive courses outside the department, but this approach has not yet been seriously considered.

Increased commitments have also led to difficulties in recruitment, and Mr MacBride claimed after he had left office that because of this, the probationary period tended to be a formality: "once your are admitted as a Third Secretary, you are there for life".[25] This was an exaggeration. Nevertheless, recruiting new staff is not easy because of the competitive market for university graduates. Five or six new appointments as third secretary are made each year,[26] and it was found necessary to extend the age limit for candidates from twenty-six to thirty years of age. To some extent, the disadvantages of a shortage of staff have been offset by the increased use of honorary consuls

[23] Dáil Debates: 117, 856.
[24] Dáil Debates: 117, 881–2.
[25] Dáil Debates: 159, 597.
[26] Between 1965 and 1969, twenty-eight appointments were made. A higher rate of recruitment may be necessary in the future because of EEC membership. Not only are the department's commitments increasing, but career opportunities in the European institutions are now open to Irish officials.

(of whom there were thirty-six in 1972)[27], who not only increase the scope of Irish representation abroad but also undertake certain administrative consular duties and sometimes take over commercial duties from those diplomatic missions which are in the same state. However, such relief as this affords is marginal, and the honorary consul, who is essentially a part-time representative, may not always be amenable to control by headquarters.

Another serious personnel problem arises from the increased range of duties and the greater demands for specialisation imposed on modern diplomatic services, particularly in connexion with the pursuit of economic objectives. In 1958, Mr Denis J. O'Sullivan remarked in the Dáil on the changing role of Irish diplomats: previously, he said, ". . . their duties were in the main directed towards advancing the recognition of this State . . . In the last few years, however, a new duty has been imposed on our missions abroad . . . we have to rely on our Ministers abroad and on the members of the staffs of our Embassies to advance our trade potential".[28]   O'Sullivan's emphasis on this aspect of the diplomats' work was an understandable reaction to the grave need during the nineteen fifties for the Irish economy to improve its export performance. In 1956, for example, when this need was especially obvious, Mr MacBride maintained that ". . . one of the chief functions which the Government expects from them in the present circumstances is to secure additional export markets,"[29] and he even proposed that bonuses should be granted to individual officials on the basis of the results they might achieve.[30] Indeed, it has been argued in recent years that the promotion of trade was not merely an important responsibility of the Department of External Affairs but that it was its most important function. In 1963, Brendan Corish, the leader of the Labour Party, claimed that he did not think ". . . it too important that they [the diplomats] should be engaged in what is regarded as purely diplomatic work. All their efforts should be directed towards getting more trade and they should regard themselves as trade attachés more than any thing else".[31] In 1964,

[27] Information supplied by the Department of Foreign Affairs.
[28] Dáil Debates: 167, 264 and 266.
[29] Dáil Debates: 159, 595.
[30] Dáil Debates: 159, 594–5.
[31] Dáil Debates: 201, 989.

Mr Jack McQuillan went so far as to suggest that the wrong criteria were being employed for the recruitment of staff: "Neither can we expect", he said, "the men in External Affairs, most of whom are trained in the arts and literature and who have only a scrappy knowledge of trade matters, to get export markets for Irish goods".[32]

Such a viewpoint, which tends to ignore the political role of the diplomat, comes only too readily to a parliament and a public which looks for tangible and easily demonstrable results from any form of government activity, but there can be little doubt that the diplomat's duties as a promoter of trade are loosely defined. Admittedly, heads of missions are instructed to give priority to trade promotion, and the economic division in Iveagh House is becoming one of the most important of the functional divisions. Nevertheless, this positive attitude towards trade is not carried as far as it might be. Most missions are poorly staffed and opportunities for increasing trade might easily be missed. In any case, the traditional diplomatic practice of transferring personnel from office to office at relatively frequent intervals does not allow officials to develop relationships with commercial organisations abroad over a sufficient length of time. Staff transfers are made at short notice (usually one month) and this does not always allow for a sufficiently comprehensive briefing of overseas personnel. But it is perhaps unrealistic to expect any significant change as long as the function of trade promotion is diffused among different branches of the whole administration.[33]

Although these shortcomings reflect the small scale of Irish diplomatic activity, they also illustrate the somewhat tardy reaction of a foreign service (which up to the end of the nineteen forties was assigned an important and almost exclusively political role) to the very different international situation of the last twenty-five years. The department, which for the first thirty years of its existence was promoting the interests of a fundamentally protectionist economy by negotiating bilateral trade agreements, had to change direction and, working in conjunction with several state-sponsored agencies such as Córas Tráchtála (the Irish Export Board) and the Industrial Development Authority, had to undertake tasks which were alien to the traditions

[32] Dáil Debates: 208, 907.
[33] See above, p. 117-118.

10

established during its formative years. Under these conditions, it is hardly surprising that the diplomat sometimes appears to neglect one or other aspect of his task, for he is asked to be simultaneously an all-rounder coping with a wide range of demands made on him and an expert capable of dealing skilfully with specialised issues.

When we consider the principal characteristics of the Irish diplomat, this element of versatility is perhaps his most striking attribute. Although specialists in various fields are employed, sometimes on a short-term basis, the burden of international negotiation, in specialised as well as in the traditional areas of diplomacy, falls mainly on the diplomat.

> He must be the all-purpose machine grinding all new subjects, however, abstruse, into neat capsules of national interest and international equity. He is faced with the necessity of acquiring expertise on the one hand and of preserving a 'generalist' approach to many related but individually complicated spheres of affairs on the other.[34]

Moreover, the representative functions of the Irish diplomat, as of all diplomats, entail a very high degree of personal responsibility and the ability to adapt to unusual conditions of work. As Mr MacBride said in 1951:

> It is essential, probably more essential in the Department of External Affairs than in any other Department, that the officers should be imbued with a spirit of national self-responsibility. They have to be prepared to work harder than in other Departments, to make personal sacrifices, even heavy sacrifices, in order to discharge their duties to this nation effectively. Most officers in the Department, but particularly those who serve abroad, have to develop a sense of initiative and a sense of devotion to duty which is not called for to the same extent from civil servants who work at home in the larger Departments . . . each individual member of our staff abroad . . . has to represent this nation for twenty-four hours around the clock. Every action of his may bring credit or

[34] *Diplomatic Service*, p. 5.

discredit on this nation because he or she will be looked upon as the representatives of this nation. By their actions and by their zeal to duty we will be judged abroad.[35]

The meticulous conduct demanded of the diplomat both inside and outside formal working hours is accompanied by what to many people might seem an inconvenient mode of life. He is moved from country to country and post to post at frequent intervals, usually of between two and four years, and must learn to adapt to the varying environments in which he finds himself. Although he relies for the most part on the somewhat stereotyped social life of the small diplomatic community, his one sure contact with his country and background is his family. Here his difficulties are multiplied: he may not be able to offer his wife the prospect of a permanent home nor his children a settled education. Although efforts are made to keep his financial circumstances consistent, by means of special allowances, certain postings may cause a relative decline in the diplomat's standard of living. Of course, there are people for whom the unsettled nature of this nevertheless conventional way of life is one of its principal attractions, but they are exceptional; not only are such people difficult to find, but it may be difficult to recognise the necessary personal characteristics in the potential recruit, whose enthusiasm may be based all too shakily on the supposed glamour of diplomatic life.

Recruitment procedures to the Department of Foreign Affairs must take account of certain aspects of a candidate's personality and capabilities which might not be a consideration in the recruitment of staff for domestic government departments. If the competition for a post is restricted to members of the civil service, there should be little difficulty in assessing the candidates, whose abilities will have already been tested and recorded. However, this type of competition has been employed only about once in every five or six years and most recruitment to the higher grades of the service (five or six posts a year) is conducted by open competitions, designed to attract candidates for the post of third secretary, the bottom rung of the ladder to ambassadorial rank. To enter such a competition, the candidate

[35] Dáil Debates: 126, 1965–6.

must either have a first or second class honours degree or an equivalent qualification. In view of the comparatively small numbers able to attend a university, let alone obtain an honours degree, this stipulation does tend to restrict entry to a small minority. A further restriction is an upper age limit of thirty; and up to 1973, women had to be either unmarried or widowed. There is no formal procedure for broadening the basis of recruitment to include candidates who do not conform to these requirements, but who might nonetheless have valuable experience in other walks of life and who might be recruited at a somewhat higher level. However, because of the increasing demands which now confront the diplomatic service, such a procedure might well be instituted in the future. For example, chairmanship of the European Community Council of Ministers, a duty falling to Ireland during the first six months of 1975, involves servicing a multitude of committees; this obligation in itself suggests a need for more flexible recruitment procedures, perhaps on a short-term basis.

At present, candidates for the third secretary posts are assessed by interview and, if there is a particularly large number of them, screening interviews are used. The main interview is conducted by a board of three members, at least one of whom is a senior official in the Department of Foreign Affairs. The interview is competitive and based on fairly rigid criteria: the candidate is marked out of 100 for his academic or professional qualifications, another 50 for any additional qualifications (such as post-graduate degrees), and 100 for "experience of value for the post". Added to this are a possible 350 marks for "general suitability", based on the candidate's actual performance during the interview. Candidates are expected to have "a good general knowledge of Irish history from 1800; a knowledge of current social and economic conditions in Ireland; world political affairs from the beginning of the French Revolution, and current world economic affairs".[36] Finally, successful candidates must pass a qualifying test in oral Irish.

Up to 1971, assessment by interview had been supplemented by a written examination. The placing of the Irish test after the interview

---

[36] *The Third Secretary in the Department of Foreign Affairs.* Career Leaflet No. 159, Careers Information Section, Department of Labour, Dublin, June 1972.

is a comparatively recent procedural change and reflects the persistent controversy over the role of the Irish examination in recruitment. In 1957, Mr Declan Costello claimed in the Dáil that he knew of people who "would have served the Government well but because they failed to pass the examination in Irish they were not even considered at the interview board".[37] Under the new arrangement, the Irish test is no longer the initial eliminating stage of the recruitment process and an effort is made to help the successful candidate in the interview to achieve the one remaining qualification for his recruitment.

On the whole, the recruitment of third secretaries provides little more than the basic raw material from which the diplomat is moulded, and the recruit's expertise as a diplomat will largely depend on his subsequent training. This training, following the traditions of the British civil service, takes place on the job, and there is no extensive formal training course at an establishment separate from the department. The training normally takes place during the first two years of the official's career and comprises six months work in four of the sections within the department. Because of the expansion of overseas missions, the additional functions undertaken by the headquarters in Dublin, and the fact that many of the first generation of diplomats have retired, the period of training may be reduced to one year. The training programme lays particular emphasis on working in the consular section so that recruits will become acquainted with the complex consular routine, and in the economic division so that they will have some experience of the problems of trade promotion and of international economic negotiations.

The first two years of service are probationary. However, in times of expansion, this stipulation may have been treated as a formality rather than as providing the occasion for a serious assessment of the official's performance. In 1956, a former Minister for External Affairs, Mr MacBride, said that he did not ". . . ever remember a Third Secretary being told that he would do no good and that he should move off and get another job".[38] Obviously, when posts are difficult to fill, the department will not lightly get rid of its probationary

[37] Dáil Debates: 163, 604.
[38] Dáil Debates: 159, 597.

officials. Nevertheless, not all ministers could claim the same experience as Mr MacBride and, if doubts about an official do arise, they are considered seriously.

After the initial period at headquarters, the training programme aims to give the official as broad an experience as possible of the wide range of activities within the department. Mr MacBride declared in 1951, "the aim is to ensure that all the officers of the Department will have a reasonable grasp of the work of all these different divisions in the Department".[39] This description attests to the varied functions which the individual official is asked to perform, especially in the small overseas office, and also acknowledges the usual policy of frequently rotating diplomatic posts. However, as Mr MacBride pointed out, it may be advisable to waive this practice for the specialist, particularly the commercial attaché who ". . . acquires a knowledge of the trade in that country and makes contacts which can be valuable to him, and [who] should be in a position to remain there as long as possible".[40]   But unfortunately, most officials who perform the function of commercial attaché—usually on a part-time basis—are not regarded as specialists and are subjected to the normal rotation of posts; thus, the skills and contacts which they have acquired are wasted.

Indeed, the principle of rotating posts at frequent intervals appears to be applied with regard to what are often contradictory criteria. Rotation is necessary if officials are to obtain the greatest possible experience, but perhaps more importantly in the short term, it is *essential* if the right man is to fill the right post at the right time. In practice, though, appointments may have to be made at comparatively short notice and, consequently, the official's training can sometimes be a rather haphazard affair.

The basic, general skills of diplomacy include principally the ability to negotiate a favourable result while at the same time sustaining good relations between the negotiating parties. They also include the ability to analyse and report a situation accurately and perceptively and to be able to do so in several foreign languages. These skills depend on innate qualities of character which can only be developed

[39] Dáil Debates: 124, 1424.
[40] Dáil Debates: 124, 1424.

through experience. Nevertheless, because the diplomat's duties demand expertise in a variety of subjects, it might be expected that practical training and experience would be supplemented by intensive formal training courses. But to date, the Department of Foreign Affairs has found it difficult to institute such courses and the individual official is often required to learn for himself. A statement in 1961 by Mr Aiken, then Minister for External Affairs, on the matter of learning foreign languages, illustrates this: "If an officer has to be changed to a country and does not know the language, he is expected to make it up very quickly. Most of them are so accustomed to picking up languages that they do not take very long to acquire one".[41] Although it may be true that officials do succeed in "picking up languages" (in 1967 Mr Aiken claimed that all ambassadors were proficient in "at least one of the languages commonly used in the countries to which they are accredited"[42]), it does seem an unnecessary burden to impose on them when modern methods of language training could be instituted systematically by the department. The Department of Finance's training section administers a course in spoken French which the official may attend during working hours if his other commitments permit, but it is often difficult for him to adapt his timetable to meet the times of the course, which is arranged for the civil service as a whole and not just for the Department of Foreign Affairs. The Department of Foreign Affairs also runs a weekly French class of its own, but this takes place outside normal working hours.

Other training courses organised outside the Department of Foreign Affairs are used informally and intermittently by officials. The Institute of Public Administration provides administrative and economics courses which may be attended by individual officials; however, the Department of Foreign Affairs has never arranged with the IPA a course specifically designed for members of the foreign service. The immediate obstacle to the provision of more courses for officials is held to be the shortage of staff within the department. Pressure of work does not permit junior officials to absent themselves for the several weeks or perhaps months which a

[41] Dáil Debates: 191, 668.
[42] Dáil Debates: 227, 2162.

worthwhile course requires, and it would be difficult for senior officials, who would have to teach such courses, to fit them into their busy programme. Given this constraint, the best that can be done is to arrange informal lectures and seminars within the department and to send probationers to the two-week general training courses for administrative officers and third secretaries organised by the Department of Finance.

A similar piecemeal arrangement exists for briefing officials before a new posting. In a short space of time, usually one month before the appointment takes effect, the official is sent for some days to other government departments, to the state-sponsored agencies such as Córas Tráchtála and Bord Fáilte, and to private firms, so that he can acquaint himself with Ireland's economic interests in the country to which he is being appointed. During this same period, he is expected to settle his personal affairs and be briefed by the various sections of the headquarters office. Since it is doubtful whether he obtains anything but the most superficial views of the task which awaits him, perhaps in future more time should be devoted to establishing firmer contacts with these organisations outside the department.

Apart from these all too hasty briefings, there is little attempt to provide regular comprehensive refresher courses for officials. In 1956, Mr MacBride suggested that it might be possible to ". . . arrange with our universities here for a course of lectures in international affairs, particularly in international economics. This course of lectures . . . could become one of the prerequisites of admission to the service; but, in addition . . . it would be helpful to the members of the existing staff. . . ."[43] However, nothing came of this idea, not least because the universities did not provide comprehensive courses of this kind. The department insists that officials returning from overseas postings report to the economics section on trade promotion, and this 'debriefing' acts as a surrogate refresher course. Anything more than this would necessitate the establishment of a permanent training section either within or outside the department and a readiness to give officials leave to attend courses.

It must be stressed that a greater use of formal training courses outside or inside the department does not invalidate the principle of

[43] Dáil Debates: 159, 598.

practical training 'on the job'; rather it supplements this training and is made necessary by the expertise demanded of the modern diplomat. Some other small foreign services appear to attach much more importance to specialised training: the Norwegian official, for example, receives a year to eighteen months special training before undergoing two probationary years working in the head-quarters office.[44] A shorter, more intensive course of three months is provided for the Australian foreign service and is also open to some other nationalities.[45] The Irish diplomatic service might find this sort of course suitable, particularly if it was repeated at fairly regular intervals during the official's career. It would demand the hiring of additional staff, but in the long-term it might be the most effective means of allowing the diplomat to lift his head above the morass of day-to-day duties in order to reconsider the broad purpose of his occupation as well as to acquaint himself with new developments.

To date, the training of the Irish diplomat has placed considerable emphasis on the ability of the individual to learn for himself, to take the initiative in equipping himself beyond the basic requirements of his job and to profit by the varied experience which he undergoes. By examining the background and careers of individual diplomats, we may obtain a clearer picture of the type of man who can 'survive' this recruitment and training to emerge as an effective member of the Irish foreign service. Unfortunately, the information on which such a survey can be based is scanty: the only detailed facts available have to do with heads of missions, the details of whose careers are announced in newspapers and in some international reference works. Even here, there are gaps in the biographical data which are readily available and, perhaps more seriously of all, there is no information about senior civil servants as a group, so that we are unable to see exactly how a career in the Department of Foreign Affairs compares with that in the domestic departments.

Nevertheless, from the information which is available, an impression can be obtained of the type of official at the highest level of the Department of Foreign Affairs.[46] The survey made here covered

[44] J. A. Storing, *Norwegian Democracy* (Allen & Unwin, London, 1963) pp. 109–112.
[45] A. Watt, *The Evolution of Australian Foreign Policy 1938–1965* (Cambridge University Press, Cambridge, 1967) p. 295.
[46] See Table 3, p. 308.

twenty officials in service in the early nineteen sixties, all of whom were either heads of missions or held posts of equivalent rank in Ireland; the variation in age between them was twenty years. We know comparatively little about the personal background of these officials and nothing about their parents' occupations; however, in view of their fairly expensive and prolonged formal education, it is safe to assume the majority of them came from well-to-do middle class families. All were male, although women have held important diplomatic posts: Josephine McNeill was appointed Ambassador to the Netherlands in 1950 and Sheila Murphy was an assistant secretary in the department. Both are now retired. Mrs McNeill was not only the first (and up to 1973 the only) woman ambassador; she was the last ambassador to be appointed from outside the career foreign service. In 1972, there were twelve women in the foreign service, the most senior being a counsellor.[47]

There is no explicit information provided about the officials' religion, but, since only one of the twenty is recorded as having attended a Protestant school, it is safe to assume that the majority of them were Catholics. Fortunately, there were data about their educational background, and it is clear that most officials received some form of higher education. The majority attended the better-known Catholic secondary schools in the Dublin vicinity; of the sixteen recorded cases, five attended Christian Brothers' Schools in Dublin and Dundalk, two went to Blackrock College, two to Clongowes and one each were students at Belvedere, Castleknock, Rockwell and the Protestant Dublin High School. Two were educated overseas. Although these facts indicate the predominance of a particular type of education, there is little evidence of any particular institution acting as a 'nursery' for diplomats.

At least seventeen of these officials are recorded as having attended a university and read successfully for a first degree. The majority (twelve) were graduates of the National University of Ireland, eight of whom were members of University College Dublin; three were graduates of Trinity College Dublin and one each graduated from the L.S.E. and Glasgow. Most of them took Bachelor of Arts degrees,

[47] This represents an increase in the number of women entering the Department of Foreign Affairs; two years previously, there were only five.

although there is little evidence of what specific academic disciplines they studied. In one case, a degree in Classics is recorded, in another a degree in Celtic Studies; the graduate from the London School of Economics had studied International Relations (this was the only recorded instance of the academic discipline being related to the subsequent career). Only in one case was the undergraduate course taken on a part-time basis. No less than twelve of the twenty individuals continued their university education and took postgraduate or professional courses. Five future officials took LL.B's and three of these eventually practised as barristers, while other postgraduate courses studied included diplomas in archaeology and Ph.D's in archaeology and history. It is significant that, of these twelve, five engaged in postgraduate work in overseas universities—in England, the USA, Spain and Germany—and three had their academic or literary work published. On the basis of this survey, the Irish diplomat appears to be highly educated and, in some cases, to have had experience of other countries before commencing his career.

It is interesting to examine the pattern of these officials' careers. Not all of them entered the civil service immediately after completing formal academic training. The three who did not were practising barristers—for periods of three, six and eight years respectively— and two of these came into the Department of External Affairs as legal advisers. So, although there is no evidence that private commercial or academic experience is regarded as mandatory by the department, the man with legal qualifications and experience may well be at an advantage at the recruitment stage. On the other hand, his promotion within the department may subsequently suffer if he is confined to the limited opportunities afforded to the specialised legal adviser.

Thirteen out of the twenty officials had some experience of working in other government departments. Of these, one was an official who had started his career in the Department of External Affairs and was then loaned for a two-year period to the Department of Industry and Commerce as head of a division. The other twelve, who had started their careers in another department, were transferred, perhaps on a temporary basis, to External Affairs and subsequently remained there. Two of these officials with experience in the Departments of Industry and Commerce, Agriculture and Supplies came into External

Affairs in the specialised post of commercial attaché, while another, who had twelve years experience in the Department of Industry and Commerce and the Department of Finance—including the post of private secretary to the permanent head of the civil service— was then transferred to External Affairs. Experience outside the department, particularly for the man with legal qualifications, was an invaluable asset both for the individual officer and for the department as a whole.

However, the transfer of officials from one department to another occurs not so much because it is regarded as desirable in itself; rather, it reflects the demands imposed on the department by increasing obligations. The fact that the phenomenon was significant among senior officials in the early nineteen sixties is a consequence of the expansion of the Department of External Affairs in the nineteen thirties. It had to catch up on the already established government departments and recruit experienced personnel from them. Although the consequences of this type of recruitment may remain for some time, the subsequent pattern of recruitment from the initial administrative level of third secretary was adopted in all but the most exceptional cases; to this extent, a 'closed shop' career foreign service has been evolving. This is in many ways advantageous for the career diplomat's future but it might give rise to a 'closed shop mentality' by which the foreign service becomes even more isolated than it would naturally tend to be. In view of the fact that increased specialisation in the promotion of economic objectives and in dealing with the press is required of the modern diplomat, this danger becomes all the more acute. If there is to be a separate foreign service, therefore, it is vital that it should be responsive to government policy as a whole and to the government service as a whole.

This seems to be yet another reason for more extensive training *outside* the Department of Foreign Affairs and, possibly, for a greater use to be made of outside experts, such as commercial and press attachés, to work with and in the foreign service. The increasingly common practice of seconding officials from other departments on a short-term basis, especially since Ireland joined the EEC, may contribute towards more open attitudes. Both the career diplomats— whose occupational obsession with status can encourage *élitism*—

and Irish-based civil servants, whose views of the foreign service may be unreasonably coloured by what appear to be the extravagance and pomp of diplomatic life, could more readily come to terms with each other's problems.

The official's career inside the Department of Foreign Affairs can de divided into two parts. First, he works his way up to the highest post—that of counsellor—which is still under direct supervision both at home and abroad. In the cases reviewed in the survey, the average period of time this took was just under twelve years, though it may take as few as six years or as many as eighteen, and in very rare cases may not be necessary at all. Obviously, the length of time depends on the man's previous experience either inside or outside government and on the opportunities for promotion. The present average age of entry to the department is nearer twenty-five than the twenty-nine which was the average of the officials in the survey (the higher age reflecting their experience outside the departments); this might prolong the initial stage when the department's rate of expansion is slow. Usually, half this time will be spent in the head-quarters office and half in overseas missions, but there is considerable variation in the individual cases.

Of the twenty officials investigated, the average age at which the second main stage of their career was reached was forty-one. This echelon is the senior or ambassadorial post where the official has considerable personal responsibilities. If his status is assistant secretary, he is in charge of a branch of the headquarters office; if his rank is that of chargé d'affaires, minister plenipotentiary or ambassador, he may be in charge of an overseas mission. Of the twenty careers surveyed, the earliest age at which this level was reached was thirty-four and the latest, fifty-one. So the senior official usually has a career of some twenty years before he retires. Since there are five senior posts overseas for each one in the headquarters office, by far the greater part of this time is spent overseas: of the twelve officials in the survey who had at least ten years service at this level, the average length of service at home was 4.8 years as against 13.1 years abroad. During his whole period of service, the Irish diplomat will generally have had experience in three or four overseas offices as well as in the headquarters office, and it seems that this policy of rotating posts is maintained in the majority of cases.

One peculiarity remains to be noted. Owing to the rotation of even the most senior posts, it is likely that, in addition to the permanent head of the Department of Foreign Affairs—the Secretary—there will be one or more senior ambassadors serving under him who have been his predecessors as head of the department; for example, in 1972, the Ambassador to the UN was the Secretary's immediate predecessor. This phenomenon highlights the diffusion of authority within the department, unavoidable because of the very nature of its work, but which could conceivably be intensified by a clash of personalities who are given nearly equal status at the highest level. If such disagreement took place and the Secretary's authority was weakened, the result might be a lack of cooperation between the offices at home and those abroad. However, there is no evidence that this arrangement does hinder either the administrative or policy-formulating duties of the highest officials in the Irish foreign service; indeed, it appears that some senior officials are as happy in charge of one of the more important overseas embassies as they would be in charge of the department itself.

★   ★   ★   ★

After fifty years, the Irish diplomatic service has developed a certain tradition, with the concomitant advantages and disadvantages. It is a professional body, commanding the loyalty and integrity of its members. It can look back on some notable achievements, such as the evolution of Ireland's constitutional relationship with Britain and the maintanance of neutrality. It has included—and includes—some notable public servants. Because of the paucity of material on Irish diplomatic history, it is impossible to assess precisely what influence Irish diplomats have exerted on the making of specific decisions, but it would be very surprising indeed if, in general, they had not played an important role.[48]

On the other hand, the department's tradition may have been a factor in its slow response to the increasing scope of diplomacy since World War II and in its fondness for procedures which work well

---

[48] The first-hand account of Irish diplomacy, such as is found in the opening chapter of C. Cruise O'Brien, *To Katanga and Back* (Hutchinson, London, 1962), is all too rare.

in a very small and intimate organisation but which are outmoded in a larger body. Yet it is only fair to point out that, although the diplomatic service can be criticised for its slowness to act or because of a certain narrowness in its approach, this is largely because it is operating in a domestic environment in which it is often regarded with suspicion and usually with indifference. The Irish people have a diplomatic service which is, if anything, better than they deserve.

PART III

THE DOMESTIC ENVIRONMENT

"All powers of government, legislative, executive and judicial, derive, under God, from the people, whose right it is to designate the rulers of the State and, in final appeal, to decide all questions of national policy, according to the requirements of the common good."

Bunreacht na hÉireann, Article 6.1.
(Constitution of Ireland)

Chapter 6

THE DOMESTIC ENVIRONMENT:
PUBLIC OPINION AND FOREIGN POLICY

"We believe the public to be their own masters, that we do not know better than they. . . ."

Noel Browne, 1963
(Dáil Debates: 199, 1145)

"I do believe that . . . the public can be led to see certain things. . . ."

Eamon de Valera, 1936
(Dáil Debates: 62, 2736)

THE state's foreign policy is made by the government; decisions are taken, formally by the cabinet as a whole, but in particular by the head of the government and the foreign minister, and, for the most part, are based on the information and advice provided by the professional civil service and in particular by the Department of Foreign Affairs. This is how policy is *made*, in so far as specific governmental decisions are taken and responsibility for them is accepted. However, this outline is altogether too simple in that it largely ignores the many factors within the state which the policy-maker must consider before taking specific decisions; these factors are often beyond his direct control since they exist outside the institutional framework of the executive arm of the government. Even in the most totalitarian state, those who govern cannot consistently ignore the demands of the governed, and are unlikely to do so for, in general, they are themselves the product of the environment in which these demands have evolved.

The domestic environment in which foreign policy is made may

163

be examined either as a very general phenomenon, existing outside any clearly defined period of time, or more especially as the interplay of specific forces within the political system, operating at a particular period of time. When analysing the first alternative, an approximate parallel may be drawn with the notion of a society's political culture: this has been defined as "the general pattern of people's attitudes and beliefs about, and their knowledge of, politics and political phenomena—including such matters as political organisation, the government, politicians and public servants, what the state should do and should not do, and the extent and effectiveness of their own participation in politics".[1] Two of the most important elements of political culture in Ireland are a distinctive nationalism based on a long struggle for independence, and the pervasive influence of Britain.[2] The consequent ambivalence towards Britain and the obsession with Anglo-Irish relations have already been remarked on,[3] although the extent to which they colour the domestic environment of Irish foreign policy cannot be stressed too often.

Two other general features of the Irish domestic environment deriving from elements of the country's political culture are the prevalence of conservatism in Irish politics and the inward-looking attitudes found at many levels of the political system. The persistence of a sizeable rural community, noted for its bias towards self-owned small farms, has produced people who are "conservative, unimaginative shrewd in the short run and individualistic".[4] Their interests rarely extend beyond their own locality and their ties with large emigrant communities in Britain, North America and Australia are essentially personal. Moreover, they are strongly attached to a Church, which although international in scope, in its Irish manifestation has been notably insular. Admittedly, it provides a view of the world which allows of certain rather simple ideological guidelines; there is thus a degree of sympathy for other states which profess similar values (in theory if not altogether in practice), and there is a broad commitment to the forces of 'the free world' in the struggle against

[1]Chubb, *The Government and Politics of Ireland*, p. 43.
[2] For a concise survey of Irish political culture, see ibid, pp. 43–60.
[3] See above pp. 5-6.
[4] Chubb, *The Government and Politics of Ireland*, p. 52.

international communism. The image of Ireland as a Catholic state is found in James Dillon's typical plea "to hear in the councils of the world one Catholic voice at least which is allowed and which has the courage to speak, which has the knowledge to speak, which has the solid ground beneath it of a Christian philosophy on which to stand".[5] Yet it may be argued that the Catholic Church is important not because it influences the specific foreign policy issues but because it colours the domestic environment in a general way, as a paternalistic upholder of traditional and inward-looking values.[6]

Of course, all these characteristics of Irish political culture are subject to change, and for the past twenty years have experienced an unprecedented pace of change. Nevertheless, they remain—and will remain for some years—pertinent to the policy-maker's domestic environment. In the first place, the policy-maker's beliefs and attitudes were formed in that environment, predisposing him to take the prevailing political culture into account in all his actions, even if he does this almost subconsciously. But at the same time he is subjected to continual pressures from individuals and groups who may not have his occupational commitment to the formulation of foreign policy but who are similarly affected by the political culture. In short, he has to be aware of, and respond to, what is commonly known as 'public opinion'.

The concept of 'public opinion' is often used to describe "the people as a whole in their political role".[7] This political role, however, is a complex one. Mr Seán MacBride, when Minister for External Affairs in 1950, referred to public opinion as ". . . that complicated interplay of forces—the Press, the radio, the speeches of public men, the statements of important organisations and so on—which at the same time, shapes the point of view of the ordinary man in the street and serves to make it articulate".[8] Thus, it is necessary to distinguish between the mass of varying and often contradictory opinions held

[5] Mr James Dillon spoke these words in 1945 when he was an independent TD. Later he became leader of the Fine Gael party. Dáil Debates: 97, 2601.

[6] See below pp. 278-283.

[7] Frankel, op. cit. p. 71.

[8] Dáil Debates: 122, 1530.

by members of the public (though not necessarily expressed in any clear or effective manner) and those institutions and organisations which embody these opinions, so that they may more effectively influence government policy. It may be argued that in the second instance we are dealing with the channels of public opinion rather than with public opinion itself, but it is misleading to stress the distinction to this extent. To describe parliament, political parties, special organisations and the communications media merely as 'channels' is to underestimate the extent to which they can create public opinion as well reflect it. Indeed, the most immediate and positive influence on the government comes from the "small attentive minority"[9] of the public which animates the behaviour of these more clearly-defined sectors of public opinion.

This is not to say that the concept of public opinion as referring to the people as a whole is completely devoid of significance. Because it is ". . . an important negative influence . . . which prescribes the limits within which foreign policy can be shaped",[10] it is less easy to identify than the pressures exerted by specific groups. Nevertheless, in the last resort, the government depends for its existence on the support of the majority of the public, and so its policies must remain within the limits which are prescribed (or assumed by the policy-maker to be prescribed) by mass opinion. As Frankel says, "power of a vague but very real nature is here wielded without any clearly defined responsibility".[11]

An examination of the influence of this mass opinion on Irish foreign policy, although an essential part of an investigation of the process by which foreign policy is formulated, is, therefore, subject to severe limitations. The difficulties are compounded by the lack of scientific investigation of public opinion in Ireland and, indeed, by the absence of the proper basis for the sort of investigation which has been executed with some degree of success in industrialised states; such factors make assumptions on this subject extremely precaiious. Public opinion polls are a very recent phenomenon in Ireland, and it is doubtful whether they are being used extensively or continuously

[9] Frankel, op. cit., p. 77.
[10] ibid., p. 70.
[11] ibid, p. 70.

enough to identify underlying political tendencies.[12] Letters to the press, reflecting at best the views of a very small, informed minority only, and at worst the attitudes of groups or individuals on the outer edge of society, cannot be a reliable guide. Therefore, assumptions about what the 'Plain People of Ireland' are thinking about any specific issue are based on intuition rather than on reason. Nevertheless, such assumptions are made, maintained, reflected in policy and tested only by the course of time and events.

However, the Irish Constitution does include one formal procedure whereby public opinion can be tested. A joint petition by a majority of the Seanad and one-third of the Dáil—with the further approval of the President—enables any bill to be referred directly to the will of the people.[13] In theory, this process of referendum has the virtue of isolating an important issue, concentrating public debate on it and arriving at a simple numerical expression of the weight of public opinion for and against it. But in fifty years, the only referendum held on an issue of foreign policy was that of May 1972, to elicit the public's approval of Ireland's proposed entry into the EEC. In a comparatively high poll of 71 per cent., 83 per cent. voted in favour and 17 per cent. voted against. In quantitative terms, this was a decisive affirmation, but the result still gave rise to varying interpretations. The vote was interpreted by some as a rejection of violence in the Northern Ireland crisis, since the proponents of violence were among those groups opposing EEC membership. It was seen by others as the only rational response to a difficult economic situation,

---

[12] The first opinion poll on a foreign policy issue in Ireland was held between 24 and 29 June 1961. A sample of 943 people, "representing all political parties, and all sections of the community aged sixteen years and over" were questioned about their attitudes to the EEC. This was the only such poll for many years (see *The Irish Press*, 12 July 1961). In April 1968, *The Irish Press* published the results of a poll on attitudes towards partition (see *The Irish Press* 16, 17, 18 19 April 1968). In May 1970, the periodical *This Week* commissioned a poll on political attitudes on a range of issues connected with the question of partition and its reverberations in Ireland's cabinet crisis of May 1970. The results were broken down by age, sex, region, and party allegiance, thus providing an interesting profile of opinion at this particular date. The campaign for EEC entry stimulated a more consistent interest in polling: surveys were conducted in May 1971 (see *This Week*, 2 July 1971) and prior to the referendum in May 1972 (see the *Irish Independent*, 3 May 1972). In addition, privately commissioned surveys were made, but the results were not published. Financial considerations still mitigate against the routine adoption of significant surveys.

[13] Bunreacht na hÉireann: Articles 27 and 47.

or, alternatively, as a positive acceptance of a European identity. But to some observers it was merely "a confirmation of the highly entrenched character of party loyalties in the Irish electorate".[14]

More often than not, the referendum in Ireland has proved to be a Pandora's box to be opened only with the greatest reluctance or in a fit of collective absent-mindedness. The EEC referendum was itself used, not to test opinion prior to the making of policy, but to ratify and legitimise policies which had been made over ten years previously. In 1963 in the Dáil, when Dr Noel Browne and Mr Jack McQuillan attempted to call a referendum before negotiations to join the EEC were completed, the Fianna Fáil government refused to countenance the possibility. Several arguments were put forward against the suggestion, including the expense it would entail and the fact that the public will on the matter had been reflected to some degree in the general election of 1961.[15] But the main obstacle consisted of a strict interpretation of the Constitution. Article 27, Section 1 of the Constitution of 1937 states that a majority of the Senate and at least one-third of the Dáil may petition the President to refuse to promulgate a bill already passed by both Houses "on the ground that the Bill contains a proposal of such national importance that the will of the people thereon ought to be ascertained".[16] This petition may then be accepted or rejected by the President after consultation with the Council of State. The President's discretionary powers and the fact that Article 27 applies to a specific bill and not to a general statement of government policy considerably limit the frequency with which referenda are held.

In 1963, the government's case as expounded by the Minister for Justice, Mr Haughey, was that the legal procedure for joining the EEC was signing the Treaty of Rome, and that while treaties had to be laid before the Dáil, they were not, like ordinary bills, subject to the provisions of Article 27. Mr Haughey pointed out that

> if the treaty involved does not bring any corresponding change in our domestic law, then that is the end of the matter. . . .

[14] T. Garvin and A. Parker, 'Party Loyalty and Irish Voters: The EEC Referendum as a Case Study', *The Economic and Social Review*, October 1972.
[15] See Dáil Debates: 199, 1140–2.
[16] Bunreacht na hÉireann: Article 27.1.

The Constitution does not contemplate or envisage in a case of this sort, . . . that the matter should be brought before the people by means of a referendum. In fact, the exact opposite is the position. The Constitution clearly contemplates that the making of such a treaty is a matter entirely for the Government and the Oireachtas. . . .[17]

The government's position was endorsed by spokesmen of the major opposition party, though for rather different reasons. Mr M. J. O'Higgins of Fine Gael claimed that "if parliamentary democracy is to function here, it must function on the basis of Deputies representing their constituencies, representing the people and being prepared to shoulder the responsibility of coming to decisions with regard to matters of this sort that come before them".[18] In effect, referenda were seen as a threat to the role of parliamentary institutions and they were regarded in much the same way by the British government, faced with similar demands following the British negotiations to enter the EEC. The fact that a referendum was eventually held in Ireland was due to the exceptional circumstance that adherence to the Rome Treaties necessitated an amendment of the Irish Con-stitution, which in turn made the popular vote obligatory. But in cases where this condition does not apply, it is most unlikely that a referendum will take place.

It is clear that, as an expression of mass public opinion, the refer-endum more often than not remains a dead letter, and it might be expected that where there is no institutional procedure for expressing political opinions, the public would have recourse to other forms of expression. One such outlet is participation in mass demonstrations. Although demonstrations derive much of their effect from their espousal by the leadership of specific groups rather than because they have any spontaneous force of their own, nevertheless they may be seen as examples of how the "predominant inattentive majority" influences the policy-maker.

The occasions when mass demonstrations have taken place in Ireland in response to an issue of foreign policy are relatively few. These

[17] Dáil Debates: 199, 1139–40.
[18] Dáil Debates: 199, 687.

protests are, on the whole, an urban phenomenon and usually occur in Dublin, the seat of government. Some of the more important of these demonstrations have indicated a widespread and intensive support for the foreign policy of the government of the day, rather than a wish to change it; in these cases, the protest is aimed at a foreign government. Notable examples were the large rallies held in Dublin during World War II, which were organised by the government, both to justify its policy of neutrality to the people and to demonstrate to outsiders, by the attendances and enthusiastic support of the crowds, that public opinion supported this policy and that plans by any of the belligerents which placed reliance on contrary assumptions could be seen to be unrealistic.

After World War II, a similar mobilisation of mass opinion was encouraged by the government and the other political parties, to attempt to demonstrate to foreign governments and their publics Irish indignation about Britain's failure to accede to the Irish government's claim to Northern Ireland. This attempt came to a peak when the British parliament, in passing the Ireland Act in 1949, in effect confirmed and strengthened Northern Ireland's status as part of the United Kingdom. In response, the Taoiseach, Mr J. A. Costello, spoke in 1949 of mobilising "all the moral energies of the Irish people, at home and abroad, towards bringing Partition to an end".[19] Although this policy was pursued abroad mainly through Irish emigrant organisations, particularly in the USA and Britain, at home there was an attempt to demonstrate that the anti-partition cause was supported by the majority of the public. Mass rallies were addressed by speakers of all political persuasions, including members of government and the main opposition parties, and funds were collected under the aegis of an organisation which aimed to represent *national* opinion—the 'Mansion House All-Party Conference'. However, these government-sponsored demonstrations had no effect on British policy, and once the Ireland Act was law, public interest was rapidly dissipated, for the Act did not materially alter the status of Irish citizens in Britain. The Irish government had clearly overestimated the strength of public opinion on this issue.

The difficulty of gauging the strength of public opinion was also

[19] Dáil Debates: 114, 3.

apparent on those occasions when an attempt was made to mobilise mass opinion in order to criticise the government's foreign policies. During the winter of 1936–1937, the government's policy of non-intervention in the Spanish civil war and its cautious attitude towards the recognition of General Franco's régime was opposed not only by the main opposition party, Fine Gael, but also by a pro-Franco group, the Christian Front, which enjoyed considerable popular support. Indeed, its leader Mr Patrick Belton, a Fine Gael TD, claimed to represent public opinion, or at least 99.9 per cent. of it;[20] the people of Ireland, he said, "have spoken on it, as over 100,000 citizens gathered in College Green to cheer for the success of the arms of General Franco".[21] He went on: "the real decision in this matter will be taken outside this House, and if the President wants to get public opinion on this matter, I will give him the opportunity of getting it by a public demonstration in College Green".[22] Mr Belton's claims and threats contributed towards an emotional debate in the Dáil on the Spanish Civil War (Non-Intervention) Bill, but did not in any degree deflect Mr de Valera's policy towards the war.

It can be argued that although Mr Belton's claims were mathematically far-fetched and unsubstantiated, he did nevertheless represent, or came near to representing, the mood of the greater part of the population. The issue at stake was generally painted in very simple and emotive colours—". . . the issue in Spain," said Mr James Dillon, ". . . is God or no God"[23]—and the Christian Front was seen as a crusade to defend the existence of the teaching and institutions of the majority church in Ireland. Collections were taken outside Catholic churches throughout the country in order to send volunteers to fight in Franco's army, and the degree of personal participation was further heightened by the fact that many Irish families had relatives in the religious orders which were suffering in the Spanish civil war itself. Directives from the pulpit and from the organisation of the Christian Front gave sympathisers specific objectives to pursue and a sense of reassurance.

It is plain that something much wider than any sectional, regional

[20] Dáil Debates: 65, 642.
[21] Dáil Debates: 65, 637.
[22] Dáil Debates: 65, 656.
[23] Dáil Debates: 65, 695.

or professional opinion was at work. It is equally clear that, even though public opinion was opposed to the government, the government was able to withstand this onslaught and maintain its policies, because of the strength of its leadership and its parliamentary discipline. In the general election of 1 July 1937—less than six months after the passing of the Non-Intervention Bill—although the Fianna Fáil government lost its absolute majority in the Dáil and had to continue with the support of the Labour Party, Mr Belton lost his seat in the Dáil. Despite the fact that the government's policy on the Spanish civil war was an issue in the election, other matters, such as the persistent economic crisis and the controversy over the new Constitution, had a greater impact.

There have been few movements of mass public opinion in Ireland with as broad a base as the Christian Front. Mass demonstrations criticising the government's foreign policy have occurred since, but while these have been a predominantly urban phenomenon, the Christian Front made its church door collections throughout the country. Apart from the nationalist rallies held during the IRA campaign of the mid-nineteen fifties, these demonstrations appealed to a narrower section of the community and particularly to students and organisations active in the universities. Up to the mid-nineteen sixties, the protests tended to be isolated events, such as the large demonstration against Russian intervention in the Hungarian rising of 1956.

Since then, however, they have taken place more frequently, perhaps because of the marked increase in the student population and by the example provided by political activism in other countries. Marches against American participation in the Vietnam war, South African apartheid or British policy in Northern Ireland, accompanied by the ritual burnings of flags and effigies and the delivery of petitions to junior embassy officials, are not uncommon. These may be interpreted as manifestations of opinion, but there is little evidence to suggest that government policy has been significantly altered by demonstrations, although, if taken in conjunction with other types of expression of opinion, they may provide the policy-maker with a keener perception of the particular issue. Sometimes if a demonstration becomes riotous, as happened at the burning of the British Embassy in Dublin on

2 February 1972, it can exacerbate an already tense diplomatic situation but this is hardly the same thing as effectively influencing long-term policy. Indeed, this particular demonstration, because of its violent outcome, may have induced a reaction against some of the objectives of those who instigated it.

The effect of mass public opinion is difficult to assess, and in Ireland, where its interpretation is more an art than a science, it is impossible to do more than hint at its significance in the formulation of foreign policy. It is, perhaps, best appreciated, not in terms of heads counted or of popular demonstrations held, for these tend to reflect transitory moods which often have less popular support than their appearance suggests, but rather in those boundaries formed by the prevailing political culture, beyond which the policy-maker will hesitate to venture. However, when calculating where these boundaries lie, the policy-maker's assumptions about the nature of public opinion, and especially about attitudes towards the international position of the state, become an important factor.

What appear to be widely differing assumptions have been made about Irish public opinion in this respect. For example, in 1946, Mr de Valera, as Taoiseach, thought "our people . . . as wise, politically, whether on national or international questions, as most people are . . . on the whole . . . they are wiser".[24] But ten years later, when holding the same office, Mr J. A. Costello took a less sanguine view of the wisdom of public opinion: "our people have had no very great interest in or indeed knowledge of foreign affairs", and, consequently, the government had ". . . a duty to educate our people in the importance of active participation in international affairs . . . to a proper conceit of themselves . . ."[25] Mr de Valera's optimistic view must be qualified by the fact that it was offered as a reason— or an excuse—for not embarking on a widespread public debate on whether to apply for membership of the United Nations Organization; and Irish public opinion had demonstrated its wisdom by maintaining him in office for fourteen years and through six general elections. Mr Costello's pessimism, while similarly coloured by his own long experience of opposition, nevertheless struck a more convincing note at the time and is not without significance in the present.

[24] Dáil Debates: 102, 1467.
[25] Dáil Debates: 159, 610–611.

When considering whether Irish public opinion is well-informed about international politics in general and Irish foreign policy in particular, there are two factors to be taken into account: first, the degree of interest shown in these matters and, second, the amount of information which is available to stimulate this interest. On the first point, there is not a great deal of evidence to suggest that the Irish people as a whole have shown a consistent or profound interest in foreign policy. This is hardly surprising, for as Mr Costello pointed out in 1956, "because for centuries we were not an independent and juristic personality no tradition of interest in foreign affairs grew up in this country".[26] The one tradition which did develop exemplified an almost exclusive interest in Ireland's relations with Britain, a preoccupation which has possibly made international politics outside the British Isles seem rather unreal, if not completely irrelevant, to most of the Irish people.

Even within this tradition, public opinion, with its scant appreciation of many of the wider implications of policies pursued by Irish governments, may be seen as of a somewhat crude and emotional character. Where physical change has been at stake, whether it was to a large degree symbolic or whether it affected the material well-being of the population, widespread public interest has been aroused. The removal of the British garrisons from the disputed ports in 1938 and the prolonged economic war following the cessation of land annuities to Britain in 1932 were two issues whose consequences were clearly seen, and the government's sensitivity to public opinion on both matters was considerable. On the other hand, the policies of W. T. Cosgrave's government, which in retrospect appear to be important landmarks on the road to constitutional independence, aroused little response and certainly did not save this administration from defeat in 1932. These policies called for subtle legal adjustments which were unintelligible to the layman; moreover, they were enacted in the distant and somewhat artificial arenas of the League of Nations and the Commonwealth, which in Irish eyes could never lose the stigma of being called 'British'. In the late nineteen forties, too, the public's initial outburst of enthusiasm during the anti-partition campaign did not outlive the failure of the government's policy of mobilising effective support from public opinion overseas.

[26] Dáil Debates: 159, 611.

However, the partition issue is not based entirely on constitutional niceties; indeed, the territorial and human dimensions are inescapable. Since 1969, the Irish public has followed the development of the Northern Ireland crisis in the press, radio and television, and its interest has been demonstrably high. An opinion poll published in June 1970 found that the 'don't know' category replying to questions on the partition issue was never higher than 8 per cent. of the overall poll, and on one question it was as low as 1 per cent.[27] As long as this issue has a direct bearing not merely on the traditional question of the Border but also on the political situation within the state, it is probable that interest will remain high. It is also noteworthy that in 1970, unlike the anti-partition campaign of the late nineteen forties, the predominant characteristic was concern and support for the quiescent policy of Mr Lynch's government.[28]

Public interest in Ireland's relations with countries other than Britain has, on the whole, been indistinct. One exception to this may be the period during World War II when the mass demonstrations in favour of neutrality betokened a more than usually keen reaction to the threat of invasion; it could be argued that military neutrality subsequently became a sacred cow of Irish policy, at least until the early nineteen sixties. A certain propensity for anti-communism— mainly because of religious beliefs—has been a staple characteristic of Irish politics; it was quite forcibly expressed during the Spanish civil war but has not been expressed so vehemently in recent years. Ireland's participation in the United Nations has aroused a measure of public pride, though perhaps this is not so much an effect of a clear appreciation of what the UN is trying to do as a consequence of the parts played by Irish personalities and Irish troops in the work of the organisation: the crowds at the funeral of Irish UN troops who were killed in the Congo aptly illustrates this communion of interests.

The possibility of joining the EEC aroused a certain public interest in the early nineteen sixties. An opinion poll, taken shortly before

[27] *This Week*, 12 June 1970.
[28] In a poll in 1970, 83 per cent. of those asked, disapproved of arms being supplied, to Northern Ireland (*This Week*, 12 June 1970). Just under two years later, following the referendum campaign during which more 'hawkish' attitudes towards the Northern crisis became associated, rightly or wrongly, with a 'no' vote on the EEC, the 'yes' vote was 83 per cent. of the total poll.

the Irish application was announced, revealed that 28 per cent. of those questioned were 'well informed' about the EEC—that is to say, they claimed to have either a 'good idea' (9 per cent.) or a 'general idea' (19 per cent.) of the Common Market; of the remainder, 36 per cent. had only a 'vague idea' and 36 per cent. had never heard of it.[29] Although this poll was not followed through, it is safe to say that ten years later, in the midst of a prolonged referendum campaign, such a degree of ignorance could hardly have existed.

In those instances where there has been public interest in issues of foreign policy, its effect on the policy-maker's range of choice has usually been imprecise and often negative. Nor is it probable that this public interest is always evidence of a rational assessment of alternative policies; rather, it may be based on simple attitudes and slogans. Although Ireland is a literate society, and by world standards highly educated, it is also noted for "a marked anti-intellectualism".[30] There is a reluctance to question conventional wisdom and to measure assumptions against the experience of other countries, even in the universities. The university system is based on the British model—but the British model of the early twentieth century, established before the social sciences were fully developed and before the academic discipline of international relations began to assume its own identity. Thus, although the study of international law has a small place in university courses (possibly sustained in part by the constitutional bias of Irish foreign policy during the nineteen twenties and thirties), it is only in the last fifteen years that the study of Irish politics has been soundly established and that the teaching of economics has prospered. As yet, however, the study of international relations—and indeed of international history—have not found a place even at the highest level of the educational system. This means that the Irish policy-maker does not operate against the background of an intellectual tradition which would enable him to broaden his perspectives, organise his ideas more systematically and compare his problems with those experienced by officials in other countries.

The absence of an intellectual tradition has also affected the presentation and dissemination of information to the public; the

---

[29] *The Irish Press*, 12 July 1961.
[30] Chubb, *The Government and Politics of Ireland*, pp. 56–57.

communications media have not always paid much attention to foreign affairs. During the greater part of the period since 1922, the communications media in Ireland have consisted principally of the press and a state-sponsored radio station. The press must be regarded as the more important of the two media because of its more extensive news coverage and the greater diversity of opinion it encompasses; nevertheless, its effectiveness as an educator of public opinion may be too easily overrated. As Frankel points out, the press is "selective, often unreliable, and is not read by all citizens even in fully literate and democratic societies".[31] In Ireland it has suffered from two serious disadvantages: a widespread reticence concerning the distribution of public information, and technical and economic difficulties brought about by the small size of its audience.

The suspicious attitude towards the distribution of information displayed by many Irish public institutions stems, perhaps, from the traditions of the nineteenth-century British civil service; its persistence may be due to the experience of the independence struggle and, more especially to the civil war, when reticence and distrust were among the principal virtues of survival. In the field of foreign policy, this suspicion was particularly evident in cases where information and discussion could be used to stir up the embers of the Treaty controversy. One consequence of this bitter conflict was the allegation of political bias made against the Department of External Affairs, which served as one of the principal whipping-boys of W. T. Cosgrave's new administration.

Because it had absorbed some of the staff and the overseas duties of the provisional government's publicity department, the new Department of External Affairs was seen in 1923 as little more than a partisan propaganda machine, or, in the words of Mr Gavan Duffy, (a former Minister for Foreign Affairs in the provisional government), as "a most unsatisfactory Publicity Department for the present Government".[32] Although Gavan Duffy was a politically isolated critic of his former colleagues, the more extreme and numerous elements of anti-Treaty opinion, shortly to cohere in the Fianna Fáil Party, echoed his sentiments until they achieved office in 1932.

[31] Frankel, op. cit., p. 72.
[32] Dáil Debates: 3, 2388. See also above, pp. 108-109.

12

In this atmosphere of distrust, it is hardly surprising that the Department of External Affairs did not develop a tradition of a frank and comprehensive dissemination of information to the public.

But the paucity of information lay not only in the natural desire of government departments to avoid joining in political controversy and allegations of bias; it also stemmed from the fact that individual newspapers were associated with one or other faction in the civil war. Under W. T. Cosgrave's government, *The Irish Times* opposed the very existence of the independent state, while the *Irish Independent*, with a much larger circulation, supported the Treaty, albeit without much passion. Neither gave much attention to Irish foreign policy. In 1926, for example, the leader of the opposition, Mr Johnson, complained of the lack of information about Ireland's policies in the League of Nations: "Beyond the statement made by the Minister in the Dáil, we have had no information except what we could glean from the British Press".[33]

When *The Irish Press* was founded in 1931, it was clearly associated with the Fianna Fáil party and, under Mr de Valera's government, was known by opposition speakers as "the kept paper of the Government".[34] De Valera maintained in 1938 that he could "from time to time give general directions as to the policy that is to be adopted in certain circumstances but . . . only . . . in a very general way, and only at rare intervals".[35] Nevertheless, the image of *The Irish Press* as a 'party newspaper' has proved difficult to eradicate. As a consequence of the real or supposed political bias of individual newspapers, the press as a whole was viewed with distrust by the government—the principal source of information on foreign policy— for as long as party politics remained embittered by the original Treaty split. Only too easily the bogey of an 'irresponsible press' could be conjured up to justify the government's withholding information; thus in 1936, Mr de Valera complained that "when even small matters went to the opposite side of the House, they were in the Press almost as soon as I was told that contact had been established".[36] It has often been the tendency of governments, there-

[33] Dáil Debates: 14, 540.
[34] Dáil Debates: 71, 184.
[35] Dáil Debates: 71, 430.
[36] Dáil Debates: 64, 1219.

fore, to release as little information as possible except in parliamentary debates, where announcements can be more easily controlled.

In addition to the reticence of governments in releasing information, the discussion of foreign policy in Irish newspapers has suffered from the technical shortcomings of the press itself. Serving a population of under three millions, even the bigger national dailies have until comparatively recently been either unwilling or unable to employ sufficient staff to report fully on special aspects of public life and have been unadventurous in their search for sources of information abroad. The fate of the Irish News Agency, established in 1949 but closed down in 1957, was a case in point. Although it undoubtedly suffered from the fact that it was a government-sponsored organisation directly associated with an unsuccessful government policy (the anti-partition campaign), the Irish News Agency was above all the victim of sectional interests which were apparently not concerned with its potential both as an improved source of overseas information and as a coherent source of information on Irish affairs for the foreign press. Attacked by the National Union of Journalists and by important press proprietors, its early demise illustrated the complacency of the communicators, an attitude which the service they provided hardly justified.

During the nineteen sixties, however, the press began to develop a more positive attitude. This was possibly a reaction to the increasing competition for news presentation, especially because of the advent of television. The circulation of the three Dublin-based national dailies (the *Irish Independent*, *The Irish Press* and *The Irish Times*) dropped from 342,400 in the second half of 1956 to 329,593 in the corresponding period in 1966, a decrease of 3.7 per cent. Despite this general stagnation—and the competition of the British national dailies which in recent years have taken up to 10 per cent. of the Irish market—the smallest of the Irish dailies, *The Irish Times*, increased its readership: circulation rose from 36,267 in 1956 to 44,563 in 1966.[37] While several reasons may be adduced for this exceptional increase, including the fact that this paper at last lost the stigma of

[37] These circulation figures are audited by the Audit Bureau of Circulations, London, and were supplied by the Association of Advertisers in Ireland Ltd. Reliable figures for the fourth national daily, the *Cork Examiner*, were not available for the period 1956–66.

being anti-national and anti-Catholic, its comprehensive and comparatively specialised treatment of Irish foreign policy and world politics in general may account for this increased readership. In the early nineteen sixties, *The Irish Times* was the only national daily which examined in detail the implications of Irish membership of the EEC. In 1964, it became the first Irish newspaper to employ a diplomatic correspondent (as distinct from a political correspondent), but since then, the other dailies have also improved their coverage of foreign affairs.

This development has not proved to be the panacea for all the ills of the Irish press. Nevertheless, a content analysis carried out at the end of 1967 showed that the percentage of coverage given to international news in the dailies compared more than favourably with the British press (See Table 4). Despite the fact that a large part of the

TABLE 4:
INTERNATIONAL NEWS CONTENT OF IRISH NEWSPAPERS
(with some British comparisons).

Newspaper	Percentage of paper given to international news	Percentage of paper given to total news
Cork Examiner	$17\frac{1}{2}\%$	46%
Irish Independent	$11\frac{1}{2}\%$	35%
The Irish Press	12%	$38\frac{1}{2}\%$
The Irish Times	$22\frac{1}{2}\%$	$41\frac{1}{2}\%$
The Times (London)	13%	$36\frac{1}{2}\%$
Daily Express	4%	$18\frac{1}{2}\%$
Daily Mirror	2%	24%
Sunday Independent	5%	26%
The Sunday Press	9%	44%
Sunday Times	13%	23%
News of the World	2%	12%

Source: B. Chubb, *The Government and Politics of Ireland* (Oxford University Press, London, 1970), Table 5.2, p. 128.

'international' category included British news, the argument that Irish papers ignore the outside world cannot be sustained, although it is noticeable that the Irish Sunday papers do not follow the same pattern as the dailies.

No information is available on the effect that international news has on people who read it, although it is possible to find out what proportion of the reading population are exposed to it. When the figures are examined, it becomes apparent that the readership of Irish national daily papers, especially the morning papers, is relatively small. In a survey made in 1968,[38] only 59 per cent. of readers aged fifteen and over had seen a morning paper, and it is these papers which carry the main coverage of international news. On the other hand, 81 per cent. had seen the less informative Sunday papers. The difference is more marked in rural communities (54 per cent. read morning papers, 82 per cent. read Sunday papers) than in urban communities (63 per cent. read morning papers, 80 per cent. read Sunday papers), which suggests that people outside the cities are less well-informed about world affairs.

For many years, the only communications medium to compete with the press was the radio; the number of radios in Ireland more than doubled in the fifteen years between 1950 and 1965, from 97.6 per thousand of the population to 209.9 per thousand.[39] Midday newscasts have an audience of nearly one half of the adult population[40], and important political events are given considerable coverage: in August 1969, for instance, the debate on the Irish appeal to the UN Security Council for a UN peace-keeping force in Northern Ireland was transmitted live from New York. Of all the media, radio has probably the widest audience, although television may have a greater impact. The expansion of the latter medium is a recent phenomenon, and the number of television sets in Ireland rose from 1.2 per thousand in 1955 to 114.7 per thousand in 1965.[41] Much of this expansion is

[38] *National Readership Survey in Ireland*, 1968, British Market Research and Social Surveys (Gallup Poll) Ltd. The results are summarised in Chubb, *The Government and Politics of Ireland*, see especially Tables 5.5, 5.6, on p. 131.

[39] Figures from *Statistical Abstract of Ireland* (Stationery Office, Dublin) and information supplied by Radio Telefís Éireann.

[40] Chubb, *The Government and Politics of Ireland*, pp. 139–140.

[41] The figures up to 1962 are based on historical evidence derived from Irish TAM surveys and other estimates. From 1963, figures are based directly on Irish TAM surveys.

a consequence of the development of the native Irish television service, Radio Telefís Éireann, although areas in the more heavily populated east of the country can receive British transmissions as well. The ownership of television sets is not yet evenly distributed throughout the country and at present there is a similar pattern of ownership to that of newspaper readership; for example, farmers, particularly in the west and north-west, own markedly fewer sets than do the people in the urban communities.[42] It might not be an exaggeration to speak of a geographical 'information barrier' reinforced by occupational characteristics.

Television programmes have a more extensive and regular political content than radio programmes: outside newscasts and some current affairs programmes often include items which are directly relevant to foreign policy issues. Figures for early 1967 showed that late evening (9.45 p.m.–10.00 p.m.) newscasts reached an audience of more than a third of the adult community and that the principal weekly current affairs programme reached an audience of 30 per cent.[43] It is probable that in the eastern, more urbanised part of the country, at least, the population is exposed to as much information about world politics as viewers in relatively highly industrialised states, although the effect which this has on attitudes towards foreign policy must remain a matter for conjecture.

Nevertheless, it certainly has *some* effect. The objectivity of programmes has become an increasingly acute problem both for the journalists who work for Radio Telefís Éireann (RTE)—the state broadcasting company—and for the government which, having established RTE as a state-sponsored body, has the power to intervene in its affairs. The degree of government control and the extent of the station's journalistic independence have become, through a series of controversial incidents, a sensitive political issue, which has important consequences for the type of information and comment which RTE feels free to broadcast.

The issue came to a head in November 1972 when the government dismissed the RTE Authority because of its alleged failure to comply with a government directive on the broadcasting of the views of

[42] Chubb, *The Government and Politics of Ireland*, p. 140.
[43] ibid, p. 141. See Table 5.13.

illegal organisations. Well before this crisis, the government had intervened in two incidents connected with Irish foreign policy. In April 1967, a news team was prevented from going to North Vietnam after government intervention—a decision defended on the grounds that the project was unnecessary and the film could, if sold to foreign television services, be re-edited and misinterpreted to reflect badly on the government's policy. In February 1968, a team from the *Seven Days* current affairs programme was called back from Lisbon while *en route* to report the Nigerian civil war from Biafra; this decision was taken because the sponsors of the project were alleged to have arranged the visit as a propaganda stunt for the secessionist Biafran 'government'.

Subsequent debate on these two incidents centred more on the implications for the freedom of RTE than on the merits of the government's foreign policy. It is only fair to make the point that, in the case of the Biafran project, the government had to protect the interests of a considerable number of Irish citizens in Nigeria, and a programme which came out strongly in support of either side in the conflict could conceivably endanger the lives of these people. In the case of the projected film on North Vietnam, however, it was never made clear what interests were at stake apart from the government's ability to avoid making a public declaration of its position on the war. In both cases, much resentment was caused by the manner of the government's intervention which occurred at the eleventh hour, following behind-the-scenes representations.

To some extent, the poor relations between the government and RTE were symptomatic of a persistent difference of opinion over the government's obligation to justify policy as well as to make it. It is not that this obligation has not been recognised by the government, but rather that it tends to be presented according to the strict letter of traditional British constitutional theory. Government policy is explained by the minister responsible, at a stated date, in the Dáil. Apart from the fact that government spokesmen tend to deviate from this practice whenever it suits them to do so, the procedure is inappropriate if strictly adhered to, because it is tied to the measured and sometimes leisurely pace of parliamentary life. The pressure of events and the need for the press, radio and television to provide instant coverage of complex issues, will lead inevitably to some degree of over-simplification and over-dramatisation and, possibly, to some distortion of government policy. In the long term, the way to minimise this is not to exercise *ad hoc* censorship, but rather to intensify the efforts made through all the communications media to explain policy accurately. Television, in particular, is a medium which enables an individual or a group to gain immediate and wide publicity for a point-of-view, and the government must compete for attention; it must correct misrepresentations and misunderstanding of its policies by frequently briefing journalists and other interested parties and holding press conferences. This may well entail employing two information officers for every one that is now attempting to cope with this task. Democratic government cannot claim to be the least expensive form of government.

★   ★   ★   ★

Public opinion remains an unsatisfactory concept, a nebulous something to which politicians appeal and which is informed by and expressed through the media of communication. When considering its effect on foreign policy, it is therefore more rewarding to examine its more active and tangible manifestations, what have been called the "leaders, intermediaries and sectional interests".[44] By examining the role of these elements of the "attentive minority", which both embody a variety of opinions and simultaneously attempt to mould and inform these opinions, we may be able to see more clearly the complexities and uncertainties of the domestic environment in which foreign policy is made.

The first such element is the parliament. In its legislative capacity, it can take certain decisions about government policy. Its individual members, representing a variety of opinions, are in a position to bring their views to the attention of the government. Then the role of the political party, acting as a link between parliament and public opinion, must be taken into account, particularly its capacity for articulating foreign policy objectives, based on its own interpretation of public opinion, and its justification of goals and policies in election campaigns.

[44] Frankel, op. cit., p. 70.

A third important area, outside the formal category of party politics, is that of the special interest groups which represent specific though exclusive opinions, but which nevertheless attempt to influence government policy directly and through the other intermediaries of public opinion.

Chapter 7

THE ROLE OF THE OIREACHTAS

"I think there is no Parliament in the world in which matters of foreign affairs are dealt with so casually as in this Parliament here."
John A. Costello, 1937
(Dáil Debates: 67, 748)

"There should be some sort of machinery created by the Government which will not affect their precious constitutional right of having the last word in policy, but which will, at least, have the advantage of telling us what is going on."
John A. Costello, 1957
(Dáil Debates: 163, 668)

IN a parliamentary democracy, legislatures are perhaps the most important single element of public opinion. However, they are at a considerable disadvantage in trying to assert their will on the formulation of public policy, for in spite of their formal powers of making and removing governments and of approving legislation and policy, the facts of representative politics in modern states lead to a degree of electoral and parliamentary organisation which tends to reinforce the position of governments. Furthermore, the need for stability and continuity in a changeable and complicated environment have usually meant that, ultimately, legislatures have given the benefit of the doubt to the government and have voluntarily waived many of their formal powers.

Even in those legislatures where favourable constitutional arrangements or a comparative lack of party discipline are found, the overall weakness of the parliament is evident, and especially its ability to influence foreign policy. For example, few representative assemblies are better equipped with either the constitutional rights to intervene

187

or the procedural means to do so than is the Senate of the United States Congress, particularly when it acts through its Foreign Relations Committee. Nevertheless, the comparatively well-informed and reasoned opinions of this body count for little beside the authority of a government which may withhold information in the 'national interest', and which may conduct diplomatic and military operations on its own initiative. It is small comfort to the parliamentarian that the only real check on the government's room for manoeuvre is its ability or lack of ability to control its intrinsic parts: 'sub-governments', such as intelligence agencies, are usually even further removed from parliamentary control than their nominal masters. The experience of a powerful representative assembly like the US Congress demonstrates the importance of two characteristics of foreign policy which will inevitably minimise the capacities of legislatures to make, or even influence, decisions.

For the individual state, international politics is often a series of *faits accomplis* to which the state must react quickly and coherently in order to survive. Because of this, united national action is a pre-requisite which a legislature, which reflects the diversity rather than the unity of the state, is ill-suited to carry out. A second feature of international politics—the necessity for secrecy about inter-govern-mental contacts—also militates against parliamentary participation in making of foreign policy. This is because, while in inter-state politics the state is a single 'person', acting ideally with a single-mindedness of which few humans are capable, in its internal manifestations the state represents an inadequate attempt to reconcile a diversity of opinions and interests. Therefore, the organs of the state will have to play two contradictory roles as they posit the fiction of national unity while recognising and attempting to adjust to the reality of national diversity.

This schism is most evident in the field of foreign policy, and governments take care to minimise its disruptive consequences. It is important to protect the external, diplomatic conduct of the state from possible disruption by uncoordinated and shortsighted manoeuvres from within. Diplomatic confidence and secrecy are not just convenient devices for power-mad statesmen, although they may serve the purposes of wicked or stupid men. But this is not a decisive argument against secrecy. When Woodrow Wilson attacked secret diplomacy as being a cause of World War I, he was avoiding the real issue, which was why that secret diplomacy was ineffective. His own concept of 'open diplomacy' often degenerated into open propaganda, although, ironically, its corollary, the international organisation, has also served on occasion as a convenient means for the pursuit of secret diplomacy. After some fifty years of 'open diplomacy', it is clear that some degree of diplomatic secrecy has been essential to help states to act as responsible members of the society of states and to communicate with each other.

It is evident that "as large clumsy bodies, parliaments cannot effectively exercise initiative and their participation upsets diplomacy".[1] This is particularly true of the British parliament and others modelled on it. In the first place, its procedure allows for the general, rather than for the specialised, supervision of government policy and, as a result, its members find it difficult to find the time to assess detailed information on particular areas of policy or the occasions on which to use effectively the information which they do possess. Moreover, the practice of ministerial responsibility means that the flow of information is not only restricted, but has to be channelled through the cabinet: often when this information reaches parliament, it is general rather than specific. Finally, party discipline (necessary for governmental stability under this system) discourages the criticism which would be most harmful to a government's foreign policy— that from its own back benches. Only where electoral or political conditions exist which favour more than two important parties, is this restraint mitigated.

The Irish parliament—the Oireachtas[2]—is modelled on Britain's Houses of Parliament and suffers from the limitations of its prototype. Nevertheless, in special circumstances, it has important responsibilities and, like the British parliament, has the power to supervise the government's foreign policy. The opportunities it has to do this are discussed in this chapter, and the uses which Irish representatives have made

[1] Frankel, op. cit., p. 25.
[2] The Oireachtas consists of the President and the bicameral legislature, composed of the indirectly elected upper house, the Seanad, and the directly elected lower house, the Dáil. However, in general usage, the term applies mainly to the parliamentary bodies and may be considered as synonymous with 'Parliament'.

of these opportunities are examined in the next chapter. However, the Oireachtas—like the British parliament—is not a single legislating body, but is composed of three parts. Although the major part— the directly elected representative assembly—is by far the most important, the President and the Senate also have some responsibilities.

In some countries, the head of the state is acknowledged as the principal policy-maker: the United States President and the French President (in the Fifth Republic) come readily to mind as examples of heads of state who hold ultimate responsibility, especially in the field of foreign affairs. The President of Ireland does not come into this category, for his activities are ceremonial rather than political and, as far as foreign policy is concerned, are confined to the formal duties of receiving ambassadors and distinguished foreign visitors and of making official visits to other states. Since he plays a passive and formal role not unlike that of the British constitutional monarch, it might be wondered what relevance his office has to an examination of the formulation of foreign policy.

The answer lies in his *potential* constitutional powers. When the office was established in 1937, the President was recognised as the ultimate safeguard of the people's interests as well as the symbolic head of state.[3] He may refer bills to the Supreme Court; he may refuse to sign bills if he is petitioned by a majority of the Senate and not less than one-third of the Dáil, and he may refuse a dissolution of the Dáil to a Taoiseach who no longer has the support of a majority of its members.[4] It is conceivable, therefore, that if the President was of the opinion that the government's foreign policy did not

[3] Before the office of President was established, Ireland, like other dominions, had a Governor-General from 1922 to 1936. The personal representative of the British monarch, he had no discretionary powers, and both Mr W. T. Cosgrave's and Mr de Valera's governments took care to ensure that none of his actions could be construed as affecting government policy. There were three holders of the office: the first two chosen by consultation between the British and Irish governments, the third by the Irish government alone. The latter, Mr Donal O Buachalla, willingly cooperated in reducing the position to an absurdity before it was abolished in 1936. See J. L. McCracken, *Representative Government in Ireland* (Oxford University Press, London, 1958), pp. 153–158.

[4] See F. B. Chubb, *A Source Book of Irish Government* (Institute of Public Administration, Dublin, 1964), pp. 30–31, and McCracken, op. cit., pp. 158–61. The specific powers referred to above are embodied in *Bunreacht na hÉireann*, Articles 26.1, 27, and 13.2.2,° respectively.

reflect the interests of the people as a whole, he could oppose it, provided the above contingencies ensued.

But these constitutional provisions have never been tested and the holders of the office have acted strictly according to the advice of the government of the day. Referring to a speech made by President O'Kelly in 1946, Deputy Davin was not making a wild assumption when he said: "I take it that that speech must have been submitted to the Minister for External Affairs and members of the Government before it was delivered".[5] Indeed, before the repeal of the Executive Authority (External Relations) Act in 1948, which transferred to the President the formal power of signing ambassadors' letters of credence (formerly done by the British Crown), it was claimed in the Dáil that, as far as external relations were concerned, "the poor President has no more functions than any funny man at a fancy fair"[6] and was in office "only for attending at football matches".[7]

Such interpretations of the President's office may now appear to be exaggerated. Nevertheless, it is difficult to imagine a President building up the necessary political support to enable him to act in any but the most unusual circumstances, for the government is in a strong position to counter the President's opposition. In 1963, when Dr Noel Browne suggested that President de Valera was opposed to the possibility of abandoning military neutrality and might refuse to sign any bill which had this effect, the reply of the Minister for Justice, Mr Haughey, was emphatic: "He cannot".[8]

The President has not as yet been a notable factor in the formulation of Irish foreign policy. The second constituent of the Oireachtas— the Senate—is perhaps in a better position to exert a more constant influence on the policy-makers, and is indeed an essential ally to the President, should the latter wish to oppose a bill. However, Irish Senates have been severely handicapped in any attempts they have made to promulgate their views effectively, and this constriction has been as conspicuous in the field of foreign policy as in other areas of public policy.

[5] Dáil Debates: 101, 2202.
[6] Dáil Debates: 101, 2235.
[7] Dáil Debates: 106, 2354.
[8] Dáil Debates: 199, 1150. The Constitution even restricts the President's movements. He is not allowed to leave the state "save with the consent of the Government", *Bunreacht na hÉireann*, Article 12.9.

There have been two Irish second chambers—the first from 1922 to 1936, the second from 1937 to the present—and both have been hindered by their different methods of composition. The first Senate, formed by nomination and by a confusing electoral system, was regarded as a sop to the pro-British, ex-Unionist minority and was never treated with much respect by the Dáil, especially after W. T. Cosgrave's defeat in 1932.[9] The second, officially called Seanad Éireann, is constituted by means of an equally complicated system of vocational representation, which, because of the nature of its electorate, reproduces the political alignments of the directly elected Dáil.[10] Neither Senate was equipped to play an influential role, since they were either 'anti-national' or mainly the repository of old and faithful party politicans.

The Irish Senate, like most second chambers, has as its principal function the right to discuss legislation or government policy in an assembly removed from the immediate partisan pressures of the lower house and, if it so wishes, to delay the enactment of legislation.[11] But, since the period during which the Senate may delay a bill is limited to 180 days, it is obvious that its role is secondary to that of the Dáil; and because comparatively little foreign policy is expressed in the form of legislation, the Senate has few ways of extracting information from the government.[12] There is no question-time, nor are there regular debates on foreign policy, as there are when the estimates are debated in the Dáil; in fact, the Senate sits for only a fraction of the time which the Dáil devotes to parliamentary business.[13] So apart from the rare occasions on which legislation on foreign policy is discussed in the House, the Senate is restricted to debating motions on specific issues tabled by senators themselves.

This is not to say that Senate debates on foreign policy are

[9] For a brief résumé of the development of the first Senate, see McCracken, op. cit., pp. 137–46. A detailed account is Donal O'Sullivan, *The Irish Free State and its Senate* (Faber and Faber, London, 1940).

[10] See the Report of the Commission on Vocational Organisation, 1943, p. 310, quoted in Chubb, *A Source Book of Irish Government*, pp. 207–8.

[11] See J. McG. Smyth, *The Houses of the Oireachtas*, 3rd revised edition (Institute of Public Administration, Dublin, 1973), p. 41.

[12] Smyth, op. cit., p. 51, estimates that approximately 90–95 per cent. of the Senate's work consists of a consideration of Dáil legislation.

[13] See Smyth, op. cit., pp. 54–56.

necessarily poor; on the contrary, they are often of a higher standard than debates in the lower house. Donal O'Sullivan is of the opinion that the first Senate "always provided a better forum than the Dáil for the discussion of external affairs",[14] and the same has been said of the second Senate. Speaking in the Senate on the important Republic of Ireland Bill, 1948, the Minister for External Affairs, Seán MacBride, congratulated senators for their approach to the debate which was ". . . in a constructive and helpful manner generally, more so than in the other House".[15] More recently, during the stalemate over the expansion of the EEC in the nineteen sixties, possibly the clearest and most informative discussion of Ireland's position occurred, not in the Dáil, but in a Senate debate in July 1966; this reminded both public opinion and the government alike that it was desirable to establish diplomatic contacts with the EEC which were at least as effective as those of the other applicant states.[16]

The reasons for the Senate's ability to provide coherent debate can be ascribed only partly to the slightly different composition of the second chamber. Although some senators, particularly the six senators elected by the universities, are not constrained by party discipline, most senators are former or aspiring deputies with clear party loyalties. Senators may, of course, have more time and money to enlarge their horizons by travelling abroad and, like members of the Dáil, may be chosen to represent the Oireachtas at the meetings of the Consultative Assembly of the Council of Europe, the European Parliament and other international parliamentary organisations. But it is the Senate's very political ineffectuality which is conducive to its higher debating standards. For in spite of his obvious partisan affiliations, the average senator may not feel the need to reiterate his party's line or to demonstrate its strength as rigidly as he would in the Dáil; knowing that what he says will receive comparatively little attention, he feels freer to divulge his own thoughts, which are often further

[14] O'Sullivan, op. cit., p. 250. He cites as an example the debates in February 1929 in the Dáil during which the Minister for External Affairs, Mr McGilligan, referred to the more pertinent discussion in the Senate (Dáil Debates: 28, 371). It was the Senate, too, which first proposed a foreign affairs committee in May 1924, and which discussed the question more fully than the Dáil ever did until 1957 (Senate Debates: 3, 29–44). See also below, pp. 233–234.
[15] Seanad Debates: 36, 252–3.
[16] Seanad Debates: 61, 1833–1920.

13

developed than the usual party programme. The Senate is capable of providing an occasional and informative debate on foreign policy, which may have some indirect effect on the public's or on the government's attitudes. Nevertheless, the major burden of 'supervising' the government's foreign policy must be borne in the Dáil.

The Dáil is the directly elected legislative assembly from which the members of the government are drawn and to which they are responsible. Although it cannot be said to have any significant policy-making powers,[17] it has powers and responsibilities which enable it to influence policy-making indirectly, by extracting information from the government and by criticising government policy. Only in extreme cases—where party discipline or the allegiance of independent deputies is weakened—will the Dáil exercise its constitutional right to reject a policy, for this, by convention, entails the somewhat drastic consequence of the resignation of the government. Thus, the Dáil must be judged by its ability to discuss foreign affairs in such a way as to reflect and educate public opinion, and also by its ability to criticise specific government policies. To carry out these responsibilities, it must be well-informed and encouraged to participate to some extent in the policy-making process; this in turn depends on the way in which its work is organised and the way in which its members approach their task. The rest of this chapter is concerned with the first of these factors—parliamentary procedure.

★　　　★　　　★　　　★

The procedure of the Dáil offers a variety of opportunities to discuss foreign affairs and to criticise the government's foreign policy. But these are not all equally effective nor do they all occur at regular or frequent intervals. The government's power to declare war, for example, is subject to the assent of the Dáil.[18] However, adoption of a policy of neutrality during World War II demonstrated that the real choice between war and peace depends, not so much on the constitutional rights of the Dáil, as on events which are largely beyond

---

[17] Nearly all policy discussed is government policy: from 1965 to 1969, only eleven private members' bills were introduced in the Dáil. See Smyth, op. cit., p. 46.

[18] *Bunreacht na hÉireann*, Article 28.3.1°.

the state's control. Indeed, the outbreak of World War II was the occasion for the first amendment to the 1937 Constitution, by which the powers of the government and of the Oireachtas were redefined to meet the less clear-cut circumstances where the state's survival is threatened by a war in which the state is not a participant—of being "in time of war".[19]

A more regular opportunity for the Dáil to effectively intervene in foreign policy (or any other policy) lies in its power to choose the leader of the government after a general election or the resignation of the previous head of the government. However, this power is usually more a question of constitutional theory than of political practice, for rigid party affiliations tend to make the Dáil's vote on this question largely a formality. But not wholly so. When neither of the two major parties has been able to reach an absolute majority, they must rely on winning the support of smaller parties or of the few independent members; even if the support of independents is not numerically vital to the actual nomination of the Taoiseach, the margin between majority and opposition is generally small enough to make a government reluctant to offend these deputies. It is, therefore, conceivable that support for a government could be won or lost on an issue of foreign policy. However, before 1961 there is little evidence that this was the case and it seems unlikely to occur, particularly as a result of the decisions of independent members, whose electoral strength and consequent parliamentary behaviour depend to a high degree on local constituency considerations.

In 1961, Seán Lemass, whose party held seventy seats out of the 144 in the Dáil, had to rely on the support of two independent deputies to form his government. Since the question of joining the European Economic Community had been one of the major talking-points of the 1961 general election which produced a potential deadlock in the Dáil, it might be argued that this was a case in which a government was chosen by two independent representatives (of a small

[19] The precise words in the Constitution are: "Nothing in this Constitution shall be invoked to invalidate any law enacted by the Oireachtas which is expressed to be for the purpose of securing the public safety and the preservation of the State in time of war or armed rebellion, or to nullify any act done or purporting to be done in time of war or armed rebellion in pursuance of any such law". *Bunreacht na hÉireann*, Article 28.3.3°.

proportion of the people) because of an important issue of foreign policy. However, a closer investigation reveals that there was no disagreement between the three main parties on joining the EEC, and the point at issue was which party would the electorate entrust to conduct the negotiations.[20]   Under these circumstances, the attitudes to the EEC of the two independent deputies must have been of minor importance in determining the way in which they voted on the nomination of the Taoiseach.

In short, the Dáil—as distinct from the people—has not yet chosen a government because of an issue of foreign policy. The debates which accompany the procedure for nominating the Taoiseach and his government do, however, provide an opportunity for discussing foreign affairs and for criticising previous policies; but the opportunity is rarely taken. These debates are supposed to be concerned with the suitability of government personnel; in practice, they cover the whole range of government policy and serve little purpose other than to indicate vaguely what a party's general approach to foreign policy will be. In 1922, Gavan Duffy inquired about the government's attitude towards the League of Nations;[21] in 1933, W. T. Cosgrave attacked ". . . the external policy which has been pursued and persisted in by the out-going Government . . .";[22] in 1959, James Dillon, leader of the main opposition party attacked the government's 'independent' policy at some length;[23] and in 1961 there were several references to Ireland's application to join the EEC.[24] These remarks were brief, expressed in very general terms, and tended to be lost in a welter of complaints about domestic policy.

Most discussion of foreign policy takes place during routine sessions of the Dáil, rather than on the special occasions just referred to. Issues are brought up not only when legislation is debated but also at parliamentary question-time, in general debate, and during the

[20] See Dáil Debates: 192, 49. An exception to this was the two-man party of National Progressive Democrats.
[21] Dáil Debates: 1,30.
[22] Dáil Debates: 46,19.
[23] Dáil Debates: 176,114–18. This was the most prolonged and intensive criticism of either a foreign minister or an issue of foreign policy during a nomination debate. The issue was the government's UN policy, and Mr Dillon, leader of the Fine Gael party, was backed up by the leader of the Labour party, Mr Corish.
[24] Dáil Debates: 192, 49 and 59.

annual debates on the estimates of government departments. Legislation forms the bulk of parliamentary work but is less prominent in the field of foreign affairs, since a great deal of foreign policy is never expressed in legal form. That which is, can be found in three special types of legislation: the ratification of international agreements and treaties, bills to implement these agreements, and special constitutional legislation which unilaterally alters the international position of the state.

The Constitution makes it clear that "every international agreement to which the State becomes a party shall be laid before Dáil Éireann" and that international agreements "involving a charge upon public funds" are only binding if approved by the Dáil (with the exception of "agreements or conventions of a technical and administrative character").[25] In so far as this involves the crude alternatives of outright acceptance or rejection of a treaty, it gives the Dáil very limited room for manoeuvre, particularly as the majority party or parties will be loath to oppose the *faits accomplis* which their own leaders in the government present to them. However, as Frankel points out, "this power usually implies the capacity to suggest amendments and often impels the governments to resort to prior consultation, in order to avoid the possibility of rejection".[26] In this way, the government's knowledge that it will have to face the public scrutiny of a full-scale debate in the Dáil prevents it from negotiating what it thinks would be an unacceptable agreement. Of course, the government may either misjudge the situation or, in the case of a multilateral treaty, may take little part in the negotiations leading up to it. When Ireland was in the loosely defined British Commonwealth, this led to acrimonious ratification debates, for important constitutional implications (and imagined constitutional implications) often under-pinned the principal aims of the treaties.[27]

The occasions on which formal ratification debates are necessary are comparatively rare, and the government has never been defeated on such a debate. However, the points at issue in the treaty may

[25] *Bunreacht na hÉireann*, Article 29.5.
[26] Frankel, op. cit., pp. 25–26.
[27] See, for example, the debate on the Anglo-American Liquor Treaty, 1924 (Dáil Debates: 6, 2917 ff.) and the Treaty for the Renunciation of War (the Kellogg-Briand Pact) of 1928, debated in the Dáil in February 1929 (Dáil Debates: 28, 277 ff.).

come before the Dáil again in the form of implementing legislation. For example, after accepting the international non-intervention committee's policy towards the Spanish civil war in 1936, the government not only had to face a difficult debate ratifying this decision (the Spanish Civil War (Non Intervention) Bill of 1937), but also had to put the Merchant Shipping (Spanish Civil War) Bill to the Dáil shortly afterwards in order to make the non-intervention policy effective. Several other important bills of this type have been necessary, usually arising from the long-term treaty obligations necessitated by membership of the League of Nations or of the United Nations.[28] Again, a government defeat on such legislation is most unlikely, but a debate does provide deputies with an opportunity to obtain detailed information and to press for government reassurances on specific aspects of the policy to be followed. However, governments always seek to reduce enabling legislation to a minimum. An important instance of this was the passing of the Defence (Amendment No. 2) Bill of 1960, which authorised the government to employ the armed forces outside the state for indefinite periods; this obviated the need for them to ask for the approval of the Dáil at regular and frequent intervals.

A third type of legislation was extremely important as far as Irish foreign policy was concerned, and allowed the Dáil much scope for expressing its views. This was the legislation between 1932 and 1948 which defined the state's constitutional position. Since Ireland's evolution in, and unilateral departure from, the British Commonwealth took place during this period, the legality of this process was an issue constantly confronting the Dáil. The Executive Authority (External Relations) Bill of 1936 was one of the two most important bills of this kind, and was the culmination of a succession of legislative acts which all had the effect of changing the state's relationship with Britain. Although the Dáil was rushed into defining its views on the bill, under the threat of the guillotine, the same cannot be said of the other vital piece of quasi constitutional legislation, the Republic of

[28] For example, the League of Nations (Obligations) Bill of 1935 (authorising Irish support of the League's sanctions against Italy) and the Defence (Amendment) Bills Nos. 1 and 2 of 1960 (authorising military support for the UN's Congo operation). The agreements with Britain in 1938 also caused a spate of additional legislation concerning the financial and commercial aspects of the new situation.

Ireland Bill of 1948, the purpose of which was to repeal the Act of 1936. For three long days in November 1948, the Dáil exercised its right to discuss the country's relations with Britain and the Commonwealth on the last occasion before this issue became part of the more usual bilateral or multilateral treaties and agreements. Whether it did so effectively is another question, and it can be argued that the House was poorly equipped to deal with the highly legalistic aspects of Irish policy towards the Commonwealth.[29]

But legislation represents no more than the visible peak of the (rather small) iceberg of Irish foreign policy; it expresses merely a portion of the government's activities and affords the Dáil only irregular and infrequent opportunities of influencing the government. On the other hand, the Dáil may more often intervene in foreign affairs through parliamentary questions and routine debates.

The parliamentary question, which may be raised throughout the period in which the Dáil is sitting, is the most readily available method by which a member of the Dáil can raise issues of foreign policy. However, there are serious limitations to this form of democratic control. In the first place, the time allowed for answering questions is restricted, and questions on foreign affairs have to compete for attention with a multitude of questions on domestic—and very often on local—politics. For example, from October 1956 to July 1957, out of approximately 1,800 questions answered, only 303 came into the category of 'miscellaneous', a category which foreign policy shared with other peripheral issues.[30]

Parliamentary questions are not normally a means of exerting direct pressure on the government, but rather are a means of extracting information which may be used *inter alia* to discredit government policy; questions thus act as an irritant, which if persistently applied— and supported by wide publicity—may in the long run make untenable a specific policy. These questions may, however, have to be asked for years rather than for months or weeks. In October 1932, Mr de Valera was placed in an embarrassing position when, in replying to a question, he was forced to admit that the King of England signed

[29] See below, pp. 230-231.
[30] See T. Troy, 'Some Aspects of Parliamentary Questions', *Administration* vol. 7. no. 3, p. 252.

the letters of credence of Irish representatives abroad;[31] in 1946, he faced a barrage of similar questions,[32] was rather less obviously embarrassed, and the King continued to sign letters of credence. This is not to say that these questions were completely without effect— for in 1948, a new Taoiseach, John A. Costello, showed a greater sensitivity to questions on Ireland's relations with Britain and the Commonwealth than Mr de Valera had done. Describing the background to his decision to repeal external association and also to leave the Commonwealth, Mr Costello professed to having been upset by questions:

> When Deputy Cowan was putting down his questions to me . . . I foresaw that there was an unending vista of barren controversy facing us and I must admit that I recoiled from the prospect of a constitutional Purgatory, wherein I should spend an indefinite period of my time in perilous pirouetting on constitutional pin-points.[33]

Another case where a government's foreign policy was reprehended during question-time occurred during the period of Ireland's neutrality in World War II. In 1944, the questions of James Dillon—the only vocal opponent of neutrality—provoked Mr de Valera to threaten to censor questions in some way:

> Questions which appear to be aimed at embroiling us with one set or other of belligerents . . . are very often tendentious in the framing and the mere putting of them on the Order Paper is dangerous. . . . If there is a continuance of questions of this sort, I shall have to ask the House to give to the Ceann Comhairle, or to some other authority, the power to exclude them from the Order Paper.[34]

But Mr Dillon stood firm in his defence of the parliamentary questions

[31] Dáil Debates: 44, 525–6.
[32] For example, between 14 February and 12 June 1946; see Dáil Debates: 99, 2090; 100, 1587–8; 101, 1595.
[33] Dáil Debates: 113, 384.
[34] Dáil Debates: 92, 1911–12.

which he described as ". . . the most potent weapon in the hand of an individual Deputy against the Executive" and, moreover, a weapon whose ". . . use with discretion is the responsibility of the individual Deputy".[35]

James Dillon's point was not denied, but the fact that he described the parliamentary question as "the most potent weapon" does not disguise the fact that, nonetheless, its potency is limited. In no case was this more clearly shown than when the Fianna Fáil government decided to join the EEC in 1961. Quite apart from the cascade of questions on the economic implications of this decision, the number of questions on the political implications was overwhelming. After the Christmas recess of 1961, Seán Lemass was faced with no less than twenty-eight such questions in one day, a surfeit of parliamentary curiosity which both detracted from the impact made by the more searching questions and gave Mr Lemass considerable opportunity to avoid many of the points in his brief and very general replies.[36] When he was asked whether joining the EEC would affect Ireland's UN policy, Mr Lemass was able to content himself—if not his questioner—with the typically vague reply that it might "be affected in some degree".[37]

One of the most serious weaknesses of the parliamentary question is that it allows the government spokesman a definite advantage. He is favoured by the rigid form in which the question must be posed, by the limited time set aside for its answer, and by the firm control of the Ceann Comhairle (Chairman) over the extent to which supplementary questions be raised. The government spokesman has been briefed by his department and has what appears to be authoritative information with which he may refute what are often no more than the hints and suggestions of the individual deputy.[38] He may plead the need for diplomatic secrecy on questions of foreign affairs: that documents are confidential to the governments concerned, that the question is still being negotiated or that the question is hypothetical—the latter being Mr Lemass's reason for not indicating

---

[35] Dáil Debates: 92, 1914–15.
[36] Dáil Debates: 193, 1–25.
[37] Dáil Debates: 193, 22.
[38] See Troy, op. cit., pp. 255–56.

the government's attitude towards a possible failure of the EEC talks nine months before the talks did fail.[39]

When challenged on this issue, in December 1962, by the leader of the Labour Party, Brendan Corish—who said that "it is not good enough for the members of the Government to say these are hypothetical questions"[40]—Mr Lemass's reply was revealing. There were two sorts of question, he said, which he did not feel obliged to answer. First, there were those "which could in any circumstances cause difficulties or complications for us in these negotiations". He continued: "The second type of question that I do not like answering is one which asks me to speculate about the possible course of events in the future. . . . It is an unwise operation for any politician to endeavour to prophesy regarding a course of events which is not under his control".[41] If silence is to be the golden rule of the government's approach to parliamentary questions, it must be left to the unborn historian to discover to what extent a government has abused its pleas for secrecy.

There is a more immediate means of counteracting an unsatisfactory reply: the deputy may ask for an adjournment debate. Although the time set aside for such a debate is only half an hour and is not followed by a vote, it is at least possible for deputies to disclose the details of the issue and to force the government spokesman to defend his case in more precise terms, which might expose its weaknesses. Furthermore, by lifting the issue out of the normal ruck of parliamentary questions, the possibility of obtaining more effective publicity is enhanced. It was on an adjournment debate on 8 March 1962 that the Taoiseach, Mr Lemass, was compelled to admit that the policy of strict military neutrality was no longer to be justified by the partition of Ireland; although he shrugged this off as 'academic', it was, nevertheless, the clearest indication made to the Dáil by that date than an important element of Irish foreign policy might be changed.[42] But such admissions are rare, and obviously only a very limited number of questions can be pursued on the adjournment.

Most members of the Dáil would probably agree with Mr Aiken's

[39] Dáil Debates: 194, 1163–6.
[40] Dáil Debates: 198, 1357.
[41] Dáil Debates: 198, 1474–5.
[42] Dáil Debates: 193, 1315–24.

words when he was questioned in 1964 on his government's attitude to the admission of communist China to the UN. After trying to explain the position, he complained: "We cannot deal with a complicated issue like this simply by question and answer".[43] However, the only alternatives to the parliamentary question are the much less frequent full-scale debates, and opportunities to discuss foreign policy on these occasions are comparatively rare. The most frequent debates in which the discussion of foreign affairs is relevant are those general debates on the whole range of government policy, which are usually held (under a variety of titles) before the Dáil adjourns for the seasonal recesses; the annual debate on the Estimate for the Department of the Taoiseach also could be placed in this category. But, although these debates theoretically offer the Dáil a periodic synopsis of national policy, in practice they provide little opportunity for anything but the general discussion of a wide variety of unrelated subjects.

Indeed, foreign policy may not be mentioned at all in these debates. When it is, it is merely referred to rather than discussed; even the more comprehensive references tend to repeat in more general terms the arguments raised on previous occasions. During a two-day debate on 2 and 3 August 1961, four speakers (including the Taoiseach and the leader of the opposition) referred in some detail to the previous day's announcement of the government's application to join the EEC; four other speakers (including two leaders of minor parties) mentioned it briefly, while the thirteen other deputies spoke as if this issue had never been raised.[44] Although this may be a reflection of the average parliamentary representative's attitude to foreign policy,[45] it also demonstrates the unsatisfactory nature of general debates. In the event, none of the eight speakers who did attempt to raise the issue of EEC membership, elaborated on the remarks they had made a month previously (during a debate on the OECD Convention and the External Affairs Estimates), but passed on to other aspects of government policy. Repetition and superficiality, it seems, inevitably tend to replace intelligent discussion on these occasions.

[43] Dáil Debates: 213, 903.
[44] Dáil Debates: 191, 2570 ff.
[45] See below, pp. 215-221.

Nevertheless, it could be argued that, by providing an overall summary of government policy, the general debate fulfils a useful role. The Dáil provides other opportunities for more detailed discussion of specific policies. Of these, the only regular one for the discussion of foreign policy is the annual debate on the Estimate for the Department of Foreign Affairs.[46] Theoretically, this is an opportunity for deputies to criticise the administration of the department, but, in order for a discussion of policy to take place, the procedure of 'referring the Estimate back for reconsideration' must be adopted. It is not difficult to do this and the procedure is by no means always strictly applied, but the result is an unsatisfactory and confusing mixture of the listing of administrative details and the articulation of national objectives. In 1931, for example, the Fianna Fáil spokesman, Mr Mullins, laced his attack on the government's Commonwealth policy with comments on the pay of officials, guest lists at receptions in London, complaints about negligent representation abroad, the lack of publicity, British police interfering with Irish Sweep tickets in the post, flags at international football matches, trade with Greece, the USA and the Soviet Union, extra-territorial limits, the medical examination of immigrants, and the Hoover moratorium.[47] Usually, only the most important issues make any impact in this amount of detail, but never exclusively so, and the minister's reply inevitably reflects the confused nature of the debate.

In fact, the minister's role in the estimate debate is of cardinal importance: he both introduces and sums up the debate and in so doing can help to gather the disparate strands of administrative detail and overall policy into a coherent pattern which may make some impact on public opinion. In this respect, parliamentary discussion is again at the mercy of the government, for as a former Minister for External Affairs, Seán MacBride, pointed out in 1953, "it is very difficult for the Opposition to serve any useful or constructive purpose

[46] There were no estimate debates in the critical years of 1927 (following the murder of Kevin O'Higgins) and 1940 (because of the situation following the fall of France). On some other occasions, estimates debates have either been little more than a formality, due to a recent change of government (e.g. 1951, 1954), or have been 'postponed' to the following year—in effect, cancelled—as, for instance, in 1966. In these cases, the vote of the department must still receive the formal approval of the Dáil.
[47] Dáil Debates: 39, 1230–47.

if the Government is silent on its policy in regard to any particular matter".[48]

Mr MacBride himself was one of the most forthcoming of ministers, but his outspokenness was not typical. Mr de Valera was sometimes criticised for his perfunctory introductions to debates,[49] but claimed that if no new issue had arisen, there was no need to expound government policy:

> The general idea, however, and what is being done by the Department is known . . . it would be a waste of the time of the House to enter into a long explanation as to what is happening and what is being done.[50]

Frank Aiken was inclined to follow this example and, up to 1959, was content to give a "factual recital merely of the departmental events . . . giving no indication of any kind as to what the Government's foreign policy is . . .".[51] After 1959, his attempts to outline government policy at the beginning as well as at the end of the debate tended to help determine the course of the discussion but, during the 1964 estimate debate, which was largely taken up by allegations of political bias in the writing of the information booklet, *Facts about Ireland*, the rational discussion of foreign policy was still the uneasy bed-fellow of enthusiastic and well-publicised attacks on the minister's administrative actions.

When Mr MacBride complained in 1953 that it was ". . . a pity that, once a year at least, we could not have a debate or discussion in the House on foreign policy . . .", he was thinking of the estimate debate, where the "Minister . . . should give at least a broad outline of the Government's policy . . .".[52] Possibly, a more satisfactory arrangement would be to have separate debates on policy and administration, for, although the two are closely related and may cover the same issues, they deserve to be examined separately. Special debates on foreign policy are not unknown, although they are certainly

[48] Dáil Debates: 136, 1171.
[49] Dáil Debates: 56, 2176.
[50] Dáil Debates: 56, 2213.
[51] Dáil Debates: 136, 1171.
[52] Dáil Debates: 136, 1171.

rare since they usually originate in private members' motions which receive a low priority on the parliamentary agenda.[53] But it is difficult for a government to refuse indefinitely a private member's motion on an important current issue. The issue of Irish unity has been debated from time to time in this way: for example, on 28 October 1954, Mr McQuillan of the small Clann na Poblachta party introduced a motion on the problem of partition, and on 23 October 1957, a different aspect of the same issue was again discussed.[54]

A more interesting example—because of its more comprehensive approach to foreign policy—was the motion of 'Disapproval of the Government's Foreign Policy' on 28 November 1957.[55] This was debated in government time, a further indication of the Dáil's dependence on the government's cooperation. The main issue was the government's UN policy, especially Mr Aiken's disengagement proposals for central Europe and his readiness to discuss in the UN the admission of communist China to that organisation. The debate itself, freed from administrative side-issues, was one of the best to take place in the Dáil on a question of foreign policy. Speeches on both sides had been carefully prepared and were well-informed; instead of the usual exchange of slogans, outside opinions were referred to in support of arguments, and Mr Aiken explained the government's policy at length and even cleared up some of the opposition's misconceptions.

No one was converted—that is not the purpose of parliamentary debate—but most deputies who were interested not only had an incentive to become better informed simply because there was a debate, but could not have failed to have been better informed because of what they had heard during the debate; indeed, the arguments put forward in the debate provided material for the parties' attitudes

[53] In 1971, for example, out of 835 hours during which the Dáil was sitting, 147 hours were devoted to private members' business—and 7½ hours of this were allocated out of government time. See Smyth, op. cit., p. 55.

[54] The first debate dealt with the admission of Northern Irish representatives to the Dáil (Dáil Debates: 147, 160 ff.), while the second concerned the failure of the government to raise the question of partition in the UN (Dáil Debates: 164, 146 ff.). Since 1969, the situation in Northern Ireland has been more extensively discussed than is usual, but the government has maintained a strict control over the timing of these debates.

[55] Dáil Debates: 164, 1168 ff.

towards the UN for the following three years. In short, the government had been compelled to defend its policy in some detail and in public; the Dáil—and, indirectly, public opinion—had been educated by the experience. Parliament was playing a positive role in the foreign policy-making process.

But this was an exceptional case, and when we examine the part which Irish parliamentary institutions play in the formulation of foreign policy, it is clear that their actions are less effective than they might be or should be. It is not a question of usurping the fundamental policy-making role of the government; rather, it is a question of ensuring that the work of parliament is effectively organised in order to facilitate its essential supervisory and educative functions. The organisation of the Oireachtas is clumsy and inadequate and may even provide serious obstacles to a full discussion of issues of foreign policy.

First, the consideration of foreign policy is at a serious disadvantage because of the competition between the whole range of issues which comprise public policy. To some extent, this is inevitable, for a parliament's main concern must be with the immediate and tangible problems which it faces; because of these, it may be difficult to justify the somewhat abstract and academic discussion which foreign policy sometimes entails. The danger is that often foreign policy is not merely put in its place but is excluded altogether, for there is a great temptation for government and opposition alike to ignore the long-term interests of the state; if foreign policy is to be anything more than a panic-stricken reaction to external events, an element of long-term planning is essential. There is all the more reason, therefore, to ensure that parliament—and the government—is given every incentive to take a long-term view of foreign affairs through the discipline of its organisation and procedures. In the Oireachtas, there is little provision for this since the consideration of administrative details and of wider objectives are confusingly entwined. Nor has there been much continuity in parliamentary attention to foreign affairs, and even with the more consistent external pressures on Ireland which have arisen since 1969, the organisation of the parliamentary timetable is unduly biased in favour of short-term considerations.

Not only does the Oireachtas set aside very little time to a consideration of foreign policy; it is also ill-equipped to obtain the necessary information to do so effectively. As we have seen, it is to a large extent at the mercy of the government, and inevitably the temptation for the government to abuse its position is only partially countered by the imperfect expedient of the parliamentary question. A lack of continuity is discernible in the supply of information, too, since the onus for obtaining it is on the private member for whom foreign policy is but one of many preoccupations; consequently, his information is often secondhand (from the press) or out-of-date (from the report of previous years' estimate debates).

The amount of information provided on the estimate debate is sparse and is restricted to financial details in the Book of Estimates. In 1949, the Minister for External Affairs, Mr MacBride, considered providing an annual report, which would include a fairly detailed outline of the government's foreign policy, to be made available as the basis for discussion.[56] Nothing came of this suggestion. Even the government white papers on specific issues, such as membership of the EEC, are rare and, although they contain much descriptive material, provide little in the way of direct argument to support the government's policy. Since Ireland joined the European Community in 1973, the practice has been adopted of issuing government reports on EEC participation every six months. The first of these reports follows the same pattern as the EEC White Papers—a descriptive summary, with the minimum of explanatory comment on background material.[58]

A third major obstacle to the parliamentary discussion of foreign policy is the actual procedure of debate. Even with a comparatively small assembly like the Dáil (at present 144 members), a full-scale debate is a clumsy affair, and because each speaker (apart from the proposer of the motion) is restricted to a single contribution, it is almost impossible to extend dialogue beyond the first few speakers on each side. Such debates do not make much impression on their audience nor do they convey a coherent argument when read in the

---

[56] Dáil Debates: 117, 945.
[57] See, for example, the White Papers on the EEC, published in June 1961 (Pr. 6106), June 1962 (Pr. 6613) and April 1967 (Pr. 9283). In April 1970, a further White Paper on 'Implications for Ireland' of EEC membership (Prl. 1110) gave little more than 1,000 words to a chapter on the *political* implications, and this was not substantially increased in the final, pre-referendum White Paper (Prl. 2064) issued in 1972.

form of parliamentary reports. Above all, they encourage a superficial approach to discussion which may become little more than a succession of unrelated and often irrelevant catch-words. For such complicated issues as membership of the EEC, this procedure is plainly inadequate. In 1961, even the Minister for External Affairs, Mr Aiken, complained when discussing this subject that a committee-style of debate (where procedure is more informal) would be more effective.[59] However, he did not suggest how 144 members might participate in such a debate, nor did he refer to any alternative arrangements.

On the whole, it is difficult to agree wholeheartedly with Mr James Dillon's assertion in 1962 that ". . . debate in Dáil Éireann is not merely a waste of time and is not . . . merely gas. It does serve a useful purpose".[60] A doubt remains about whether debates serve as useful a purpose as they could or should do. Parliament is a means of expressing and educating public opinion only in so far as its own members are educated by their participation in the work of government; if its members find it difficult to learn, or if they are unwilling to learn, their existence as parliamentarians is futile. The members of the Oireachtas clearly find it difficult to learn about foreign policy, but what makes their predicament—and that of their constituents—more serious, is that not very many of them appear to have the inclination to learn.

[59] Dáil Debates: 191,665.
[60] Dáil Debates: 194, 1394.

14

Chapter 8

PARLIAMENTARIANS AND FOREIGN POLICY

"I do not wish to interfere in debates of this class at all".
T. Kelly, during the External
Affairs Estimate debate, 1936.
(Dáil Debates: 62, 2706)

Mr O. J. Flanagan: *"May I direct the attention of the Chair
to the fact that there is a Deputy asleep in the House? Is that in
accordance with Standing Orders?"*
Mr Dillon: *"He is here in any case."*
Debate on membership of the United Nations, 1946.
(Dáil Debates: 102, 1337)

THE effectiveness with which parliaments play their limited role
in the formulation of policy depends both on the ways in which
their activities are organised and on the ability and inclination
of their members to make positive use of the facilities which they
possess. As we have seen in the previous chapter, the Irish parliament—
the Oireachtas—is not organised in such a way as to encourage
deputies or senators to participate in the policy-making process,
and opportunities to question and debate occur infrequently. However,
even with such clumsy instruments, it is possible for the individual
legislator to make his mark upon parliamentary deliberations by
bringing his knowledge of foreign affairs to bear upon the government's foreign policy, whenever the chance arises. When considering
the role of the Oireachtas as a whole, therefore, it is important to
examine the role of its individual members.

There is no precise indicator of what constitutes positive or negative
participation by a member in the parliamentary discussion of foreign
policy, apart from the obvious and extreme cases where there is no
participation at all and where the individual is completely engaged

as, for example, in his capacity as Minister for Foreign Affairs. There are several criteria for assessing the success of deputies and senators as representatives: the frequency of their participation in debate or at question-time, the manner of this participation (which can range from a closely reasoned and well-expressed speech to a facile and thoughtless interjection), the effort made to argue a case rather than to repeat a formula, and the ability to approach a problem from a national point-of-view rather than to provoke a partisan squabble. In general, these criteria are insufficient evidence for reaching definite conclusions about particular cases, but they do give an overall picture of the attitudes which parliamentarians have to their part in the policy-making process.

However, before examining the attitudes of Irish parliamentarians to foreign policy, it is as well to comment briefly on their opinions about the whole range of public policy and the part which they feel they can usefully play in its formulation and execution. The distinction noted by Edmund Burke between the representative's two main functions—first, to represent the interests of those who actually elected him and, second, to represent the interests of the nation as a whole—are particularly important here. Foreign policy almost always falls within the latter function, since it is essentially concerned with inter-state relations; local constituency considerations affect the representative's treatment of foreign affairs only in those cases where specific commercial policies or the problems of ethnic minorities arise. Indeed, Burke maintained that on most policies the representative ought to be a national rather than a local spokesman, a contention which would favour the discussion of foreign policy in any assembly where it was widely believed. But Burke is a prophet without honour in his own country.

The Irish representative has been called ". . . primarily a local consumer representative, an advocate and expediter of affairs for his constituents and his locality"[1]; his position as a national legislator is generally a secondary matter. A subsequent study confirmed this view.[2] A traditional suspicion of bureaucracy is responsible for the

[1] Chubb, *A Source Book of Irish Government*, pp. 157–8.
[2] J. Whyte, *Dáil Deputies: Their Work, Its Difficulties, Possible Remedies* (Tuairim Pamphlet, no. 15, Dublin, 1966).

hesitancy of many Irish citizens to do business with any branch
of the government without first eliciting the support of their
representative—the TD (*Teachta Dála*). It is no coincidence that
most TDs were born or are resident in their constituencies, are members
of well-established families in the area and serve on locally elected
bodies. Even the surprisingly large number of TDs who owe much
of their reputation to their sporting activities are participants or former
participants in sports which are based on local rather than on national
loyalties.[3]

All of this suggests that the representative is inclined to give a high
priority to his constituents' interests. If he should wish to detach
himself from his constituency, he would undoubtedly risk his parliamentary career. The multi-member constituency is also responsible
for this, for it ensures that electoral competition is based on the
provision of practical (and easily publicised) services for constituents.
When the TDs belong to the same party, this competition to provide
personal services is, if anything, more acute because they cannot
identify themselves with different party programmes.[4] While serving
as an intermediary between the individual elector and the administration, the deputy is bedevilled by poor secretarial and office facilities,
the lack of an alternative body to listen to individuals' complaints,
and the need to give some attention at least to his permanent occupation
and family. It is little wonder that, as Senator Michael Hayes remarked
in 1962, ". . . Deputies, instead of being in the Dáil, are in the
Library writing piles of letters to their constituents".[5]

In these circumstances, it is difficult for the representative to devote
the necessary time or effort to the consideration of national policy.
This is a serious shortcoming in a parliament which is not organised
to educate him in matters beyond his immediate experience, but
which relies on him to educate himself. The problem is probably
not as serious as it was up to the nineteen fifties, for the level of
academic education enjoyed by TDs has risen significantly since then:
in 1965, 30 per cent. of the total membership of the Dáil had university
or professional training (as opposed to 22 per cent. in 1944); 50 per

[3] ibid. especially p. 32.
[4] ibid. pp. 19–20.
[5] Seanad Debates: 55, 1688.

cent. had secondary education (29 per cent. in 1944); and the percentage of those with only primary education fell from 48 per cent. in 1944 to 20 per cent. in 1965.[6] A secondary or university education is not, of course, a guarantee of a high level of intelligence or of a special knowledge of government policy; and, in any case, formal education in the social sciences is a rarity among those deputies who are university graduates. However, some passing acquaintance with the workings of government is more likely at the advanced stages of education and the more highly educated representative should have a clearer notion of how to educate himself yet further—always provided that he finds the time to do so.

It is difficult for the Irish representative to play the role of legislator, either in the narrow sense of commenting on actual legislation or in the broader sense of criticising the administration of government policy and thereby influencing future legislation; the demands of constituency work make specialisation in national policies something of a luxury. However, it could be argued that a certain degree of specialisation does exist in the Dáil because of the varied occupations of its members. At first sight, since these occupations present a cross-section of the country's activities, policies which demand special skills and professional expertise to formulate may benefit from the informed comment of groups of deputies who have special interests to protect or special knowledge to offer. In 1965, for example, 24 per cent. of TDs were full-time farmers whose expertise enabled them to influence agricultural policy; at the same time, there were eight full-time teachers in the House to discuss education.[7] However, it is doubtful whether this crude form of vocational representation introduces a significant degree of expertise on questions of national policy, in view of the small scale and local basis of the great majority of Irish occupations. At best, the government will be encouraged to counter the narrow expertise of its critics with its own broader, national point-of-view.

Irish foreign policy suffers because of a lack of expertise among parliamentarians in the Dáil. Special knowledge about breeding pigs may be a useful electoral aid in a pig-breeding constituency,

[6] Whyte, op. cit., pp. 24–25.
[7] ibid. pp. 27–29.

but special knowledge of foreign affairs is not a qualification that recommends itself to Irish electors. If a TD is knowledgeable about foreign affairs, it is coincidental, and generally his constituents do not press him to make use of his proficiency; indeed, if he is seen to be using it to the apparent detriment of his constituency work, he may well be regarded as wasting his constituents' time—and their votes. So the parliamentary discussion of foreign policy does not even benefit from that small degree of expertise which is guaranteed in some other important areas of policy by the crude occupational structure of the Dáil; on the contrary, with a few exceptions, the 'experts' in foreign affairs are in the Department of Foreign Affairs, and consequently advise the government.

On the whole, the general conditions under which the Irish parliamentary representative works render him comparatively ineffective in the field of foreign policy. Both the lack of facilities through which he may inform and educate himself and the burden of constituency work tend to disincline even the most enthusiastic deputy to become a regular contributor to the discussion of foreign affairs in the Dáil.

In view of this "comparatively passive role, so far as legislation and the scrutiny of the conduct of business are concerned",[8] it is hardly surprising to find among deputies a certain degree of apathy about foreign policy. The often remote and abstract nature of the subject constitutes a temptation to 'leave it to the government', even in those states where foreign affairs are more significant than in Ireland; in small states on the margin of world politics, it is a temptation to which the average representative is almost bound to succumb. In Ireland, the temptation to steer clear of foreign policy has been particularly strong because the country has only a slight tradition of participation in international politics. Where such a tradition has developed further, it has been related to the national obsession with Britain. Other questions of foreign affairs have been regarded as incidental and are generally ignored.

Any broad view of Irish foreign policy has been treated by many Irish representatives with indifference or hostility and, although these attitudes are less pervasive in the early nineteen seventies than during

[8] Chubb, *A Source Book of Irish Government*, p. 157.

the early decades of the state, they are still favourably received in the Dáil. A general indication of TDs' indifference to foreign affairs is the comparatively small numbers speaking on the infrequent foreign affairs debates. Mr J. A. Costello maintained in 1946 that "certainly since I became a member of this House, the one debate that attracts the least attention of Deputies is the debate on our foreign affairs".[9] The attention of deputies does not seem to have changed significantly since then; ten to fifteen speakers is normal for the debate on the Estimate for the Department of Foreign Affairs, and since the same names recur year after year and there are few complaints from the silent deputies, it is safe to assume that the other 90 per cent. of Dáil members have little direct interest. An illuminating remark by Mr T. Kelly in 1936 reveals a government backbencher's attitude to his own duties and those of the opposition:

> The job of the members opposite evidently is to obstruct the business, to keep it going with talking and talking. . . . Our job is to see that the business is done as quickly as possible and in as business-like a way as possible. Very few of us ever trouble the House with long speeches. We are perfectly satisfied to leave the administration and conduct of affairs here in the hands of the Executive Council [i.e. the Cabinet] . . . we do say that the business could be got through much more quickly and much more effectively if there was less talk, but we cannot control that.[10]

Those issues which have made an impact on public opinion have produced greater activity in the Dáil. For instance, the public *furor* over the Spanish civil war was reflected in a turnout of twenty-five impassioned speakers on the second reading of the Spanish Civil War (Non Intervention) Bill of 1937;[11] the corresponding stage of the Republic of Ireland Bill of 1948 took three days, and forty-two deputies spoke—nearly one-third of the total membership.[12] But such occasions are rare, and seem to depend on mass public opinion influencing the Dáil, rather than the converse. For the important

[9] Dáil Debates: 101, 2209.
[10] Dáil Debates: 62, 2706.
[11] See Dáil Debates: 65, 597 ff.
[12] See Dáil Debates: 113, 347 ff.

debate on the government's foreign policy on 28 November 1958, there were only eight speakers.[13] A small number of speakers does not necessarily mean a less effective debate—often the contrary is the case—but does indicate the general reluctance of the back bench TD to take an interest in foreign affairs.

To some extent, the passivity of the majority of the TDs towards foreign affairs is based upon the best of intentions. In 1949, Deputy Davin of the Labour Party claimed that he ". . . always took it that it was proper for a back bencher to sit tight and make it appear to the world . . . that there is unity amongst all Parties on the foreign policy of the Government of the day . . .".[14] However, there is a danger that such a commendable desire for a bipartisan policy might be a convenient excuse for not thinking about foreign affairs, let alone not discussing them. In the last resort, such compliance, reinforced by the exigencies of party discipline, may cause the representative to forsake his duties as a critic.

It is impossible to say whether the majority of Irish parliamentary representatives would agree with this explanation for their silence, for their views on foreign policy (if they have any) are rarely heard. The infrequent interventions of backbenchers in debates on foreign affairs do not, however, convey the impression of a Dáil full of well-informed deputies manfully restraining a wide range of opinions on foreign policy for the sake of bipartisan unity. Their comments are usually brief, superficial and sometimes totally unrealistic;[15] the deputies tend to emphasise the more tangible aspects of foreign policy, particularly where it affects trade policy, for usually they participate as mouthpieces to their constituents' special interests. Such remarks as are made about the broader aspects of foreign policy, especially those to do with issues arising outside the field of Anglo-Irish relations, tend to be repetitive, uninformed and ineffectual. Although there are notable exceptions,[16] the contribution of the majority of TDs is minimal and nebulous; perhaps this is hardly

[13] See Dáil Debates: 164, 1168 ff.

[14] Dáil Debates: 117, 799.

[15] An example of one of the more imaginative interventions by a backbencher occurred in 1925 when Mr Connor Hogan suggested that Ireland should try to "get a slice of Africa" to start an Irish colony as an outlet for its surplus population and exports! (Dáil Debates: 11, 1448–49).

[16] See below, pp. 221-227.

surprising in view of the burden of their constituency work which only occasionally brings them into contact with the administration— let alone the formulation—of foreign policy. "Every day we are in touch with the other Departments, because we are made conscious of their existence by our constituents . . . we are rarely called upon to interview the Department of External Affairs . . ."[17], remarked Mr Baxter in 1925 and his point remains valid. The representatives' indifference towards foreign affairs reflects that of their constituents.

However, the insularity of Irish representatives is not confined merely to a passive indifference towards foreign affairs, which, after all, is found in most legislatures, although it is usually not as pronounced as it is in Ireland. On occasion, some deputies have held an attitude of outright contempt for the outside world and its influence on Ireland, and have been proudly and self-consciously isolationist. Although this isolationism finds expression in comparatively few parliamentary representatives, it has certain attractions in a country which has been geographically and culturally insulated from the mainstream of world politics.

One of the principal elements of Irish isolationism is a somewhat exaggerated inferiority complex. Dr Noel Browne remarked in 1960: ". . . one of the difficulties in talking about foreign affairs in the Dáil is that one always talks in the shadow of the *Skibbereen Eagle;* one feels one has no right to comment on things which concern large Powers, that one can be tossed aside as a small nation without being allowed any say".[18] A crude conclusion to be drawn from this fatalistic attitude is that it is not only presumptuous but a waste of time to formulate foreign policy or to take any initiative in international affairs, and this argument found some support in the first decade of the state's existence when its international status was uncertain. In 1923, D. J. Gorey, attacking the existence of a Department of External Affairs, claimed that "we are concerned with no foreign affairs. We have no colonies and have no interests to clash with any other

[17] Dáil Debates: 11, 1447.
[18] Dáil Debates: 183, 1898. The *Skibbereen Eagle* was an Irish provincial newspaper notorious for its imperious pronouncements denouncing the foreign policies of Tsarist Russia in the latter part of the nineteenth century. It has since become synonymous with a pretentious and unrealistic attitude towards the place of Ireland in world affairs.

nation. I think it is ridiculous to be playing with theatricals like this".[19]

Even when it is recognised that the "theatricals" have some purpose, they are seen as a distraction from the real needs of the state. In 1929, Mr T. Sheehy asked: "Would it not be much better for us in this Dáil to be talking about drainage schemes, development schemes, and other schemes for the building up of the nation instead of all the arrant nonsense we have to listen to here".[20] The "arrant nonsense" which upset Mr Sheehy was the debate on the Treaty for the Renunciation of War. In 1955, the isolationist view was put at greater length by Mr Jack McQuillan:

> as far as Ireland is concerned she should keep her nose out of the business of other nations and try and look after her own business first. There is no question or doubt that we are not doing that and if we are able to put these brilliant minds, who are setting their brains to solve international problems, to solving the problems affecting the country here we would be doing much better and would be doing a very good day's work for the country from any viewpoint.[21]

The isolationist TD criticises not only the time spent on discussing foreign policy, but also takes exception to the expenditure incurred; particular resentment is expressed about the need to keep up diplomatic appearances. In 1928, Mr Corry regretted that salaries had to be paid to Irish representatives abroad ". . . so that they might squat like the nigger when he put on the black silk hat and the swallow-tail coat and went out and said he was an English gentleman".[22] In 1956, Mr McQuillan echoed this attitude: "I think that a little bit of the Spartan outlook would be no harm at all when it comes to the question of alleged prestige",[23] and he dismissed cultural contacts as being ". . . portrayed by the clinking of glasses and long sessions at diplomatic parties".[24]

[19] Dáil Debates: 5, 940.
[20] Dáil Debates: 28, 317.
[21] Dáil Debates: 152, 575–6.
[22] Dáil Debates: 27, 482–3.
[23] Dáil Debates: 159, 430.
[24] Dáil Debates: 159, 429.

This suspicious isolationism was given a not untypical twist in Mr McQuillan's case by his acceptance of diplomatic activity for one specific purpose—the ending of partition. Indeed, barely a month before complaining that the debate held in November 1957 on Ireland's policy in the United Nations was a waste of time, he had sponsored a motion of his own, demanding that the UN's support should be sought to bring about the reunification of Ireland.[25] In 1961, he continued to maintain that, until Ireland was united, any broader foreign policy objectives were worthless. Jack McQuillan was a frequent participant in foreign policy debates, yet one of his principal concerns was to repudiate the idea that Ireland had any part to play in international politics. His attack on the government's policy towards the UN intervention in the Congo was typical: "You are able to settle the problems of every country in the world except your own. Let us look after our own back garden first".[26]

Irish isolationism is based on several factors, including an over-simplified (though not entirely inaccurate) view of diplomatic practice and the feeling that the great problems of world politics are no concern of Ireland's. But it must be stressed that it is not expressed forcefully by many TDs: Mr McQuillan, for example, was no ordinary representative and to a large extent his isolationism was conditional. Nevertheless, isolationism may be latent in the passivity and indifference of most representatives, and when difficult and complex questions on foreign policy have to be answered, it can be a convenient excuse for doing nothing.

At times, isolationism has been an important element in Irish foreign policy: it was explicit in the policy of military neutrality during World War II and was perhaps partly implicit in the post-war policy of concentrating on the anti-partition campaign rather than on developments in Europe. In the first case, it was justified by events; in the second case, its limitations were gradually exposed. Thus, as long as Ireland has remained comparatively untouched by external events and as long as there is a "back garden" demanding attention, an isolationist attitude may be sustained by the indifference of the majority. For no matter what the limitations of this attitude

[25] See Dáil Debates: 164, 146 ff.
[26] Dáil Debates: 192, 171–2.

might be in the long term, in the short term it is an inexpensive and simple answer to complicated problems.

★   ★   ★   ★

If the majority of Irish parliamentary representatives are either indifferent or sometimes positively inimical to the content and conduct of foreign policy, it is clear that such influence as the Dáil exerts in the formulation of foreign policy derives from a comparatively small number of its members. These come from certain clearly defined groups in which some degree of specialisation in foreign affairs is an asset, even though it is not actually called for.

The first group of parliamentary representatives who play an important role is the most obvious one—the government. We are concerned here not so much with the overall executive responsibility of the members of the government as with one particular aspect of that responsibility—their obligation to discuss and defend their policies in the houses of the Oireachtas. In practice, this generally means that two people are directly concerned: the head of the government, and his foreign minister who usually takes the main burden of parliamentary work.[27]   The importance of the contribution by members of the government to the parliamentary discussion of foreign policy cannot be stressed too often, for the role that parliament as a whole is allowed to play depends to a large extent on these particular parliamentarians. Through their control of the parliamentary timetable, their stranglehold on the supply of information, and their ability to take the initiative, government ministers are responsible for establishing the direction and tone of parliamentary proceedings.

The cooperation of the government is, therefore, essential if parliamentary discussion is to serve any useful purpose. In normal circumstances, the government will try to cooperate with the Dáil, since in the long run this will weaken the force of their opponents' criticism and ensure their survival. However, during the first fifty years of the Dáil, the cooperation offered to it by the individual heads of government and their ministers has varied considerably.[28]

[27] For exceptions to this—as when the head of the government is his own foreign minister, or when another minister is called in—see above, pp. 55-60 and 91-94.
[28] The effect of the Dáil's early difficulties on its role with regard to foreign policy is discussed below, pp. 228-230.

The sporadic discussions of their policies, favoured by some ministers, left those few members of the Dáil who were interested in foreign affairs floundering in a vacuum in which they could complain but not debate. A reticent minister does little but encourage the indifference of the majority of members. On the other hand, if the minister takes the lead in debate and defends his case in detail, he will force his opponents to do likewise and, in the presence of a true dialogue, the indifferent may even be stimulated to form their own opinions.

The government is one essential part of any parliamentary dialogue; the other is its 'shadow'—the opposition front benches. In the Dáil, in the face of comparatively secretive governments and disinterested backbenchers, the principal focus of the parliamentary discussion of foreign policy has often been the leadership of the alternative government: in effect, this has been either the Fianna Fáil party, or more often the Fine Gael and Labour parties acting together. Even where more than one party is concerned, very few individual TDs are directly involved; there are usually two from each party—its leader, and a party spokesman who is given the special responsibility of criticising foreign policy.

Several factors combine to make the opposition front benches the most fruitful source of discussion. Their occupants are well-established members of their parties and will probably enjoy a high reputation among party workers and in their constituencies, which they will generally have held for some years. So, although they will neglect constituency work at their peril, the pressures on them to compete with the other representatives in their constituency will not be so great. Their arrival on the front benches is in most cases an indication that they have been able to cope successfully in the past.

By virtue of his position, the front bench spokesman is expected by his parliamentary colleagues to play a prominent role in debate. He does not have to fight for attention; on the contrary, he is looked to as an expert in his subject and as the principal source of alternative policies. Before 1932, opposition parties, whether Labour (up to 1927) or Fianna Fáil (from 1927 to 1932), had little experience of parliamentary politics and none of government; but since that date, the degree of expertise and experience of foreign policy spokesmen has been comparatively high.

The Fine Gael spokesmen during Mr de Valera's sixteen years or government from 1932 to 1948 included two former Ministers fof External Affairs, Desmond FitzGerald and Patrick McGilligan, whose intimate knowledge of the intricacies of Ireland's constitutional position and of the administration of foreign policy made them well-informed and authoritative critics of the government. They were supported by John A. Costello, former Attorney General and member of Ireland's League of Nations delegation, and James Dillon. The former's experience of international politics in the League and clear appreciation of the nature of parliamentary government was beneficial, and Mr Dillon's striking parliamentary personality made him an effective spokesman. After the change of government in 1948, Mr de Valera himself was the opposition spokesman on foreign affairs and, because of the immense authority he had acquired as leader of his party, head of the government and as an international statesman, his presence in debates was remarkable. Indeed, during the estimates debate in 1948, he found it necessary to point out to another deputy: "It is no good addressing these questions to me. I am not now in a position to determine them".[29]

Subsequent opposition spokesmen on foreign affairs may not have had the stature of Mr de Valera, but they were effective nonetheless. Although Mr Aiken played a subsidiary role when Mr de Valera was in the Dáil, as Minister for External Affairs he had to face John A. Costello, Liam Cosgrave and Seán MacBride (his predecessors), James Dillon and Patrick McGilligan, as well as some well-informed and indefatigable Labour spokesmen. Of the latter, Dr Conor Cruise O'Brien, a former official in the Department of External Affairs, was particularly well-qualified to speak with authority when he entered the Dáil in 1969. A Fine Gael spokesman at that time was Dr Garret FitzGerald, who had already established a reputation as a foreign affairs specialist in the Senate. Indeed, there is a strong element of continuity and experience among this small group of TD's who, no matter what their party affiliations are, have an intimate knowledge of parliamentary politics, of governmental responsibility for foreign affairs, and of the course of Irish foreign policy. The background of these deputies—a professional career (often in law), or a

[29] Dáil Debates: 112, 1005.

full-time political career based in Dublin—is hardly typical; their position has been strengthened by the fact that if anyone is brought into the government's confidence and can interpret the behaviour of their governmental counterparts, it is they.

Taken together, the few individual parliamentary representatives who have played the interchangeable roles of governmental and opposition foreign policy specialists since the inception of the state may be seen as an *élite*, but if they are an *élite*, they are so largely by default, for it is possible (though difficult) to make a positive contribution to debates from positions other than the front benches of the major parties. In the first place, the backbenchers of the major parties who do wish to devote a large part of their energies to foreign affairs have opportunities to participate in discussion within the limitations imposed by party discipline. Although in most cases this leads to a superficial repetition of the party line, there are rare examples when an individual backbencher attempts to bring his special knowledge to bear on issues of foreign policy. Thus in 1961, during the debate on the Convention of the OECD, a government (Fianna Fáil) backbencher, Mr Lionel Booth, spoke knowledgeably and articulately on European integration,[30] and in 1962 an opposition backbencher, Sir Anthony Esmonde (Fine Gael), gave his own view of Ireland's EEC application, based on personal contacts with EEC officials.[31] Both speakers displayed an appreciation of the complexity of international politics and a more comprehensive knowledge of foreign affairs than the average TD.

But if these examples show that it is possible for a TD to be well-informed about foreign affairs, they also emphasise the fact that the typical TD is unlikely to be so. Mr Booth and Sir Anthony Esmonde were untypical in at least two respects: they came from cosmopolitan backgrounds and were sufficiently wealthy to gain direct personal knowledge of the world outside Ireland. Sir Anthony Esmonde was partly educated in Germany and Mr Booth was a director of a company (large by Irish standards) which assembled British motor vehicles. Like most of the front bench spokesmen, they were highly educated and widely travelled.

[30] Dáil Debates: 191, 243–53.
[31] Dáil Debates: 198, 1389–95.

Indeed, the lack of opportunities for the ordinary TD to travel abroad has been an important cause of his insularity. Generally, neither his constituency work not the nature of his occupation justify long and expensive trips abroad, and the opportunities for him to travel in his capacity as a member of the Dáil are rare. However, apart from visits to inter-parliamentary conferences (which are the preserve of the party *élite*), since 1949 members have been chosen (in effect by the party) to represent Ireland at the Consultative Assembly of the Council of Europe. If a TD feels that he can spare the time away from his constituency and work, he may put himself forward as a candidate for the panel of four representatives and four substitutes. When most of the places have been filled by prominent members of the three major parties, by a representative of the Senate (usually, but not always, chosen) and by a representative of the small parties and independent TDs, there may remain two or three places for backbenchers. These are often filled by the Booths and the Esmondes.

Since the beginning of 1973, representation on the European Community's European Parliament, in which Ireland has ten seats, has increased the opportunities for the TD or senator to gain expertise in foreign policy. But again, the seats may be allotted on the basis of services rendered to the party rather than on the grounds of any interest in foreign affairs; and in any case, the greater demands which the European Parliament makes on its members' time is inhibiting for the constituency-bound Irish parliamentarian.

Usually, deputies representing small parties, or independent TDs, have more scope than the ordinary parliamentarian to make their opinions tell. Although small parties and individual TDs do not usually command the respect which the major parties enjoy, at times they may be vital to a government's survival. In addition, they are not subject to the same strictures of party discipline as is the ordinary backbencher. The classic example of the small party enjoying parliamentary influence out of all proportion to its size is that of Clann na Poblachta, the radical republican party, whose leader, Seán MacBride, was Minister for External Affairs from 1948 to 1951. During the same period, the influence of the backbencher in this type of party was demonstrated by a Clann na Poblachta TD, Captain Peadar Cowan, whose question in 1948 on the issue of republican and Commonwealth status could not be ignored by the government.[32] Mr MacBride proved that a small party could play a decisive, negative role when, from 1954, he held the second coalition government to ransom with his party's conditional support, which he eventually withdrew in 1957. His threat to table a motion against the government led Mr Costello to request a dissolution; although MacBride's motives were ostensibly economic, the crisis took place at a time of IRA guerilla activity on the border, and the government claimed that their firm response to this was also behind the Clann na Poblachta leader's withdrawal of support. The claim was not substantiated, the IRA was even more firmly suppressed by the succeeding government, and Mr MacBride's move proved to be a phyrric victory for his small party.[33]

On the other hand, when there has been a more stable distribution of power among the major parties, the parliamentary members of the small parties have rarely participated in the discussion of foreign policy. Some, notably the farmers' parties, have not shown much inclination to try to exert influence, but an exception to this was the National Progressive Democratic Party. This was a splinter group which broke away from Clann na Poblachta. It consisted of a former Minister for Health, Dr Noel Browne, and Mr Jack McQuillan, and both were extremely active and vocal on a variety of foreign policy issues during the early nineteen sixties. They supported the followers of Lumumba in the Congo on every possible occasion, criticised Ireland's application to join the EEC, asked nearly all the questions posed in the Dáil on the government's attitude to nuclear disarmament and racial discrimination, and staged a walk-out over what they alleged was the government's failure to support Dr Conor Cruise O'Brien after his resignation from the UN in 1961. Mr McQuillan also made frequent attempts to revive the partition issue. These tactics introduced alternative points-of-view and may have performed the invaluable function of keeping the government on its toes, but, in the long term, they made little appreciable impression on government policy.

[32] Dáil Debates: 113, 374.
[33] See Basil Chubb, 'Ireland 1957' in D. E. Butler (ed.) *Elections Abroad* (Macmillan, London, 1959) p. 194.

One further instance must be mentioned of an independent TD who took a truly independent line on foreign policy. In 1942, James Dillon was expelled from the Fine Gael party for publicly opposing the policy of neutrality which had been accepted by both the government and the other parties. During the general debate on the Estimate of the Department of the Taoiseach in that year, Dillon showed himself a true disciple of Edmund Burke by upholding the independence of the parliamentary representative in the face of the demands of his constituents and of another form of discipline which Burke would not have recognised—his party. "We, the elected representatives of the people", he said, "are under no bond of honour or obligation to follow one policy or another. Our only duty is to follow the policy which we, the elected representatives of the people, believe to be right".[34]   The reply of Mr McGilligan—a former party colleague— was significant:

> . . . as a private citizen I may have views which might coincide with those which Deputy Dillon has in certain aspects of the war; but, as a representative of a huddled, densely-populated part of this almost defenceless city, I would have to pause before I began to consider that, as a Deputy, I might announce here in public some of the views which, as a private citizen, I might be bold enough to hold.[35]

In abnormal, as well as in normal conditions, the representatve is generally the servant of his constituency, and while this is probably less true of the indirectly elected senator than of the TD, the limited opportunities which the former has to discuss foreign policy nullify much of the influence which he might otherwise exert.[36]

It is clear, therefore, that the public discussion of foreign policy at the highest level—in the houses of the Oireachtas—is in the hands of relatively few men: mostly party leaders, with the occasional intervention of advantageously placed members of small parties or independents, and a handful of enterprising backbenchers. On the

[34] Dáil Debates: 88, 670.
[35] Dáil Debates: 88, 702.
[36] See above, pp. 192-194.

other hand, the prevalent attitude in both the Dáil and the Senate is one of apathy. This inertia strengthens the position of the government, whose policies are not therefore subject to a continuous, comprehensive and searching criticism.

★   ★   ★   ★

Apart from this general apathy towards foreign affairs, two other factors have bedevilled the role of the houses of the Oireachtas in the formulation of foreign policy. Although both factors have to do with the peculiar circumstances pertaining during the first three decades of the state, they have, nevertheless, done much to encourage the continuing neglect of foreign affairs in the Irish parliament.

The more important of these factors was the abnormal development of the Irish parliament as a result of the civil war of 1922–1923. From 1927, when the principal parliamentary division came to reflect this fratricidal struggle which was based on an issue of foreign policy—the state's relations with Britain—,the atmosphere in which foreign affairs were discussed was anything but sweet and reasonable. As late as 1949, the Minister for External Affairs, Seán MacBride, replying to the External Affairs Estimate debate, said that he had ". . . seldom listened to a debate that made [him] feel more despondent about this Parliament. . . ."[37] Referring to the civil war controversy, he went on: "Is it on that basis that we are to run our Parliament— on bitterness, on hatred, on personal prejudices? Are we going to continue that for ever? Or, are we going to begin to have a normal political development? . . . and to consider issues on their merits?".[38] Although there were fundamental differences between the major parties, Fianna Fáil and Fine Gael, over the 1921 Treaty, these became increasingly irrelevant, since each party, when in power, worked towards the same objective—asserting the political independence of the state, particularly in its relations with Britain.

Indeed, as the differences in policy between the two parties diminished, the differences between personalities showed a distressing tendency to linger on, like the disembodied grin of the Cheshire cat.

[37] Dáil Debates: 117, 1036.
[38] Dáil Debates: 117, 1038.

Mr Aiken remarked in 1953: "One of the reasons why debates on external affairs sometimes get into a rather personal sphere is that there are in fact very few differences between us and they are differences only of personality".[39] So the pattern continued, a pattern in which parliamentary manners were often uncivil, and debate was marred by irrelevancies. This was a parliament where even the most correct of its members, Mr Dillon, could refer to an opponent as ". . . the fastidious little Minister for Local Government . . . mincing in his place making his vicious, wicked little speech . . .",[40] and this during a debate on a motion to condemn communist persecution of Catholic prelates in central Europe—hardly an issue to divide the Dáil.[41] It was a parliament where Mr Dillon's questioning of the policy of neutrality in 1941 could provoke the retort from a back-bencher: "I say the Deputy should be removed out of the House. I will put him out —— quick, the corner-boy. If he does not shut his —— mouth we will shut it for him".[42] All parliamentarians lapse occasionally, but the frequency with which personal abuse reduced the level of debate in the Dáil to "the Biddy Moriarty standard"[43] during this period was remarkable. The discussion of foreign policy—with its emphasis on thwarted national objectives—suffered to a particularly high degree.

Another legacy of the civil war years was the large measure of irrelevant matter introduced into debates. This usually took the form of passionate and lengthy personal interpretations of the recent history of the civil war and sometimes the not-so-recent history and legend which had preceded it. This quasi historicism, and the abuse which it provoked, often made the specific issue under consideration a minor feature of the discussion. Mr James Larkin remarked during the debate on the Republic of Ireland Bill of 1948: "At times it seemed to me as if the republic had almost been drowned in a spate of oratory. I think it would have been much better . . . if we . . .

[39] Dáil Debates: 138, 881.
[40] Dáil Debates: 103, 1394.
[41] See Dáil Debates: 103, 1322 ff. There was even a division at the end of this debate on 21 November 1946, which, in view of its non-controversial subject-matter, was one of the most striking examples of the failure of party cooperation and the pettiness to which the Dáil could descend.
[42] Dáil Debates: 84, 1867. The blanks are in the official report of the debate.
[43] Dáil Debates: 113, 623.

did not indulge in retrospective history".[44] (As if to demonstrate the shortcoming about which he had just complained, Larkin immediately proceeded to give his own version of Irish history since 1916).

Time has healed most of the civil war wounds, but as long as those who suffered directly or even indirectly from its ravages are sitting in the Dáil, the temptation to refight the civil war rather than to discuss policy remains. In 1963, Mr Dillon may have looked on President Kennedy's state visit as symbolising ". . . the closing of a chapter and its relegation to the hands of the historians . . .",[45] but the estimates debates in 1964[46] made him revise his opinion. Although such incidents are harmful enough, the acceptance as normal of a greater degree of mutual suspicion between the major parties than is justified by their real differences on public policies has been even more injurious. This mistrust is undoubtedly an important factor in the reluctance of governments to divulge information about their foreign policies, which in turn is a major reason for the failure of the Dáil to play a more significant role in the formulation of foreign policy.

As well as the damage which the civil war and its aftermath inflicted on the parliamentary discussion of foreign policy, a second unusual feature made the task of the Oireachtas more arduous than might otherwise have been the case, until 1948 at least. This was the pre-dominantly legalistic nature of Ireland's relations with Britain. During the government of W. T. Cosgrave, this legalism manifested itself in the subtle and complex assertion of independence by establishing precedents with regard to formal treaty-signing powers and the like; too subtle, perhaps, for a novice parliament to understand fully. As Mr Joseph McGrath, the Minister for Industry and Commerce, complained during the constitutionally-involved debate on the Anglo-American Liquor Treaty in 1924—"Is there not a great deal of confusion?"[47]

But if the Dáil was confused in 1924, it was floundering in 1936 when Mr de Valera's government took advantage of the British

[44] Dáil Debates: 113, 673.
[45] Dáil Debates: 208, 865.
[46] See Dáil Debates: 208, 845 ff.
[47] Dáil Debates: 6, 3073.

abdication crisis to remove the Crown from the Free State Constitution and establish that most subtle of relationships with Britain—
external association. The two bills rushed through the Dáil on 11
and 12 December 1936, the Constitution (Amendment No. 27) Bill
and the Executive Authority (External Relations) Bill, met with a
bewildered response. Mr J. A. Costello pointed out during the debate
on the former bill that ". . . the real reason Deputies are so shy about
speaking on this Bill is that they are quite unable to understand it".[48]
Mr de Valera himself did not seem very sure of some of the detailed
legal implications, remarking: "I shall have to leave the lawyers to
argue it out at the end".[49]

It was not without justification that Jack McQuillan in 1948
described the External Relations Act of 1936 as "simply a lawyers'
feast".[50] Repealing the act in that year, Mr J. A. Costello, head of
the so-called 'lawyers' government', justified his action by hoping
not merely to "take the gun out of Irish politics" but by taking the
constitutional lawyer out of Irish foreign policy. There had been,
he claimed,

> rather too much in the last 25 years of constitutional law and
> constitutional lawyers. For 25 years, we have arid futile and unending
> discussions as to the nature and character of our constitutional
> position and our constitutional and international relations with
> Great Britain, with the other members of the Commonwealth of
> Nations and with other foreign nations . . .[51]

At the end of the final stage of the Republic of Ireland Bill of 1948—
one of the longest, most bitter and cliché-ridden debates on Irish
foreign policy—Mr Costello said that "if there were any justification
required for the passing of this Bill, the purgatory that we have
gone through in the last few days justifies it."[52]

★   ★   ★   ★

[48] Dáil Debates: 64, 1292.
[49] Dáil Debates: 64, 1388.
[50] Dáil Debates: 113, 523.
[51] Dáil Debates: 113, 348-9.
[52] Dáil Debates: 113, 1013.

The discussion of foreign policy has been neither easy nor popular in the Irish parliament. It is unlikely to be any easier now that Ireland is a member of the EEC; the mysteries of international economic negotiations supplement those of constitutional law, which, because of the European Community's essentially legal nature, will again enjoy a certain standing. Foreign policy is still largely the preserve of those who have special obligations to formulate and comment on it and of those few individual representatives in the Dáil and the Senate who are interested and well-informed about its consequences. If one of the main purposes of a parliament is that, in Mr Dillon's words,

> the ordinary Deputies of this House constitute a two-way channel that not only brings, or ought to bring to this House, the feeling of the people at large, but ought also be able to channel down from this House to their own constituents certain essential information about the vital business of this State[53]

then it is clear that neither the parliamentary discussion of foreign policy nor the behaviour of the majority of parliamentary representatives in the Dáil contribute as effectively as they might towards this end.

The remedy for this unsatisfactory state of affairs is two-fold. First, the role of the parliamentary representative must be reformed, both to protect him from and wean him away from the overwhelming demands of his constituents. It may be unrealistic to expect that the abolition of multi-member constituencies (where the representative may compete over-zealously with his colleagues to run constituents' errands) would be acceptable, but the provision of alternative channels for voicing grievances against the administration might prove worthwhile.[54] At all events, if the TD is to be a legislator rather than an errand boy—and this applies not merely to foreign policy but to all public policy—something must be done to enable him to consider the international and national consequences of public policy as well as the effects it might have in his constituency.

[53] Dáil Debates: 163, 662.
[54] See Whyte, op. cit., pp. 15–23.

The second reform that should be instituted is particularly important for the formulation of foreign policy. This is the reorganisation of the work of the Dáil in order to educate its members and provide them with more regular opportunities to examine foreign policy in detail. James Dillon pointed out in 1957 that the TD cannot educate his constituents if he is not himself educated—if he is not given "the facts". He went on to claim that "it is not necessary to adopt a special procedure to get that information for them about the vast majority of business transacted in this House because debate to and fro here ordinarily provides a Deputy with all the factual information he requires";[55] but he might well have gone on to point out that for foreign policy—where there often is manifestly little or no "debate to and fro"—there might well be need for a "special procedure". The most effective special procedure would be a standing committee on foreign affairs.

Proposals for such a procedure can be traced back to the earliest years of the state. Most of these had little effect, though two at least did produce *ad hoc* committees of a quasi parliamentary nature; but the persistent failure of the Irish parliament's attempts to reform itself are a further demonstration of its marginal role in the development of foreign policy.

The first proposal for a standing committee on foreign affairs came from the Senate in May 1924 when Senator Douglas advocated a committee of five members from each house of the Oireachtas to "consider the position of the Saorstát in relation to foreign affairs, and to report thereon to the Oireachtas from time to time . . . .".[56] In the brief debate which followed this recommendation, more serious consideration was given to the idea than at any other time until 1957; senators stressed the need to educate a public largely innocent of international politics, drew comparisons with similar institutions in the USA and France, acknowledged the need to provide a permanent staff and chairman, and rejected the cross-questioning of civil servants. Only one speaker out of nine disagreed and a message was sent to the Dáil, but met with no immediate response from the lower house which had little respect for the second chamber.[57]

[55] Dáil Debates: 163, 662.
[56] Seanad Debates: 3, 29.
[57] See O'Sullivan, op. cit., pp. 122–3.

Some months later, in July 1924, the Minister for External Affairs, Desmond FitzGerald, said that he had "no objection" to a committee of this kind and ". . . would welcome it to a large extent, but of course it will be recognised that we could only cooperate and put the material of our Department at the disposal of such a committee to a limited extent".[58] But this rare instance of ministerial generosity was not seized upon and when Major Bryan Cooper referred to the idea in February 1926[59] during a private member's debate on the supply of information on foreign affairs, his was a voice in the wilderness. It was probably no coincidence that Major Cooper, an independent TD of 'ascendancy' affiliations, was usually in the political wilderness; reform is often the product of such circumstances.

This was also true of the nineteen thirties, when renewed proposals came from the Fine Gael party, then in opposition. In 1936, John A. Costello, discussing the League of Nations sanctions against Italy, claimed that:

> if we had something like a foreign relations committee, some non-party committee of this House . . . we would, I have no doubt, be enabled to put upon an issue of this kind what the attitude of the Irish nation is to be in the future . . . we could have had a common united policy on this particular issue, which has no relation to Party politics or internal politics in this country, but which affects the welfare of the State as a whole. . . .[60]

Further pleas for a standing committee were put forward by James Dillon in 1937,[61] and by Mr Cogan in 1939,[62] but de Valera had made his attitude clear in April 1938 when he observed that a formal bipartisan arrangement was unlikely to work in a deeply divided parliament: "We in this House . . . have been working under conditions which are not altogether normal in Parliaments . . . there has been the Civil War . . . these things are not easily

[58] Dáil Debates: 8, 838.
[59] Dáil Debates: 14, 568–9.
[60] Dáil Debates: 62, 2775–6.
[61] Dáil Debates: 67, 812–3.
[62] Dáil Debates: 75, 1459–60.

forgotten . . .".[63] He preferred, he said, to rely on informal contacts with opposition leaders and cited an instance of this before he negotiated the Anglo-Irish agreements in 1938:

> I did say to a prominent Deputy on the Opposition Benches that I was going to London. I met him casually and I said: 'I hope you will understand the seriousness of this position and that nothing will be done by your people to cause unnecessary embarrassment'.[64]

However, the outbreak of World War II was responsible for the first genuine bipartisan approach to foreign policy in the history of the state, and the first tentative steps towards institutionalising this common viewpoint resulted in the formulation of the Defence Conference in May 1940. This body consisted of "three members of the Government, three of the principal Opposition, and two of the Labour Party, to meet each week and at such other times as may be necessary, to consult and advise on matters of national defence".[65] In view of the fusion of defence and foreign policies in time of war, this committee might conceivably have acted as a foreign affairs committee; however, this does not appear to have happened. One of its original members, Mr James Dillon, opposed the policy of neutrality but, on his expulsion from the Fine Gael party in 1942, he ceased to be a member of the Conference, and once the immediate threat of the country's defence had passed, the Conference ceased to function.[66] It seems to have interpreted its terms of reference rather narrowly and there was no suggestion that it should formulate policy objectives for post-war conditions.

In 1948, the opposition parties came into power and, as a result of the frustration they had experienced out of office, showed some sensitivity to the idea of bipartisan cooperation on foreign affairs. Although the Minister for External Affairs, Mr MacBride, did not have much personal experience of parliamentary bickering over

[63] Dáil Debates: 71, 455.
[64] Dáil Debates: 71, 454–5.
[65] Dáil Debates: 80, 1169–70.
[66] Between the end of May 1940 and the end of November 1943, it met eighty-three times, an average of once every two weeks (Dáil Debates: 91, 2339); but between the end of November 1943 and the end of April 1945, it met only twice and was wound up shortly afterwards (Dáil Debates: 96, 2498–2508).

foreign policy, he nevertheless referred cautiously to the existence of committees in other states: "I do not know whether it would be possible within the existing framework of our Parliamentary institutions to make such a provision here. It is a matter that might well be considered at some future date".[67] But this "future date" was to be indefinitely postponed since the government and the Dáil became encumbered with normal day-to-day business. Furthermore, the upsurge of bipartisan feeling towards one particular aspect of Irish foreign policy—that of partition—was in 1948 diverted into a second *ad hoc* quasi parliamentary committee, the Mansion House All-Party Conference. This, like the Defence Conference, represented an attempt to cope with a special contingency but, unlike the Defence Conference, it was not even a formal parliamentary institution but rather an anti-partition pressure group enjoying the official support of the political parties, including those which formed the government.

Mr MacBride returned to the idea of a standing committee shortly after he left office in 1951. His proposals, though more detailed, were still vague: he did not see the committee as a formal council, but rather as "one or two members of either the Dáil or the Seanad . . . with whom he [the Minister] could consult from time to time".[68] He pointed out that the panel of members of the Oireachtas chosen to represent the two houses at the Council of Europe might provide a basis for the selection of the committee, or else it would be chosen by the minister himself in consultation with the leader of the opposition. MacBride emphasised that this committee should not have "any special powers or any special functions: it should be available to the Minister whenever he wishes to consult it . . .".[69] In his opinion, the main purpose of the committee was that the minister

> might find it useful to be able, very often, to explain certain matters privately to the Opposition . . . and thus to ascertain the views of the House. It might very often save embarrassment caused unwittingly by casual questions . . . also . . . it would probably be of help to the Opposition to be kept abreast of any particular developments that might be taking place.[70]

[67] Dáil Debates: 112, 902.
[68] Dáil Debates: 126, 1967.
[69] Dáil Debates: 126, 1967.
[70] Dáil Debates: 126, 1967.

This proposal met with little response from other speakers and with none from the new Minister for External Affairs, Mr Aiken.

In 1957, the first serious proposal for a committee, initiated in the Dáil, was debated. The motion was for

> a Select Joint Committee, consisting of eighteen Deputies and seven Senators, of which the quorum should be eight, with power to send for persons, papers and records . . . for the purpose of inquiring into and reporting to the Dáil and Seanad on the following matter, namely:—the economic consequences for Ireland likely to follow the participation or the non-participation by this country in (a) the proposed Free Trade Area, and (b) the European Economic Community.[71]

Two points are remarkable in this motion put forward by John A. Costello, leader of the opposition and former Taoiseach, and James Dillon, deputy leader of Fine Gael. The first is that, although the proposal was concerned with Ireland's position in a rapidly changing Europe, it did not recommend a genuine standing committee on foreign affairs—indeed, it was limited by its terms of reference to consider the *economic* aspects of the question. However, had the committee come into existence, it is difficult to see how it could have avoided the political implications of participation. Second, this was to be a committee with 'teeth'—with the power to investigate the workings of the government departments concerned—and it was this, above all else, that provoked the government's rejection of the idea.

Mr J. A. Costello's speech emphasised that it was "the duty of the Government . . . to seek views where it can . . . to bring into close cooperation, consultation and effort every section of the community and every Party represented in the House".[72] The committee, he said, was to be educative:

> a committee that will work and work hard to educate each member of that committee and through that committee educate each

[71] Dáil Debates: 163, 629–30.
[72] Dáil Debates: 163, 637.

member of the Dáil . . . so that when the ultimate proposals come before the Government it will not be a case of people saying: 'The Government have the means of ascertaining the facts. They have the diplomats, the financiers, the economists who should know what they are doing and we will just walk in behind them'.[73]

The government, on the other hand, saw this plea for a "fully informed and fully educated"[74] parliament as a threat to its constitutional position. After citing the government's short-term objections —that the establishment of a committee would give the public "a wrong impression by conveying a suggestion of urgency that is not justified"[75]—Seán Lemass, then Minister for Industry and Commerce, produced the traditional arguments against the committee system. What worried him most was whether

this committee . . . should have the right to ask the officers of my department, or of the Department of External Affairs, or the Department of the Taoiseach, or the Department of Agriculture to come before them and to express personal views there, or to reveal the instructions they get from their Ministers, or to answer questions designed to find out whether they are of a different viewpoint from that expressed by their Ministers in the Dáil. Any such arrangements would undermine the whole theory of ministerial responsibility.[76]

Mr Lemass went on:

Ministers are here responsible to the Dáil, entitled to be questioned by any Deputy on any matter affecting their administration. Members of the Dáil have the right to table motions for debate here. That is the way that democratic Governments should work and not that private members of the Dáil should have the right of access to departmental files, the right to examine into the processes by which ministerial and Government decisions are taken.[77]

[73] Dáil Debates: 163, 638.
[74] Dáil Debates: 163, 638.
[75] Dáil Debates: 163, 643.
[76] Dáil Debates: 163, 646.
[77] Dáil Debates: 163, 646.

Therefore, the traditional, late nineteenth century theory of the government's responsibility to parliament was upheld at a time when the freedom of the individual parliamentarian had all but vanished because of party loyalties, and when the work of government was of an immensely more detailed and complicated nature than when the theory evolved. Mr Dillon complained that the civil service was capable of giving unbiased, factual information (and was already accustomed to presenting it to the Committee of Public Accounts),[78] but he did not press the matter further. Indeed, in his brief references to the committee systems of the USA and France, he showed a rather lukewarm attitude: "The fact that it is done elsewhere does not necessarily mean that we should do it here, but the fact that it is done elsewhere in democratic Parliaments . . . is worth considering before we reject as unfavourable the terms of this proposal".[79] In the event, Mr Costello and Mr Dillon withdrew their motion.

In 1961, the avalanche of questions on Ireland's application to join the EEC demonstrated the clumsiness of the traditional approach to the organisation of parliament, and in November 1961 Mr Dillon asked:

> . . . would it not be eminently desirable that there should be some committee representative of the Oireachtas which, from time to time, could inform itself in a more detailed way than is practicable by Parliamentary Question and answer, through having the power to send for administrative heads of Departments or Ministers and discussing specific aspects . . . ?[80]

The Taoiseach, Mr Lemass, replied that "the course suggested . . . requires very careful consideration because it has some doubtful implications . . . ".[81] and quickly changed the subject. Subsequent pleas both inside and outside the Oireachtas met with little response from the government. For example, in 1969, the new Minister for External Affairs, Dr Hillery, while admitting that "the Dáil can play

[78] Dáil Debates: 163, 662–3.
[79] Dáil Debates: 163, 663–4.
[80] Dáil Debates: 192, 149.
[81] Dáil Debates: 192, 149.

a big part",[82] stressed that the ultimate responsibility lay with the minister and concluded that "there are areas in which Opposition and Government are quite apart, so I do not think at this stage it could come about that a committee of the Dáil would determine our foreign policy".[83]

However, the increased work arising from the bewildering crisis in Northern Ireland and the continuous and complex questions consequent on the EEC negotiations led to a greater note of urgency after 1969. In 1972, the spokesman of the major opposition party, Fine Gael, stressed that

> Fine Gael are only too anxious for the establishment of a foreign affairs committee in this Parliament. In fact, we gave a specific undertaking that in the event of Fine Gael being in power we would establish such a committee as an essential part of democratic and parliamentary procedures here.[84]

The spokesman, Mr Richie Ryan, expressed particular concern about the inadequate information and the absence of specialised knowledge associated with traditional Dáil procedures in the face of "the complexity of international relations" and more particularly the consequences of membership of the European Community.[85] On this occasion, the government's reaction was non-committal, but not unsympathetic; the Minister, Dr Hillery, claimed that he "was interested for a long time in having a committee of the Dáil but the Opposition did not do anything about it".[86]

Later in 1972, when full participation in the European Community became imminent, the possibility of making procedural changes in order to adapt to the new circumstances received much more serious consideration from government and opposition parties alike.[87]

[82] Dáil Debates: 242, 128.
[83] Dáil Debates: 242, 129.
[84] See Dáil Debates: 260, 427.
[85] Dáil Debates: 260, 426–429 and 458–461.
[86] Dáil Debates: 260, 427.
[87] EEC membership was not the only stimulus to change. In May 1972, an inter-party committee of the Dáil was established to examine the implications of Irish unity, but its temporary nature and terms of reference suggested that it was seen as an *ad hoc* measure along the lines of the Defence Conference of the early nineteen forties, rather than the beginning of a new development in parliamentary procedure.

During the debate on the European Communities Bill 1972, there was general agreement that some form of committee should be established in order to cope with the flood of draft regulations, directives, proposals and so on which was flowing in from Brussels.[88]

Mr Liam Cosgrave's coalition government, which came into power in March 1973, persisted with this scheme which appeared in a more detailed form in the summer of that year.[89] The proposed committee was to be a joint committee of the Dáil and Senate composed of the ten deputies and senators who are appointed to the European Parliament together with sixteen others—ten from the Dáil and six from the Senate. The joint committee, which will be provided with secretarial assistance, will be able to intervene at three stages of the legislative process consequent on EEC membership. It can examine proposals and report its views to the government; these will not be binding on the government, but obviously the committee would have an influential consultative role. It can also report its views on the implementation of EEC directives and, finally, it is envisaged that it should "have the authority, by majority decision, to put down a motion for the annulment" of government regulations consequent on EEC legislation.[90] The first chairman chosen by the committee was an opposition TD, Mr Charles Haughey, who had been a member of Fianna Fáil governments between 1961 and 1970.

This proposed committee could well prove to be an important departure from traditional Dáil procedures, but time alone will tell whether it is a sufficient response to the considerable challenge of EEC membership. There may be initial reservations about its capacity to deal with the sheer volume of proposals, directives and regulations which will pass through it. In the original six member states of the European Community, this function is not performed by one committee but by a series of specialised committees which deal with specific areas of public policy. Where 'European Affairs' committees exist in these states, they act either as an initial filter, to separate

[88] The Bill was debated in the Dáil between 25 October and 15 November 1972. See Dáil Debates: 263, 90 ff.

[89] The proposed committee was first introduced by the Minister for Foreign Affairs, Dr Garret FitzGerald, in the Senate on 20 June 1973. At this stage, a total membership of twenty was envisaged. See Seanad Debates: 75, 161–164.

[90] Seanad Debates: 75, 163.

the technical details from the broad issues and to assign legislation to other committees, or as a body which is designed to stimulate interest in the further development of the European Community system.[91]

It is possible, therefore, that the proposed joint committee will be overburdened and will have little time to devote to an examination of those issues which are not often expressed in the form of legislation but which are nonetheless fundamental to the development of the European Community.

For example, the attempts to coordinate the foreign policies of the member states, in the regular meetings of officials and foreign ministers, are unlikely to receive much consideration; indeed, a narrow interpretation of the joint committee's terms of reference could exclude them altogether. A 'European affairs' committee of the type envisaged, subjected to the whole range of the EECs' legislative output, can hardly be equated with a foreign affairs committee as such; and in any case, many facets of Irish diplomacy, such as policies on decolonisation put forward in the United Nations, or bilateral aid programmes, would not necessarily arise in a European context. The new committee may establish a far-reaching precedent, but in itself it seems to be only a partial reform of parliamentary organisation.

★   ★   ★   ★

Apart from the sheer inertia of government or opposition, the reluctance of the Dáil to reform its procedures in order to play a more effective role in foreign affairs has four main sources. The first stems from the fact that Irish parliamentary practice is closely modelled on the British tradition, which has tended jealously to shield the permanent administrators and advisers from parliamentary interference. It is no coincidence that the House of Commons does not yet have a standing committee on foreign affairs, but rather has "evolved methods of exercising sporadic pressures through foreign affairs debates and question time".[92] Second, there is no doubt that, up to and including 1948, there did not exist a sufficiently bipartisan

[91] See M. Niblock, *The EEC: National Parliaments in Community Decision-Making* (Chatham House: P.E.P., London, 1971).
[92] Frankel, op. cit., p. 28. See also Niblock, op. cit., pp. 97–101.

approach to foreign policy to make a committee work, mainly because of the real and imagined divisions between the two major parties about Ireland's relationship with Britain. However, party differences no longer appear to be so acute as to be disruptive.

A third difficulty has been that, on the whole, the proposals for reform inevitably have been associated with political parties in opposition, and the notoriously unbalanced swinging of the political pendulum in Irish politics has meant that the committee is unfairly regarded as the child of the Fine Gael party. Usually, these proposals have not been advocated with a great deal of conviction; they have not been discussed in detail and too often have been tossed out as debating points by people who had little faith in their implementation. Finally, of course, there is the government. What government will readily agree to throw more light on its activities and thereby expose its mistakes and hesitations? The firm grasp of one party, Fianna Fáil, on the reins of power has generally meant that it has had too little experience of opposition to realise the long-term advantages which might accrue to it, were it to cooperate in establishing a foreign affairs committee. However, the fact that the usual roles of Fianna Fáil and Fine Gael were reversed in the general election in February 1973 may lead to a revision of attitudes by the leaderships of these parties.

An examination of legislative procedure in other small parliamentary democracies suggests that the specialised committee is a normal and often significant institution in the shaping of foreign policy. States such as Sweden, Norway, Switzerland, Australia and New Zealand— whose parliamentary procedures are in many respects quite dissimilar— have in common some form of foreign affairs committee. These vary in importance. The Australian committee seems to possess insufficient powers to make its presence felt,[93] while the Swedish body has been handicapped by its restrictive terms of reference and the lack of interest of the political parties, although it nonetheless contributes to the Swedish parliament's "steady contact with all important matters".[94]

[93] Watt, op. cit., pp. 310–311.
[94] N. Andrén, *Modern Swedish Government* (Almqvist and Wiksell, Stockholm, 1961) p. 148. For an account of the role of the Riksdag (Parliament) in influencing foreign policy, see pp. 143–48.

On the other hand, the foreign affairs committee in Switzerland (where as in Ireland, the idea of a committee, had been resisted until 1936 and was effectively put into practice only in 1945) is now "regarded as one of the most important" standing committees.[95] Among the benefits it provides is the fact that

> the government rationalises its decisions, and has a forecast of public reactions to them, and neutralizes criticism. The Assembly has much more information (seeping out to confidential sessions of the fractions [i.e. parliamentary parties]) and some of its members have the chance of putting questions to Federal Councillors and officials.[96]

In New Zealand, the external affairs committee's

> primary purpose has been to enable its members to be informed and to exchange opinion on current international developments. Documentation is provided by the Department of External Affairs, which services the Committee, and usually designates an officer to initiate discussion or answer questions on matters of current interest. While, therefore, the Committee is in no way responsible for the framing of policy, it has frequently served a valuable consultative purpose.[97]

The reluctance to establish a similar system in Ireland partly stems from the notion that a standing committee would somehow *replace* the executive arm in deciding policy—Dr Hillery referred in 1969 to the possibility of a Dáil committee "determining" foreign policy. But the foreign affairs committees in Switzerland and New Zealand do not do this and yet are regarded as performing a useful role. It would be impossible for a committee to determine foreign policy, in the sense of dealing with the day-to-day crises of international politics. What it can do is to help determine the broad objectives

[95] C. Hughes, *The Parliament of Switzerland* (Cassell, London, 1962) p. 150.
[96] ibid. pp. 150–51.
[97] A. D. McIntosh, 'Administration of an independent New Zealand foreign policy' in T. C. Larkin (ed.) *New Zealand's External Relations*, (Oxford University Press, London, 1962) pp. 52–3.

of the state's policy and to review closely the execution of policy by the executive arm of the government. A committee should not (and could not) make 'today's policy', but it could examine the advantages and mistakes of previous policies and so provide the policy-makers with clearer guidelines for the future.

This, it may be argued, is one of the most important functions of any parliamentary body; through the review of policy formulation and implementation, the public's needs and wishes and the government's actions and resources are most effectively brought together in pursuit of the 'national interest'. This function is incoherently pursued in the Irish parliament. It is noticeable that the tentative moves away from the simple procedures inherited from nineteenth-century British parliamentary tradition tend to induce a fragmentary rather than a comprehensive view. Thus, in the past, many of the proposals for reform emphasise only one type of issue—'defence', 'partition', 'the economic implications of EEC membership' or 'the surveillance of EEC legislation'.

But all of these issues are part of foreign policy, and the articulation of national objectives and the establishment of priorities can be discussed effectively only in a body which can consider them all. Ideally, such a body would be one committee in a comprehensive structure of specialised committees dealing with the major sectors of public policy—finance, industry, agriculture, social welfare, and so on; but even without this structure, the case for a foreign affairs committee deserves consideration.

Of course, it may be argued that such a committee would only formalise the position that already exists and would restrict active participation in foreign affairs to a few front benchers. On the face of it, this argument has some truth: among the committee members would presumably be those very TDs who are already foreign policy specialists, although others could be included as well. But in the long term and in a more indirect way, the committee might stimulate the interest of the houses of the Oireachtas and educate its members. Were it to provide a more regular and more plentiful supply of information, this could be disseminated through regular reports or more fully-informed debates. And if it were successful in this, it would acquire a certain prestige both inside and outside parliament, thus stimulating competition for its membership. There is, of course, no guarantee that this would happen, for there would be many problems to do with its composition, the extent of its powers, the nature of its work, let alone the vulnerability of committees to personal and partisan ambitions. But unless some structural reform is made, the Irish parliamentarian will find it increasingly difficult to come to grips with his responsibility to watch over the formulation of foreign policy.

Chapter 9

THE POLITICAL PARTIES AND FOREIGN POLICY

*"The best thing that political Parties, that differ so widely
as ours do, can hope for is that they will be content to submit
their differences and to submit their different policies to the
people and to accept the people's judgment."*

Eamon de Valera, 1934
(Dáil Debates: 53, 281)

*"Fundamentally, there is no difference of policy between
the Parties in the House in relation to our external policy."*

Seán MacBride, 1949
(Dáil Debates: 117, 850)

PARLIAMENTARY institutions, with all their shortcomings, nevertheless may be seen as important channels of communication between the policy-maker and his public, in so far as they provide an arena in which popularly chosen representatives may seek to examine and modify the content and execution of policy. However, a further dimension is added to the process by the existence within this arena and amongst these representatives of competitive groups— the political parties. Although, where electoral conditions are favourable, some political parties may survive on the basis of clearly defined minority interests and may function as little more than 'protest groups', most parties, because of their pursuance of the responsibility of government, seek to reflect the desires of the public over as wide a range of opinion as is consistent with the economic, social or ideological basis on which the party is formed. Hence, such parties attempt to act as agencies which ascertain these popular desires, promote them and, to some extent, translate them into practical policies.

In this way, it is argued, government policy may remain relevant to the wishes of the people. But, as is frequently pointed out,[1] this is but one aspect of the political party's function in a modern democracy, for the party is not only ". . . necessary as a means to explain the people to their rulers . . .", but is also ". . . a device to explain the rulers to the people".[2] In other words, because of the range and complexity of political issues, the political party does not so much bring the people's demands to the notice of the government, as select, for the attention of the people and their approval or rejection, those issues which it feels are relevant both to the people's needs and to the party's well-being. In order to comment on the role of political parties in the formulation of foreign policy, it is therefore necessary to examine the way in which these parties present foreign policy issues to the people, as well as to consider the attitudes towards these issues which parties adopt because of public opinion.

Elections are the most obvious way by which political parties act on issues of policy. Therefore, it is important to see how parties promote or obscure issues of foreign policy during election campaigns and to assess the significance of these efforts. It must be remembered, however, that a general election is usually a poor indicator of public feeling on specific issues, for, in the last resort, only one answer can be given to a multiplicity of broad questions covering the whole range of public policy. Dr Noel Browne's comment about the 1961 general election is important:

> we were talking about all sorts of things: unemployment, emigration, agricultural policy, health policy, social welfare policy, education, the failure of one group and the success of another group, and a thousand and one things. Buried deep in that was the whole idea of the Common Market.[3]

Even when foreign policy appears to constitute an important part of a party's programme, without the use of opinion polls there is no sure means of ascertaining the part it plays in influencing the voter.

[1] For example, see F. B. Chubb and D. A. Thornley, *Irish Government Observed*, (Irish Times Ltd., Dublin, 1964) pp. 4–7.
[2] ibid. p. 5.
[3] Dáil Debates: 199, 1147.

Of course, elections are not the sum total of the political party's activities. It is also important to consider the role of the parties between elections—or rather, as they prepare for the next election. Here, the structure and organisation of the party may provide some indication of the extent to which it formulates and promotes policies during this period. Unfortunately, the available information on the activity of any one Irish party is limited, but a survey of the general elections since 1923 and a brief examination of the organisation of Irish parties may provide a tentative assessment of the importance of political parties in the making of Irish foreign policy.

★   ★   ★   ★

The first general election under the Constitution of the Irish Free State was held in August 1923 and the principal issue of that election, an issue which left a lasting imprint on the two largest parties and indeed on the whole tenor of Irish party politics, was that of the Anglo-Irish Treaty of 1921. The issue of the state's constitutional and international standing, unresolved by the civil war, was to be the outstanding issue in party politics for over a decade. The electoral system—proportional representation by the single transferable vote— was expected to produce a multiplicity of parties based on a variety of sectional interests, but, in fact, only two such parties emerged in the 1923 election (Labour and the Farmers' Party), and their limited success (23.1 per cent. of the total vote) indicated the importance which the electorate placed on the Treaty issue, which was the major platform of the other two parties. Indeed, one of these parties— Mr de Valera's Sinn Féin—fought the election solely on the constitutional issue and took its stand against the Treaty, a position which earned it 27.6 per cent. of the total vote and 44 seats out of 153 in a Dáil which it boycotted until 1927. The pro-Treaty party, Cumann na nGaedheal, won 39.2 per cent. of the total vote and 63 seats in the Dáil and, in the absence of Sinn Féin, the leader of the party, W. T. Cosgrave, formed a government. The result of the 1923 election was a comparatively clear indication of the public's attitude towards the Treaty issue: it reflected a preference for the moderate constitutional position of the pro-Treaty group as opposed to the more radical position of Mr de Valera. It was an election result which had important implications for the development of the state's foreign policy.[4]

For the next fifteen years, the attitudes towards the Treaty provoked a schism in Irish party politics and the Treaty became the most important single issue in general elections during this period. Nevertheless, it was by no means the only issue to confront the electorate and it cannot be said that the electorate's divergence of opinion on this important aspect of foreign policy was reflected clearly in the results of elections. In the election of June 1927 the results were "utterly inconclusive".[5] The two major parties, Fianna Fáil (formed from the followers of Mr de Valera who left Sinn Féin in 1926) and Cumann na nGaedheal, emphasised the issue of the international position of the state during the campaign, the latter defending its policy of evolution within the Commonwealth and the former stressing a more radical assertion of independence. In spite of this, the smaller parties, formed on sectional rather than on national interests, provided the feature of the election and won 40 per cent. of the seats. This stalemate was followed by another election in September 1927 in which the smaller parties lost seats and the government party, appearing experienced and stable during a period of grave civil disturbances, remained in power. Although these two elections ultimately resulted in a Dáil which was fundamentally divided on the issue of relations with Britain (the smaller parties had to make tactical alliances with one or other of the major parties on the question[6]), it is difficult to claim that this was a consequence of an unequivocal expression of the electorate's views on foreign policy alone.

Similarly, although the Treaty issue was predominant in the 1932 election which brought Fianna Fáil to power (with the support of seven Labour deputies), it would be facile to overestimate the signific-

[4] For the 1923 election, see Cornelius O'Leary, *The Irish Republic and Its Experiment with Proportional Representation* (Notre Dame University Press, Notre Dame, 1961), pp. 16–21.

[5] W. Moss, *Political Parties in the Irish Free State* (Columbia University Press, New York, 1933), p. 156. The June 1927 election is covered in pp. 141–58. See also O'Leary, op. cit., pp. 21–24, for the 1927 elections.

[6] See J. Hogan, *Election and Representation* (Cork University Press, Cork, 1945), pp. 26–31.

ance of the issues of foreign policy in this election. Undoubtedly, Mr de Valera made a great deal of his proposals to achieve full independence: in an advertisement which his party put in the *Irish Independent* on 11 February 1932, the first three points had to do with the removal of the parliamentary oath of allegiance to the Crown and the abolition of outstanding annual payments, notably the land annuities, to Britain.[7] Cumann na nGaedheal failed to point out that its policy of evolving a more independent position within the Commonwealth had borne fruit in the Statute of Westminster in 1931, and, against a background of serious economic crisis, its inferior electoral organisation allied to an inability to mark out the lines of future policy, made its defeat not altogether surprising.[8]

In January 1933, less than a year after the previous election, Mr de Valera dissolved the Dáil and another general election took place.[9] His timing was shrewd, for he not only caught the other parties in a state of disorganisation, but contrived to avoid making his foreign policy a critical electoral issue. Had the election been held later, de Valera's foreign policy might well have told against him, for his policy of constitutional evolution from a unilateral rather than from an intra-Commonwealth basis had resulted in the British government's imposition of punitive tariffs on Irish agricultural imports. The economic war was under way. However, its full implications had not yet been felt by the general public and its anti-British emphasis was still popular.[10] Mr de Valera won a slight majority in the Dáil and was given breathing space in which to develop his constitutional policies.

Although de Valera had avoided the constitutional issue—or rather had fought it on ground of his own choosing—the major parties were still divided on foreign policy. The successor to Cumann na nGaedheal, Fine Gael, remained diametrically opposed to Fianna Fáil's prosecution of the economic war and to Mr de Valera's negative attitude towards the Commonwealth. At the time, it seemed that this division would remain a feature of future election campaigns. In

---

[7] Reprinted in Moss, op. cit., pp. 206–209.
[8] The 1932 election is discussed in Moss, op. cit., pp. 173–188.
[9] The 1933 election is covered in O'Leary, op. cit., pp. 27–29 and Moss op. cit., pp. 189–94.
[10] Moss, op. cit., pp. 192–193.

1934, rejecting the notion of a bipartisan policy in the Dáil, Mr de Valera claimed that the final decision on the main lines of foreign policy lay with the electorate.[11]

Mr de Valera's philosophical attitude was put to the test in 1937, by which time the constitutional aspect of his policy towards Britain had been shown to be feasible: the constitutional implications of the Executive Authority (External Relations) Act of 1936 had been tacitly accepted by Britain without any sanction. As Professor James Hogan points out, this removed the constitutional issue from electoral politics, thus leaving the economic aspect of Fianna Fáil's foreign policy for the voters to judge.[12] Only three parties—Fianna Fáil, Fine Gael and Labour—contested the election and, at the same time, a referendum was held on the new Constitution which embodied Mr de Valera's policy of external association with the Commonwealth. Although the Constitution was accepted by 57 per cent. of the electorate, only 45.3 per cent. voted for Fianna Fáil, which lost its overall majority and relied on Labour support until the next election.[13] Fine Gael included in their programme a less ambiguous policy towards membership of the Commonwealth, but it is more likely that Fianna Fáil's set-back reflected the dissatisfaction caused by the harmful effects of the economic war, then approaching its sixth year. Criticism of government policy towards the Spanish civil war, although bitter less than a year previously, did not seem to have been important, and the main critic, Mr Belton, lost his seat.

However, Mr de Valera's foreign policy was more consequential in the next general election in 1938, and he regained—with interest— the ground lost in the previous year. On this occasion, the success of his policy towards Britain effectively silenced the opposition. By the time he was given an excuse to dissolve the Dáil after a snap defeat in the House, de Valera had negotiated the agreements with Britain which settled all outstanding disputes with the exception of the Northern Ireland question, and had initiated a beneficial trade policy; in short, the economic war had been ended on comparatively favourable terms for Ireland. The conclusion of economic hostilities

[11] See Dáil Debates: 53, 281.
[12] Hogan, op. cit., pp. 29–31.
[13] For the 1937 election, see O'Leary, op. cit., pp. 29–30.

had been one of the most important aims of Fine Gael's foreign policy since 1932; now this had been achieved by its rivals and W. T. Cosgrave's party could do little else but criticise the trade agreement with Britain ". . . apparently for no better reason than that it had been negotiated by Fianna Fáil".[14] Such a negative approach, along with the deaths and retirements of several Fine Gael leaders and the party's inability to establish a sound local organisation to attract young voters,[15] led to its winning only forty-five seats in the election against Fianna Fáil's seventy-seven and indeed the latter party held an overall majority of sixteen seats in the Dáil. The 1938 election was a clear indication that the sharp division on the signing of the 1921 Treaty was no longer to play a dramatic role in elections, and when the issue was settled in 1948, it was not a consequence of an election.

As it happened, John A. Costello's repeal of the Executive Authority (External Relations) Act of 1936 took place less than a year after the 1948 general election, which (superficially) might suggest that the government was acting in direct response to the public's will as expressed in that election. This was not the case, however.[16] Seán MacBride, leader of the new radical Clann na Poblachta party, was the only politician to raise the issue during the election campaign and, in the event, his party won only ten seats; he himself admitted that this hardly represented a mandate for a change in foreign policy. Furthermore, although MacBride was Minister for External Affairs in Mr Costello's government, the decision does not seem to have been made on his insistence alone, for Costello was equally determined to follow this policy. The Treaty issue, originally the main line of division between the major parties and at least an implicit factor in election campaigns in the nineteen twenties and thirties, became a matter of the past; although it had created traditional (or historical) party loyalties, in itself it no longer reflected a serious split between the foreign policies of the major parties.

In fact, it is 1938 rather than 1948 which marks the watershed between a period when an issue of foreign policy—the evolution of

[14] O'Leary, op. cit., p. 31.
[15] ibid, pp. 35–36.
[16] ibid, pp. 40–43.

Anglo-Irish relations—loomed large in election campaigns, and the subsequent period when a high degree of bipartisanship towards foreign policy (among the major parties at least) kept foreign policy out of electoral politics. The worsening situation in Europe assisted this disinclination to be partisan. In 1938, speaking on defence, Mr de Valera admitted to the Dáil that ". . . in so far as it is practicable the Government will be very anxious to get assistance from other Parties in the House".[17] By the time he enforced Ireland's neutrality policy in 1939, agreement had been reached between all the parties and was maintained throughout World War II. However, this was not accomplished without some heart-searching among the Fine Gael leadership, for neutrality necessitated an implicit repudiation of the party's support of the Commonwealth, whose other member states, in the event, all fought alongside Britain. Mr James Dillon, the deputy leader of the party, opposed the neutrality policy and in consequence was expelled from the party in 1942. Apart from this incident, neutrality was not an important divisive issue in election campaigns, although it may well have influenced the voter to maintain the *status quo* during the war.

There were two elections during the war, in 1943 and 1944. The first took place in what Hogan refers to as "normal conditions"— that is to say that neutrality had been widely accepted as the country's policy, rather than that of any particular party; moreover, the threat to it—from either side—had receded by 1943.[18] Thus, "considerable sections of the electorate were now moved mainly by economic considerations and voted along economic rather than political lines".[19] A clear-cut division on foreign policy did not arise and the polarisation of votes between the two main parties did not occur; both lost heavily, to the advantage of the smaller sectional parties.

Mr de Valera continued to head the government with the support of Clann na Talmhan, but his precarious parliamentary position prompted him to call another election after a snap defeat in May 1944.[20] The circumstances of this campaign were much more favourable to Fianna Fáil than they had been a year before. To some extent, it was

[17] Dáil Debates: 72, 705.
[18] Hogan, op. cit., pp. 31–32. The election of 1943 is discussed pp. 31–36.
[19] ibid. p. 32.
[20] The 1944 election is discussed in Hogan, op. cit., pp. 70–78.

the story of 1937 and 1938 all over again, for the success of the government's foreign policy once more attracted a large number of voters and left the opposition without an effective platform. The future of neutrality had been raised just before the dissolution of the Dáil by a British and American request that the Irish government should break off diplomatic relations with Germany and Japan; the question of possible participation in the war had to be answered. The government's positive confirmation of neutrality proved a popular move and Fine Gael, as principal opposition party, could hardly make an issue out of this decision, for by "discreetly dropping the Commonwealth for the duration of the War, it fell in behind Mr de Valera, a party without a policy".[21] In fact, the opposition was reduced to silence in the face of what a Labour deputy, Mr Richard Corish, referred to as ". . . the issue put before the people . . . that the only person who was able to keep the bombs from falling on the people of this country was Deputy de Valera . . .".[22] Admittedly, the other parties were disorganised and the Labour Party was split. Nevertheless, the 1944 election demonstrated that, where a bipartisan attitude existed, any success in the field of foreign policy would benefit the government's party.

The acceptance of military neutrality both during and after World War II had been one pillar of this bipartisan approach; the disappearance of the Treaty as an issue was another. Indeed, by 1949, Mr Seán MacBride was largely justified in claiming the absence of any important differences on foreign policy between the political parties.[23] Certainly, in the elections of 1951 (won by Fianna Fáil) and of 1954 (won by an anti-Fianna Fáil coalition), there was no disagreement over foreign policy; indeed, foreign policy was hardly discussed. The 1951 election has been described by one observer as ". . . the first genuine 'pork-barrel' election in Ireland"; the same commentator maintained that in the 1954 election "foreign affairs were completely ignored".[24]

The serious issues of the nineteen fifties were economic, and this was particularly evident during the election of 1957. In spite of the

[21] ibid. p. 34.
[22] Dáil Debates: 94, 1462.
[23] See Dáil Debates: 117, 850.
[24] O'Leary, op. cit., pp. 44–45.

IRA campaign on the border, which encouraged the re-emergence of the Sinn Féin movement in electoral politics, the established parties avoided the irredentist issue (the sole remnant of the old Treaty controversy) and fought the campaign on the economic crisis, the weakness of coalition governments and on the claims of the various agricultural interests.[25] Sympathy for the IRA campaign was evident in some northern constituencies where Sinn Féin gained three out of the four seats which they won overall, but this success proved to be short-lived and, in any case, Sinn Féin deputies did not take their seats.

However, the 1957 election returned Fianna Fáil to power, and Fine Gael abandoned their tacit bipartisanship in an extremely trenchant denunciation of the new government's policy in the United Nations, particularly its independent attitude towards the issue of the admission of communist China and its military disengagement plan for central Europe. In the autumn of 1957, the Fine Gael foreign policy spokesman, Mr Declan Costello, maintained that there was "a sharp conflict between Opposition and Government,"[26] but the party's attempt to raise the issue in an election paid few dividends. An opportunity to do this did not arise until the Presidential election of 1959 and, by that time, Fine Gael's rigidly anti-communist attitude had been somewhat blunted. Moreover, the personal qualities of the Fianna Fáil Presidential candidate, Mr de Valera, and the concurrent debate on the electoral system itself were enough to occupy the voters' minds.

Fine Gael did not subsequently attempt to make foreign policy an electoral issue and most parties assumed a bipartisan attitude in the general election of 1961, held a few months after Seán Lemass had announced his government's intention to apply for membership of the EEC. Only one small party, the National Progressive Democratic Party, opposed entry to the EEC on left-wing and neutralist grounds but it won only two seats in the election and was based on a skeletal organisation which did not enjoy national representation. There was, therefore, little chance that opposition to the government's EEC policy would affect the election results

---

[25] The 1957 election is discussed fully by Basil Chubb in chapter 3 of D. E. Butler ed.), *Elections Abroad*, (Macmillan, London, 1959). See also O'Leary, op. cit., pp. 46–48.
[26] Dáil Debates: 164, 1194.

significantly; yet the government party claimed that their victory granted them a clear mandate to join the EEC.[27] By the time the next general election was held in the spring of 1965, entry to the EEC, thwarted by General de Gaulle's veto of January 1963, was no longer an issue and the campaign was fought mainly on domestic politics.

The 1969 election campaign was also mainly concerned with domestic issues, leavened by a clash of personalities as Fianna Fáil repelled the Labour Party's attempt to promote itself as a distinct socialist alternative to the conservatism of the other two parties. One of the more remarkable new personalities to appear was Dr Conor Cruise O'Brien, standing as a Labour candidate. His advocacy of a more explicitly independent UN policy and his defence of neutrality were clearly reflected in the Labour Party's 'Outline Policy', a policy statement which represented a fairly comprehensive alternative to the inchoate foreign policies of the other parties. Nevertheless, in spite of this document, the persistent public concern about the Nigerian civil war, and the increasing possibility of EEC membership (which Labour also opposed), foreign policy remained on the periphery of the election campaign. An anti-communist smear campaign against Labour, occasioned by a comment of Dr Cruise O'Brien's about the rationale of diplomatic representation with extreme left-wing and right-wing régimes, may have helped cause confusion among Labour voters in some country constituencies; but this campaign can hardly be represented as a debate on foreign policy.

The occasion for a debate came about with the referendum on EEC membership in 1972. As we have seen,[28] there was a high level of public interest in the referendum and a decisive vote in favour of entry, a policy supported by both Fianna Fáil and Fine Gael. By its very nature, this referendum was an electoral contest about foreign policy although, ironically, the close association between this issue and that of the government's policy towards Northern Ireland blurred the debate in which, in any case, the economic aspects of entry were by far the most pressing. But perhaps the most striking feature

---

[27] See, for example, the speech in the Dáil of Mr Haughey, Minister for Justice, on 6 February 1963. Dáil Debates: 199, especially 1140–42.

[28] See above, pp. 167-168.

of the referendum campaign was that, although the political parties
played a formal electoral role in the closing stages, the direction and
the groundwork of the campaign, (which in effect lasted over eighteen
months) came primarily not from the parties but from groups which
had been established for this particular purpose.[29]

Only nine months after the EEC referendum, Mr Lynch called a
snap election in February 1973. If he was hoping to discredit his
main opponents, Fine Gael and Labour, by pointing to their differences
over EEC membership, he was to be disappointed. The Labour Party
had accepted the electorate's decision on this issue and had adopted
a role of critical participation in the European Community. In spite
of some internal differences over policy towards Northern Ireland,
Labour was in a position, by the time the election was announced,
to join with Fine Gael to campaign as a coalition alternative. The
election was fought largely on the credibility of this alternative
and on economic and social issues; foreign policy objectives were
not important and the main parties were divided only in their claims
to be better equipped to pursue their objectives. The victory of the
National Coalition, with 73 seats (Fine Gael 54, Labour 19) against
Fianna Fáil's 69 seats and 2 Independents, thus followed what can
be seen as the usual pattern with regard to foreign policy.

Indeed, if we summarise Irish electoral history, it is clear that,
apart from the constitutional and irredentist issues affecting Anglo-
Irish relations, foreign affairs have hardly been a significant feature
of the parties' electoral struggles. Even in cases where external relations
were a factor, the results do not indicate clearly the division of opinion
on any one issue; at most, it can be said that the parties made more
or less correct assumptions about public feeling on foreign policy
issues, and, in this respect, reflected rather than led public opinion.
Nevertheless, the assumptions made by the two large parties, Fianna
Fáil and Fine Gael, have been (the Treaty issue apart) very similar.
If any consistent difference between them can be found, it lies probably
in the degree of ideological content in their attitudes towards the large
issues of world politics.

On the questions of sanctions against Italy in 1935, on the Spanish
civil war between 1936 and 1939, and on the cold war—especially

[29] See below, pp. 288-291.

from 1957 to 1960—the bogey of atheistic international communism was much more readily invoked by Fine Gael politicians than by those of Fianna Fáil. But, of course, the latter were in power and possibly because of this were more likely to take a 'realistic' and pragmatic line on such issues. Since 1960, even Fianna Fáil seemed less inclined to play a flamboyantly independent role in the United Nations. In any case, none of these issues—even where there seemed to be sharp division in parliament, as over the government's intervention in the Spanish civil war—has had any demonstrably significant effect on Irish parties' electoral performance.

The smaller parties, which do not presume to be potential governments, have not always been any readier than Fianna Fáil or Fine Gael to propose alternatives to the government's foreign policy. Those with a sectional basis, such as the Labour Party and the various farmers' parties, have generally trimmed their sails to take advantage of the light and intermittent breezes provided by one or other of the major parties. However, some small parties were founded primarily on a commitment to nationalism and their objectives thus impinge directly on foreign policy. One such party was Clann na Poblachta, whose doctrinaire republicanism was a factor in the 1948 election, although its foreign policy objectives were achieved as much by a Fine Gael initiative as by the fact that they, alone of all small parties, established (very briefly) an electoral position from which their leader could receive the portfolio of external affairs. In the 1957 election, Sinn Féin, relying almost completely on the public's emotional support for the irredentist issue, won four seats, but its abstentionist policy meant that these gains were not translated into parliamentary activity from which further progress might have been made.

With the split of the party into two factions in 1970, Sinn Féin re-emerged as a new factor in electoral politics. The 'official' wing of Sinn Féin dropped the abstentionist policy, while the dissident 'provisional' wing retained the traditional view that any political system deriving from the Treaty of 1921 was beyond political redemption. Although nationalist issues were still emphasised in the programme of the 'officials', they became part of a more comprehensive radical programme. Indeed, the stereotype of the small 'one issue' nationalist party was more strikingly represented in Aontacht Éireann, formed in 1971 mainly from dissident Fianna Fáil supporters and led by a former government minister, Mr Kevin Boland. Neither Sinn Féin nor Aontacht Éireann won a seat in the 1973 general election and it is thus impossible to say how their attitudes to foreign policy would develop in a parliamentary environment. One small radical party which did establish a precedent for an active parliamentary role was the National Progressive Democratic Party which, during the early nineteen sixties, in the persons of Dr Noel Browne and Mr Jack McQuillan, provided alternative points-of-view on the UN's Congo operation, apartheid in South Africa, nuclear disarmament, NATO and the EEC. However, such an energetic approach to foreign affairs could not disguise the fact that the NPD's existence as a party was little more than a façade for the activities of its two parliamentary representatives, who were in effect two independents.

The organisation of Irish parties must also be taken into account when considering the electoral importance of foreign policy issues. Even when these issues appear to be an important part of a party's national electoral campaign, there can be no guarantee that they will be given equal weight in individual constituencies and they may well be replaced by purely local considerations and prove to be less important than the party headquarters would wish. Indeed the control of constituency campaigns by party headquarters is extremely limited, mainly because of financial and personnel restrictions. The 1957 election, for example, was fought in ". . . local campaigns with the party central organisations in only a supporting role".[30] In circumstances like these, it is probable that foreign policy issues are among the first to be jettisoned by local party organisations, unless they affect the constituency in a direct and tangible manner. Moreover, party programmes are not always clearly defined or forcefully expressed. In 1957 they had

> . . . a shadowy existence . . . sufficient to be able to refute opponents' charges of having no programme, but not so precise, or readable, or publicised that there could be much danger of their making an impact or embarrassing a candidate in his own locality.[31]

[30] The assessment is Basil Chubb's in Butler, op. cit., p. 195.
[31] ibid. p. 198.

The highly emotional nature of the Treaty issue is an exception to this generalisation and most of the elections of the nineteen twenties and thirties may be described at least in part as 'foreign policy' elections. Nevertheless, the lack of any scientific assessment of the voters' motivations in these, as in all, Irish elections must leave the relationship between specific issues, campaigns and results imprecise and a matter for conjecture.

★   ★   ★   ★

The activities of Irish political parties *between* elections are also important indicators of the way in which a party acts as intermediary between the government and the people. At first sight, it appears that local constituency organisations, represented in an annual party conference (the *Ard Fheis*), enable the discussion of policies to take place at all levels of the party organisation and, in this way, the party leadership may be influenced in the formulation of party policy. However, such an assumption gives altogether too much weight to the formal structure of the party organisation, which hardly exists (even formally) for some of the smaller parties and which, for the larger parties, may give a misleading impression. In practice, many local party branches are dormant between elections and those that are concerned with questions of policy tend to be mainly interested in domestic issues. Moreover, if there are non-conformist opinions at constituency level, it is by no means certain that they will have any profound influence on the leadership of the party. Dr Noel Browne, speaking of his experience at meetings of Fianna Fáil *cumainn* (branches) claimed that they were

> stimulating occasions . . . the rank-and-file consisted of some of the finest people in rural Ireland, independent and dedicated party workers . . . but . . . usually the officer board were of a different class altogether—fairly well-to-do middle class—damping down the radical sentiments and the iconoclasm, ensuring that policies and leadership were kept moderate. This policy prevailed throughout most of the *cumainn* and the higher committees.[32]

[32] *The Irish Times*, 12 October 1967.

This tendency for the party officials to impose moderation and compromise is particularly evident at the annual party conferences. During the two days of the conference, the delegates are faced with an agenda including—in the case of the biggest party, Fianna Fáil— a total of approximately eighty resolutions sent in by the branches. Consequently, the resolutions are phrased in broad and innocuous terms and often attempt to yoke together disparate points-of-view: in effect, they guarantee little more than the presence on the agenda of a general issue rather than specific attitudes towards that issue.

The conference usually concentrates on three or four topical issues which have become urgent and unavoidable problems and from which the party hopes to derive some tangible advantage. Issues of foreign policy rarely fall into these categories and, even if written into the agenda, are not likely to be discussed at the conference. Thus, although the Fianna Fáil *Ard Fheis* of 1967 had on its agenda a resolution on the Irish government's attitude towards the Vietnam war, the issue was not discussed. The sponsors of the resolution, mainly from the universities *cumainn*, represented a comparatively radical minority element in the party; they found little sympathy from the more conservative delegates and their resolution was circumvented without much difficulty by the procedural control of the conference which was in the hands of the party leadership. However, policy on partition is an exceptional matter. Yet, even where there is a strong division between the conference delegates, as occurred in the Fianna Fáil *Ard Fheis* of 1971, the party leadership usually contrives to maintain control.

It is probable that of the three main parties, the Labour Party suffers least from this tendency to side-step or ignore the discussion of foreign policy at their annual conference. One reason for this is that Labour, unlike Fianna Fáil or Fine Gael, has not usually been a 'government party' and therefore is marginally less concerned about appearing cautious and 'responsible'. The more radical elements within the party meet with more encouragement—or rather with fewer obstacles—in putting forward their opinions: the views of these radicals on questions of international affairs are often based on the ideological origins of international socialism. Although this tradition appeared to weaken after the nineteen twenties, it was revived to some extent in the late nineteen sixties. In 1967, the Irish Labour Party rejoined the Socialist International, following an earlier conference resolution, and subsequently the conference was a platform for the discussion of foreign policy issues such as the Vietnam war and the implications of EEC membership for Irish neutrality, shunned by both Fianna Fáil and Fine Gael.

Nevertheless, in Labour Party conferences, as in those of the other parties, it can hardly be claimed that the discussion of branch resolutions plays a major role in policy formulation; indeed debate may even be little more than an opportunity for branch delegates to approve of the leadership's policy, which on external issues is usually stated in the most general terms.[33] Even where there is disagreement and outspoken criticism of party policy, as was the case in 1972 over the party's policy towards the crisis in Northern Ireland, the conference ultimately serves as a means of formal reconciliation in which policy is usually confirmed rather than rejected. On the whole, therefore, "the resolutions of these conferences are no more than guides to party opinion for the attention of the real policy and decision makers who are in fact the leaders of the parliamentary group in the party . . ., perhaps reinforced with a few members of the central executive committee not in the Oireachtas".[34]

Most of the parliamentary members of Fianna Fáil and Fine Gael play a passive role in the discussion of foreign policy, and it seems likely that these policies are formulated by a small group under the supervision of the foreign affairs frontbench spokesmen—or even the spokesmen alone—in the opposition parties, and by members of the cabinet in the government party or parties. If there is dissension within the party, the public is rarely aware of it. Exceptions to this were Mr James Dillon's disagreement over neutrality which led to his expulsion from Fine Gael in 1942; and the opposition of Mr Gerry Boland, a former Minister for Justice in the Fianna Fáil government, to that government's policy on the admission of communist China to the United Nations. Boland stressed the fact, however, that he had not been a member of the government at that time.[35]

[33] Examples are quoted in Chubb, *A Source Book of Irish Government* pp. 242–48 and 256.
[34] ibid. p. 213.
[35] Dáil Debates: 176, 603–604.

A Fine Gael deputy, Patrick McGilligan, tartly remarked, "I suppose the Deputy is only breaking out now because he is about to retire possibly".[36] Mr Boland's admission of an independent view was untypical; up to 1969, in the two larger parliamentary parties at any rate, members generally remained loyal to the party's declared foreign policy.

In 1969, however, the Northern Ireland crisis caused a decided split within the most disciplined of all Irish parties. Fianna Fáil party members may have seen this as an issue of national rather than of foreign policy, but the fact remains that at all levels of the party structure from *cumann* to *Árd Fheis* there was heated discussion of the government's stand on events in the North and, after the cabinet crisis of May 1970, the debate was focussed on private meetings of the Fianna Fáil parliamentary party. The leader of the party was forced to defend his policy as few Irish parliamentary leaders have had to do. The Labour Party, too, experienced a certain amount of internal discord over Northern policy, which came to a head in the autumn of 1972 when the party spokesman on Northern Ireland, Dr Conor Cruise O'Brien, published a book on the subject.[37] The subsequent debate was more overt than that in Fianna Fáil, the more so since some of the leading critics came from outside the Labour Party, particularly from the Social Democratic and Labour Party in Northern Ireland.

Under more normal conditions, considerations of loyalty have served to drive the formulation of party policy behind closed doors, away from such formal party organisations as may exist. Indeed, only the biggest party, Fianna Fáil, has a formal committee of its parliamentary party which deals specifically with external affairs. This foreign policy committee is composed of four senators and four TDs, chosen on the basis of special knowledge, experience and interest by a subcommittee of the parliamentary party responsible for introducing a degree of specialisation among its members. Its members meet in private at least once every two months and appoint their own chairman. There is little evidence of precisely what this committee does and, in any case, its experience has been limited. Nevertheless,

[36] Dáil Debates: 176, 607.
[37] *States of Ireland* (Hutchinson, London, 1972).

while Fianna Fáil was the government party, this committee represented a useful guide to parliamentary opinion within the party for the Minister for Foreign Affairs, who was invited to all meetings and who usually cooperated closely with its members. Late in 1972, the Minister, Dr P. J. Hillery, described the party committee as "very useful" and "a hard-working, interested committee".[38]

The foreign policy spokesman of Fine Gael and Labour, on the other hand, are not influenced or informed by committees such as this. Full meetings of the parliamentary party called to discuss specific foreign policy issues are rare and, when held, are comparatively powerless in the face of the specialised knowledge of the party leadership. The party meeting is poorly equipped to discuss policy on its own merits and may do little more than introduce considerations of electoral tactics into the formulation of policy.[39]

On the whole, the part played by Irish political parties in the formulation of foreign policy has been muted since the disappearance of the constitutional issue which originally provided the only real ideological distinction between the two major parties, Fianna Fáil and Fine Gael. Nowhere has this been more clearly seen than in the Council of Europe (and during other inter-parliamentary gatherings) where the representatives of the two major parties (which form the greater part of the Irish delegation and which before 1973 had no significant connexion with other European parties) act closely together to support Ireland's national position. Again, the Labour Party is the only one which has tended to display a modicum of independence, as was the case in 1967 when a Labour member of Ireland's delegation to the Council of Europe, Mr Frank Cluskey, opposed his Fianna Fáil colleague, Mr Seán MacEntee, on the issue of military commitments in a politically united Europe.[40]

Participation in the European Community may well encourage Irish parties to adopt more distinct attitudes to issues of foreign policy. Of particular importance is the association of each of the three main

[38] Dáil Debates: 263, 917. In opposition, Fianna Fáil retained this external relations committee of the parliamentary party, and in the summer of 1973 it was supplemented by a "support group" of outside advisers. See The Irish Times, 28 July 1973.

[39] However, in the case of the parliamentary Labour Party, whose relatively small membership means that it is almost equivalent to the party leadership, it is probable that more scope exists for a wider discussion of foreign policy.

[40] The Irish Times, 6 October 1967.

parties with party groups in the European Parliament. Fine Gael and Labour joined the Christian Democrats and Socialists respectively at the beginning of 1973, while some months later Fianna Fáil joined the French Gaullists and some independents to form the European Progressive Democrats. These contacts will be more frequent and intensive than any previously enjoyed by Irish political parties. But as yet, apart from the Labour Party's opposition to EEC membership up to the 1972 referendum, signs of fundamental party differences on most foreign policy issues have been rare.

In spite of an electoral system designed to reflect fine shades of political opinion, Irish parties have developed as electoral organisations rather than as policy-formulating bodies; in so far as they do formulate and articulate policy, a large measure of agreement has been reached on the broad issues of foreign policy. Often this has had the effect of suggesting considerable public support for Irish foreign policy— support which may be illusory, for bipartisan agreement is not necessarily reached after extensive public discussion and the clear approval of the electorate. Indeed, in 1963, Dr Noel Browne argued that Fine Gael's bipartisan attitude to Ireland's European policy deprived the public of the means of expressing its views. "I can appreciate", he said, "that Deputy Dillon has always wanted European association . . . but I believe, in the interests of democracy, he had a responsibility to put the other side of the question to the public and let them decide on its merits".[41]

No party which has serious hopes of being an alternative government can oppose merely for the sake of opposing, but must indicate, while in opposition, the sort of policies it would put forward if it came to power. Where an opposition party is in broad agreement with the government, other means must be found to advocate alternative policies: Dr Browne's own party, with its minority basis, was an active example of this. Where a small party such as this finds it impossible to survive, there remains a further channel between the government and the people—the interest group, whose place in the domestic environment must now be considered.

[41] Dáil Debates: 199, 677.

Chapter 10

INTEREST GROUPS AND FOREIGN POLICY

*"If . . . the public wishes us on any issue to give greater
weight to the moral values to which it holds, as against its
immediate interests, then it is right for public opinion to make
this concern clear through its articulate spokesmen . . .",*

Dr P. J. Hillery, 1972
(Dáil Debates: 260, 389)

IN the domestic environment, the policy-maker is confronted with
expressions of public opinion on specific issues which cannot be
ignored. He must be aware not only of the general mood of the
people—which manifests itself at elections under a representative
system of government—but must also assess, and accept or reject,
the clearly defined proposals which he is continually given. These
proposals emanate from two main sources apart from the formal
governmental institutions: the political parties and interest groups.
The political parties, by formulating broad policy programmes
which they hope will appeal to as wide a section of the public as
possible, are attempting to select and articulate the most important
aspects of the public mood.[1]

However, in trying to formulate policies that will attract a majority
of the electors, the political party is usually too conscious of electoral
considerations and too aware of the search for consensus to develop
clearly defined attitudes on specific issues. It is only to be expected
that, in attempting to behave as potential (or actual) governments,
most parties seek to represent a broad coalition of interests rather
than one particular interest. Irish experience suggests that (the Treaty
issue apart) foreign policy interests have received comparatively
little attention from the larger parties, which have acted on the

[1] See above, chapter 9.

267

assumption that such issues arouse little response from the public. Thus, the sustained expression of interest in specific issues of foreign policy is more often found in the smaller parties or, through an alternative channel, in the 'interest group' or 'pressure group'. Together with parties, such groups "are the chief institutions managing the flow of influence between government and society . . .[they] articulate and aggregate policy demands arising from the interests and principles of their supporters . . .[and] also receive and transmit influence from the government to their supporters".[2]

Interest groups are particularly difficult to identify and define. One possible starting-point is to regard them as "organised groups possessing both formal structure and real common interests, in so far as they influence the decisions of public bodies".[3] In this way, we can restrict the area of investigation by excluding the informal cliques within government departments and the influence of those government departments which are public bodies and engaged in the 'making' rather than the 'influencing' of policy. Likewise, the party may be excluded in circumstances where its objective is not merely to influence the government but to replace it. When this purpose is not conspicuous (as, for example, in the various 'farmers' parties which have emerged from time to time in Ireland), some of the smaller parties may be indistinguishable from interest groups which use the fairly expensive and not always effective method of direct participation in legislative politics.[4]

But, even outside these categories, there is a wide variety of groups which embrace most aspects of political, economic and social activity and which resort to a wide range of methods in order to influence government policy. Although the comparative simplicity of Ireland's economic and social organisation and the small size of its population has meant that the number of interest groups is far fewer than in larger and more complex states, the variations between the aims, methods and effectiveness of the groups are considerable.

[2] R. Rose, *Politics in England* (Faber and Faber, London, 1965), p. 126.
[3] W. J. H. MacKenzie, 'Pressure groups in British Government', *The British Journal of Sociology*, vol. vi, no. 2, 1955, p. 137.
[4] It could be argued that even a small nationalist party, such as Aontacht Éireann, is, in spite of its stated objectives on public policy, more akin to an interest group because of its concentration on a narrow, if important, interest.

For example, the methods employed by Irish groups since the inception of the state have ranged from the collection and publication of information in order to support a particular point-of-view, to the display and use of physical force in order to blackmail the government to accept that view as part of its policy. Influence is exerted on all sectors of the policy-making process, from the electorate to the individual minister who is ultimately responsible for policy. As far as foreign policy is concerned, it is important to emphasise that influence may be exerted not only on the government department which has a formal responsibility for foreign policy. Indeed, this influence may be more effective if it is exerted on *several* government departments in order to stimulate inter-departmental discussion— for example, where trade policy is concerned, on the Departments of Industry and Commerce or Agriculture—or on one or more of the political parties, or on the public. The channels of influence are many, and the use made of them is of prime importance in the interest group's tactics.

The use made of the Irish parliamentary representative to act on behalf of a special interest, either in the houses of the Oireachtas or (more usually) as a delegate to the department or departments concerned, is remarkable. The TD is especially vulnerable to such pressures, since in a multi-member constituency he may be competing for popularity against members of his own party, and the need to toe the party line is a poor excuse for not advocating the interests of groups in his constituency.[5] However, foreign policy, which has generally been remote from constituency interests, has not usually constituted an important part of the TD's representations. Nor have senators been called upon to intercede often on such matters. Although most senators are elected by supposedly vocational panels, the Senate is not notably vocational in its behaviour, and its comparative lack of political power makes it a secondary channel of influence.[6] A much more disturbing feature of Irish sectional politics has been the traditional use of extra-constitutional and violent methods to achieve extreme nationalist objectives; however, other groups,

[5] See above, pp. 213.
[6] However, the Senate is sometimes used. In 1966, a debate in the Upper House helped to encourage the government to intensify its contacts with the EEC. See Seanad Debates: 61, 1833–1920.

while not averse to demonstrating strength, have stopped short of expressing their frustrations by violence.

The effectiveness of interest groups varies as much as the methods which they use and is usually difficult to assess. There can be little doubt that, in general, interest groups provide information and ideas which contribute to the formulation of government policy and, perhaps more important, act as a sounding-board for ideas originating within the government; but it is rare to discover evidence of any obvious and direct influence by a particular group. Indeed, an analysis of the process which eventually results in a specific governmental decision is likely to reveal the activities of several interest groups, often competing against each other, none of whom achieve all their original aims. Where a group is effective, it is likely that its success will be achieved by methods that are subtle or rational (or both), and, in any case, the government will take every step to maintain its position as the final arbiter between sectional interests and the national interest.

This point was made in 1947 by Mr de Valera, who was then Taoiseach, when he was asked by Mr Blowick, a member of Clann na Talmhan (a farmers' party), whether a trade agreement which had been negotiated with Britain would be ". . . submitted to the farming community who are most directly concerned". In reply, Mr de Valera said:

'Here in Dáil Éireann we have representatives of the Irish people . . . they are the people who are going to decide whether any agreements between this country and any other country are good or bad in the interests of the community.'
Mr. Blowick: 'May I take it that producers are not experts in their own line and are not worthy of consultation?
The Taoiseach: 'The Deputy can take it from me exactly as I gave it.'[7]

Although it is difficult to draw a more precise picture of the relationship between government policy and interest groups, because of the differences in the methods and effectiveness of these groups,

[7] Dáil Debates: 108, 529–30.

it is possible to examine in more detail the activities of those groups which have attempted to influence Irish foreign policy. These organisations can be conveniently classified according to their overall purpose (economic, religious, nationalist, and so on), a classification which, although oversimplified and arbitrary, does serve to emphasise the principal types of sectional interest with which the maker of Irish foreign policy is concerned. However, before attempting such a survey, it is worth mentioning two unusual types of sectional influence, one of which lies outside this classification, while the other lies outside the area where interest groups usually operate.

The first type of influence is that exerted by locally elected bodies such as county councils and county borough councils; it is difficult to regard them as interest groups (as defined above) since they are public bodies,[8] and in any case their attempts to influence foreign policy have no connexion with the functions which they were legally elected to perform. Nevertheless, Irish local councils, even before independence, established a tradition of making known their views on broad constitutional issues; since independence, this tradition has impinged on foreign policy, and most notably on the question of partition. A resolution is passed, sent to the government and commented on in the press and in the houses of the Oireachtas. In many cases, particularly during the IRA campaign of violence on the border in the late nineteen fifties, these resolutions were implicitly or explicitly opposed to the government's policy. There is no evidence to suggest that these declarations had direct effect; nevertheless, in so far as they encouraged extremist groups and weakened public support for the government's policy, they were an irritant which could not be completely ignored. It may be argued that the local council is not so much an interest group as a convenient platform from which politically active individuals may expound their views on no-matter-what issues; nevertheless, when their protestations influence public opinion, at least some of this influence derives from the impression that it is the council—with such corporate prestige as it enjoys—which has spoken.

The second type of influence emanating from outside the usual sphere of interest group activity is that exerted by *expatriate* interest

[8] See above, p. 268·

groups. Because of the existence of large and cohesive Irish communities in the USA and in Britain and the tradition of strong
nationalist sentiment found in them, it is hardly surprising that groups
within these communities hold and voice definite opinions on issues
of Irish foreign policy which affect their image of the international
position of the mother country. Indeed, during the nineteenth century,
the Fenians and other Irish nationalist groups were financed mainly
by sympathetic associations in the USA, and this tradition has by no
means disappeared.

The issue of a united Ireland has proved the common ground on
which expatriate groups attempt to influence Irish foreign policy.
Often, this influence is in support of government action, as in the
case of the intensive campaigns carried out by anti-partition groups
in Britain and the USA in the years immediately preceding and
following the Republic of Ireland Act of 1948. Here pressure was
being exerted not on the Irish government but on the governments
and people of the United States and Britain, and was discreetly
encouraged by Irish governments as a supplement to their diplomatic
activities.[9]

More unusual, perhaps, than this type of group activity are the
cases where groups outside the state have attempted to *directly* influence
the policy of the Irish government. Although the *de jure* position of
Northern Ireland is a matter of controversy, there is little doubt about
the *de facto* position and, in this sense, groups of Northern Irish citizens
may be classified as expatriate. Following the Belfast and Derry riots
of 1969, representatives of various citizens' defence groups, lacking
confidence in local police and army protection, made direct approaches
not only to the Minister for External Affairs but to any member of
the government whom they thought would be in a position to help
them. This is not to say that the groups were successful in obtaining
all they asked for, particularly with regard to commitments concerning military help; here, as in most other cases of interest group
activity, the groups exert influence (sometimes considerable) but
remain but one factor in the making of policy.

However, expatriate groups do not always support Irish foreign

---

[9] See Dáil Debates: 104, 803–4 for Mr de Valera's expression of personal sympathy for,
and official disassociation from, anti-partition groups in Britain in 1947.

policy. The criticism aroused by the government's willingness to discuss the admission of communist China to the United Nations from 1957 provoked Irish-American groups to take action, after what a member of the Irish UN delegation later called the "theo-political approach" of the Archbishop of New York, Cardinal Spellman.[10] Criticism by Irish-Americans found expression in a number of journals quoted in subsequent debates in the Dáil, but this disapproval was effectively resisted by the Minister for External Affairs, Mr Aiken.[11] In 1959, a Fianna Fáil backbencher, Mr Booth, referred to the possibility that ". . . our foreign policy would be dictated by any group of American people who might gather together, pass resolutions and send telegrams or letters to our Embassies in America, or to our Department of External Affairs at home",[12] but this would only seem likely to occur where expatriate opinion was in sympathy with public opinion in Ireland.

The greatest part of interest group activity takes place among domestic interest groups, and it is these which are likely to exert the most significant influence on government policy. If such groups are classified according to the overall aims which they pursue, an initial distinction can be made. On the one hand are those groups, such as agricultural or industrial organisations, with tangible, material interests which depend to some degree on protection or promotion through government policy; on the other hand, there are groups whose main concern is with the promotion of certain values and whose purpose is moral rather than material. The latter are sometimes referred to as 'cause' groups, an obvious example being the anti-apartheid movement.

But it is the former type of group—the economic interest group— that exerts the most consistent and possibly the most successful type of influence. That these groups are numerous and comparatively highly organised is largely a reflection of the state's increasing intervention in the regulation of their affairs in the interests of the economy as a whole. This intervention is frequent and important as far as foreign policy is concerned, since the health of both the agricultural and industrial sectors of the Irish economy depends to a large degree on

[10] See C. Cruise O'Brien, *To Katanga and Back* (Hutchinson, London, 1962) pp. 22-25.
[11] See, for example, Mr Aiken's speech during the Estimates debate in 1959, Dáil Debates: 176, 701–716 especially.
[12] Dáil Debates: 176, 639.

18

trading relationships with the country's principal external customers, notably the United Kingdom. The sensitivity of Irish economic groups to the trading conditions negotiated by governments on their behalf has resulted in a persistent lobby for more advantageous terms, not only during the period leading up to actual negotiations for trade agreements (usually renewable at regular intervals), but also *between* negotiations, particularly by groups whose objectives have not been attained in previous agreements.

Since healthy trading relations depend on favourable political relations, on the whole the wishes and needs of economic groups will tend to counteract the friction caused by disputed political issues. It could be argued that this did not happen from 1932 to 1938 during Ireland's economic war with Britain, for the interests of the economy as a whole and of some of the most important economic groups (some farmers, especially cattle producers) were subordinated to the government's constitutional objectives. However, to interpret this as a successful resistance by the government to the power of all economic groups is to over-simplify, for some economic interests, such as the new industries, actually benefited (in the short term at any rate) from the measure of protection which was introduced independently of the economic war policy. Moreover, they were largely successful in maintaining this protection after 1938.

The most widely used method of influencing government policy is regular and detailed consultation with those government departments responsible for trade, especially the Departments of Industry and Commerce and Agriculture and Fisheries, and—on the provision of facilities abroad—the Department of External Affairs. Generally, consultation has been informal and follows no rigid procedure. During the first decade of its existence, the state was hampered by the lack of organisation among the various interests. Mr McGilligan, Minister for Industry and Commerce and for External Affairs, remarked in 1929: "The difficulty all along has been to get organisations to deal with in this country instead of individuals".[13] Three years later, his successor as Minister for Industry and Commerce, Mr Lemass, had to point out that the initiative in consultation rested with the interest group rather than the government: ". . . we certainly did not go

---

[13] Dáil Debates: 30, 805.

round asking every trader if he knew of any little matter that he wanted to have rectified . . . obviously the Department cannot know until someone directly concerned brings the matter to its notice".[14]

But coy and poorly organised interest groups are no longer the norm. In 1947, the composition of the Irish delegation to a conference of the Food and Agriculture Organization was criticised because it did not include any representative of agricultural interests. Mr Hughes (a 'farmers' TD) maintained that ". . . it is quite possible to find farmers capable of speaking here on agricultural matters in the international sense . . .", and said that he did ". . . not object to civil servants acting in an advisory capacity . . . but in an advisory capacity only".[15]

Ten years later, in 1957, the idea was being raised that the government should not merely make itself available for consultation but should take the lead in proposing frequent and regular consultations, mainly on account of the economic implications of possible Irish participation in the new European trade blocs. A government circular was sent to agricultural and industrial associations in 1957 asking for their views, although in 1961 a front bench opposition TD, Liam Cosgrave, deplored the fact that "with the exception of occasional references in debates on Estimates and speeches by the Taoiseach or Ministers to Chambers of Commerce, no specific consultations or discussions were entered into between the government and the organisations concerned".[16] Likewise, a request by the National Farmers' Association that the government should establish a committee including the representatives of economic groups in order to examine developments in European trade was turned down in 1961.[17]

This does not mean that economic groups were necessarily unsuccessful in making their point; indeed, the NFA's insistence that Ireland should join the EEC probably played no small part in the government's decision to apply for membership later in 1961. At the same time, the Fianna Fáil government's casual approach to consultation with economic interests changed with the establishment of a formal consultative body, the Committee on Industrial Organisation, on which were represented the Federation of Irish Industries, the Irish

[14] Dáil Debates: 45, 819.
[15] Dáil Debates: 107, 65.
[16] Dáil Debates: 191, 255.
[17] *The Irish Times*, 28 April 1961.

Congress of Trade Unions, and the Federated Union of Employers, in addition to the Departments of Finance and Industry and Commerce.[18] In 1963, the National Industrial Economic Council was set up, and in 1967 the National Agricultural Council. Although the former was disestablished in 1971, the coalition government which came into power in 1973 proposed the creation of a National Economic Council, representing industrial, labour and agricultural interests; this may be seen as an attempt to simplify and rationalise the channels of influence between the government and the principal economic interests in Ireland. To the extent that these bodies play a significant role in the formulation of overall economic policy, they will constitute a vital element in determining the economic substance of Irish foreign policy. Although it is too early to do more than indicate how they might do this, at least the formal machinery of consultation appears to provide the policy-maker with a clearer view of the major sectional interests.

Of course, this tendency for the government to institutionalise the main channels of influence through which economic groups operate has not replaced informal methods of maintaining contact. Informal consultations with smaller groups and even with individual firms still take place, although they do not directly affect the shape of foreign policy. Influence is exerted still by individual TDs and senators: from 1956 to 1964, the persistent advocacy in the Dáil of the Irish fishing industry's interest in the extension and protection of Irish territorial waters is a case in point. However, the idea of representing an economic interest *directly* in the Dáil has lost ground. Certain farming interests, though not the agricultural industry as a whole, actually formed political parties and fought and won elections to the Dáil. Throughout the nineteen twenties and thirties, they were an important element in the balance between the major parties, and in 1943 two of them, the Farmers' Party and Clann na Talmhan, held fourteen seats between them. But since that date, their representation has steadily dwindled to a handful of independent TDs or has been subsumed by the major political parties.

Until 1967, the Labour Party could not be said to have represented a clearly defined economic interest, because of its uncertain relationship

18 See Dáil Debates: 192, 147.

with the trade union movement. Indeed, as long as the Labour Party and the Irish Congress of Trade Unions remained unaffiliated, the trade union movement could speak with a separate voice and was not necessarily supported by the Labour Party in the Dáil. For example, in November 1962, it was not the Labour Party but the National Progressive Democratic Party (Dr Noel Browne and Mr McQuillan) which brought to the attention of the government the Irish Congress of Trade Union's resolution supporting an independent and neutralist foreign policy.[19] With the affiliation of the Labour Party and the ICTU in 1967, the former's views on issues of foreign policy reflected more clearly sectional preoccupations. Thus, during the campaign before the EEC referendum of 1972, the Labour Party stressed the dangers of redundancies under EEC conditions. Nevertheless, unlike its British counterpart, the Irish Labour Party did feel able to accept the verdict of the referendum and was prepared to participate in the European Community.

It is difficult to assess the effectiveness of the efforts of economic groups to influence Irish foreign policy, since much of their behaviour is either secret or informal and their influence is diffused throughout a wide range of government departments and through interdepartmental contacts, of which the formal links, such as the foreign trade committee or the committee of secretaries dealing with the EEC, may be only a part. It must be stressed that these groups are acting in competition with each other and are unlikely to achieve total success by the time their claims have been measured against those of their rivals and of the government. Furthermore, their consultations with the government indicate not merely a one-way process of influencing government policy, for they also provide the government with an opportunity to put forward its view and to persuade sectional interests to adapt their aims. Nevertheless, if no precise conclusion can be drawn as to their influence, there can be little doubt that in the long run the activities of economic groups, by virtue of their importance to the overall policy of any government, will represent a significant factor in the shaping of foreign policy.

Less continuously active and less closely enmeshed with the machinery of government are the cause groups, which seek to ensure

[19] Dáil Debates: 197, 1136-7.

that the more obviously political aspects of foreign policy are consistent with the values which they promote. One such association is the religious group; in Ireland, this generally means what is sometimes loosely referred to as the Catholic church, a body of which nearly 95 per cent. of the state's population are members.[20] This church is international in scope and united by a common system of belief; it is characterised by centralised systems of authority, both in the Vatican and in the national hierarchies. Although the effect is often over-emphasised, membership of an organisation of this nature has undoubtedly affected Irish attitudes to a variety of international political problems. In the first place, when the Catholic church—or a part of it—is directly threatened, it attempts to act internationally to counter the menace, not merely through the medium of Vatican diplomacy but, in so far as it is possible, by way of the foreign policies of governments which may be influenced by the church and its supporters. The Catholic church is continually concerned to obtain diplomatic protection (in the broad sense) for its branches and missions overseas.

An obvious example of this was the Spanish civil war in which the interests of the Spanish Catholic church—effectively attacked in republican Spain—lay in the early recognition of General Franco's government by other states and more direct forms of military or economic aid, all of which were contrary to the policy of the international non-intervention committee to which Ireland subscribed. There was considerable urgency among the Irish public for the government to support the Spanish church. This agitation came to a head in two heated debates in the Dáil in 1936 and 1937 and persistent parliamentary questions from 1936 to 1939, when Franco's military success made the issue an academic one.[21] Nevertheless, while the issue had remained unresolved, Mr de Valera's government was accused of being opposed to the church's interests; the Pope had

[20] Minority religious groups have also attempted to influence Irish foreign policy, e.g. the representations of the Jewish community urging the Irish government to protest against the withdrawal of the UN peace-keeping force (UNEF) on the Egyptian–Israeli border prior to the Arab–Israeli war of 1967. The Protestant churches are also concerned with the partition issue, and the Society of Friends has an interest in defence policy and international peace-keeping.

[21] For the debates, see Dáil Debates: 64, 1194–1226 and 65, 597–639; 642–868; 895–1024.

denounced the Spanish republicans, albeit in rather general terms which betokened a much more wary attitude to Franco's cause than that of the Spanish hierarchy and possibly also of Franco's Irish supporters.[22] The Irish government held in good faith to the non-intervention policy adopted by most European states (though flouted by some) and, although small numbers of Irish volunteers fought on both sides, the government adopted a neutral position in spite of the ideological commitment of most of its people.

The activities of religious groups have not been confined to issues where the Catholic church is as directly engaged as an established organisation as in the Spanish civil war; these groups are also diligent when the Catholic church (or some of its members) holds strong views on the moral aspect of international politics. In 1935, a Mr Kent, speaking in the Dáil "as an Irishman and as a Catholic . . .", opposed the government's support of sanctions against Italy's Ethiopian adventure on the grounds that Italy was ". . . going out to civilise and to Christianise a pagan race".[23] Since World War II, a similar attitude has been evident to the cold war which is interpreted in rather simple terms as a struggle between Christ and anti-Christ. Although many policies of Irish governments have suggested a degree of sympathy with this view, when they have been compelled to take a position on a specific cold war issue, these governments have been criticised by sections of the Catholic church. The most notable example was Ireland's affirmative vote on the question of discussing the entry of communist China to the United Nations, an issue which caused intermittent controversy between 1957 and 1960.

The intensity of polemical debate on matters like this is not altogether surprising in a predominantly Catholic state such as Ireland. However, it would be a mistake to suppose that the relation between church directives or suggestions and the formulation of public policy is always a direct and clear one. Certainly, it is not difficult to find evidence of individual politicians professing to follow the church's teaching to the letter. One such apologist, Mr McGovern, said during the debate on the Spanish Civil War (Non-Intervention) Bill in 1937: ". . . the

[22] See Hugh Thomas, *The Spanish Civil War* (Penguin Books, revised edition, Harmondsworth, 1965), p. 449. It was only after the defeat of Franco's Catholic opponents—the Basques—that the Vatican recognised Franco's government.
[23] Dáil Debates: 59, 530.

Church has spoken. All the Catholic Bishops of Ireland and the Archbishops and Bishops of Spain have spoken. What is the use of their speaking if we, the Catholic section of this country, are not prepared to accept their teaching".[24] Similar views have been expressed on issues where a conflict existed between church and state, particularly when the moral and social teachings of the church were involved.[25]

The social and moral teachings of the church are often relatively explicit. On the other hand, even when issues of foreign policy directly affect the church, it does not usually speak with a single voice about specific policies to be followed. The Vatican's international policy is usually expressed in general terms and its interpretation and application in the separate branches of the church may vary considerably. Nor does the Irish Catholic church always speak openly or clearly through its formal leadership, the hierarchy; indeed, when the methods which the church employs to propound its views are examined, it is evident that individual bishops, sympathetic journals and lay religious organisations take it upon themselves to act.[26] All of these may express the church's overall attitude, but they do so with different degrees of emphasis and precision, and even the most receptive audiences may have to resort to their individual consciences in order to choose between specific policies.

On those occasions when the church opposes Irish foreign policy, Catholic interests are expressed in a number of ways. The sermons of a bishop or of any popular cleric reach not only their immediate audience but are widely reported in the local and national press and, as the debates on the Ethiopian crisis of 1935, on the Spanish civil war, and on the 'Red China question' exemplify, there is no lack of support for religious views in the Dáil, where a direct confrontation with the government can take place. However, to 'play the clerical card' may prove to be a double-edged weapon in a parliament where government and opposition alike profess to be predominantly Catholic and in a country where church and state profess to keep to their

[24] Dáil Debates: 65, 829.
[25] See, for example, Mr Brendan Corish's comment in 1953 on the controversial mother and child welfare scheme, Dáil Debates: 138, 840.
[26] So, of course, do churchmen outside the state, notably missionaries seeking diplomatic support after becoming embroiled in international crises, as was the case, for example, during the Nigerian civil war of 1967–1970.

own somewhat ill-defined spheres of authority. A more extreme advocacy of Catholic interests, which occurs not infrequently, leads to a degree of emotionalism which often proves transitory and unconvincing.

In 1937, an independent TD, Mr MacDermot, after listening to the leader of the Christian Front, Mr P. Belton, ". . . quoting a whole series of pastorals and episcopal letters and indulging in self-glorification because of his intimate association with Cardinals . . ." remarked that ". . . if anything could conduce to the creation of anti-clericalism, it would be [that] kind of speech".[27] It was significant that the Irish hierarchy and most of the well-established Catholic journals carefully avoided any direct or unconditional commitment to the Irish Christian Front. Nevertheless, Mr Belton's organisation achieved a small measure of success for, although he may have exaggerated when he spoke of ". . . over 100,000 citizens gathered in College Green to cheer for the success of the arms of General Franco",[28] the Christian Front collected considerable funds. Some of these were used to send some 600 volunteers under General Eoin O'Duffy (a former Commissioner of the Garda Síochána and later leader of the quasi fascist 'Blueshirt' movement) to fight in Franco's army, although these martial ambitions were hampered by the government's adherence to the non-intervention policy. The prolongation of the Spanish civil war discouraged the further development of the Christian Front, and it had lost most of its impetus by the time the 1937 general election took place.

There has not been a wide mobilisation of public opinion on a religious aspect of Irish foreign policy since the nineteen thirties. The question of the admission of communist China to the United Nations—despite the legacy of bitterness following the expulsion of Catholic missionaries in the late nineteen forties—was a more abstract issue which did not encourage interest groups to undertake and sustain a serious campaign. Although the Fine Gael party adopted clerical criticisms of the government's UN policy from 1957 to 1959 and the controversy appeared in the press, there was no Christian Front, and the issue did not become electorally important. The allegations of the church's supporters in the Dáil were moderate—with

27 Dáil Debates: 65, 687–8.
28 Dáil Debates: 65, 637.

the noticeable exception of Mr McGilligan whose lengthy quotations from clerical authorities were reminiscent of the nineteen thirties.[29] In 1959, one of the principal Fine Gael spokesman, Mr Declan Costello, summed up the dispute with the brief remark that ". . . we should pay attention to the religious groups and the individual churchmen who have expressed strong disapproval of what we did";[30] but he then went on to play down the religious aspect of the issue.

From 1967 to 1970, certain Irish Catholic missionary orders were implicated in the Nigerian civil war. Although these bodies were given considerable financial help by the Irish public and despite the fact that there was much sympathy for the secessionist Biafrans, repeated attempts by missionaries to encourage active political intervention on behalf of the Biafran régime met with little response from the Irish government. Of course, the issue was less clear-cut than in Spain during the nineteen thirties, for it was the government's task to protect the interests of missionaries working in the territories held by both sides in the dispute.

To what extent, then, can the activities of religious groups be said to have influenced Irish foreign policy? There can be little doubt that in the long term the general aims of governmental policy reflect the basic values of the Catholic church, but these are often indistinguishable from the values professed by non-Catholic, or even non-Christian, states. Nor would it be true to say that the church, in its various manifestations, has exercised a strong influence on specific policies over which it has found itself in disagreement with the government. From 1936 to 1939, Mr de Valera refused to recognise Franco's government, until external realities forced a change. Even if we believe, like Dr Noel Browne, that in 1961 the government abandoned its 'independent' position in the UN because Mr Aiken, the Minister for External Affairs, was "frightened . . . by the campaign carried on against him for his decision in relation to Peking, China . . .",[31] this was only one and perhaps a minor reason among many; the lives of Irish troops were endangered in the Congo, the government was seeking admission to the European Economic Community, and

[29] For Mr McGilligan's speech in 1959, see Dáil Debates: 176, 605–624.
[30] Dáil Debates: 176, 680.
[31] Dáil Debates: 186, 861.

the composition of the United Nations was changing drastically with the introduction of the new states which were to form the 'afro-asian bloc'.

The theory that the church enjoys a direct hold on Irish foreign policy is difficult to maintain. Mr Belton's admission of his failure to stop de Valera supporting sanctions against 'Catholic' Italy in 1935 provides an eloquent illustration:

> I thought the President [of the Executive Council] would hesitate when the Rector of the Irish College in Rome spoke. I thought he would hesitate when his friend, Archbishop Mannix, spoke. I thought he would hesitate when Father Coughlan of the United States spoke. Evidently he did not listen to them.[32]

The Irish Anti-Apartheid Movement which, unlike the church, is unashamedly and exclusively an interest group existing to promote a specific cause, is also partly motivated by religious considerations. Considerable missionary work in African colonies and states, combined with a tradition of anti-colonialist feeling arising out of the identification of Ireland as a former colony, have provided a wide base for the support of the Movement's views; indeed, it touches on the whole range of Irish political opinion from the clerical, conservative right to the progressive socialist left. During the early nineteen sixties, Dr Noel Browne and Mr Jack McQuillan were the two main deputies to express anti-racialist opinion in the Dáil, and although a boycott movement had been formed in 1959, it was not until 1964 that the Irish Anti-Apartheid Movement was founded.[33]

The Movement conducts a continuous campaign to educate public opinion through regular meetings and bulletins, school talks and letters to the press. This has borne fruit on the few occasions on which the Movement has had an opportunity to campaign on specific issues. Attempts to boycott South African goods have not been an unqualified success, but the visits of South African sports teams have occasioned

[32] Dáil Debates: 59, 1685.
[33] For a survey of the background and activities of the Irish Anti-Apartheid Movement, see Kadar Asmal, *Irish opposition to Apartheid* (UN Department of Political and Security Council Affairs: Unit on Apartheid, notes and documents, no. 3/71, February 1971).

well-publicised condemnatory action. The most striking example was the South African rugby tour of 1969–1970 which provoked large demonstrations, extensive picketing of football grounds and the players' hotels, the threat of trade union action, and the unusual absence of the President and members of the government from the principal match.

The President's absence indicates that the Movement is taken seriously by the government, and this can be substantiated to some degree by examining government policy. In 1970, for example, a proposed mission to South Africa by Córas Tráchtála, (the Irish Export Board) was cancelled by the Minister for Industry and Commerce. In the United Nations, the Irish delegation, while by no means in the vanguard of the anti-apartheid activists, has nonetheless been among the leading west European states in supporting UN resolutions condemning the South African government's apartheid policy. This may be taken as a measure of the relatively favourable conditions in which the Irish Anti-Apartheid Movement operates, but it also testifies to the success of its operation. Particularly impressive is the manner in which the Movement has avoided serious sectional or political divisions so that it has been able to pursue its aims consistently, despite its slender financial resources.

One of the forces from which the Anti-Apartheid Movement in Ireland derives its strength is the tradition of anti-imperialism, a tradition which is directly and compellingly manifested amongst those groups which may be termed 'nationalist'. They owe their existence to the dispute over the Treaty of 1921 which determined the dividing lines between the two major parties until the nineteen fifties. Although this dispute was originally concentrated on the status of the new Irish Free State, by the late nineteen thirties the outstanding unresolved issue was the partition of the island, by which Northern Ireland remained inside the United Kingdom. An issue with such pervasive emotional overtones is not likely to remain exclusively within the bounds of normal party politics, particularly since no single party policy has brought about a satisfactory solution of the problem. Therefore, outlets for these frustrated nationalist sentiments have been sought in organisations outside the party structure which seek to supplement the activities of the parties or try to impose their own (generally more radical) solutions.

An example of the former type of nationalist interest group was the Mansion House All Party Anti-Partition Conference, established after the British parliament passed the Ireland Act in 1949, thereby confirming the constitutional position of Northern Ireland within the United Kingdom. As the name suggests, this organisation sought a national basis, and leading personalities from the political parties were among its principal sponsors. The Conference collected funds, organised demonstrations and meetings and cooperated with like-minded groups such as the Ancient Order of Hibernians in Ireland, the League for an Undivided Ireland and the Éire Society in the USA, and the Anti-Partition Leagues in Scotland, England and Wales. However, the Mansion House Conference was based on over-optimistic assumptions concerning the power of public opinion and, in spite of its initial effect as a focus of nationalist sentiment, it failed to support effectively the policy of the Irish government and to influence the British government.

Much smaller groups have attempted to influence the policies towards Northern Ireland of both British and Irish governments by recourse to more violent methods. The long history of physical action against British occupation of Irish territory has made extremist republicanism a persistent feature of Irish political life. For convenience sake, these republicans may be described as the IRA (Irish Republican Army), although it is important to note that this title is an over-simplification, characterising a succession of small groups engaged in persistent debate over aims, methods and personalities.[34] Nevertheless, there is a strong element of continuity both in their revolutionary posture and in their influence on Irish foreign policy.

The heroic tradition of these revolutionary groups has generally discounted both the ends and the means of diplomacy. The failure of diplomacy in the Peace Conference of 1919 is regarded by these groups as leading inevitably to the failure of Irish nationalists to negotiate a satisfactory settlement with Britain in 1921. The extent of that failure was such that a compromise statelet—the Irish Free State—was bought at the cost of abandoning Northern Ireland. Diplomacy is thus associated with betrayal. Although the IRA has

[34] See J. Bowyer Bell, *The Secret Army: A History of the IRA* 1915–1970 (Anthony Blond, London, 1970) and T. P. Coogan, *The IRA* (Pall Mall, London, 1970).

sought aid from expatriate groups—mainly in the USA, and on occasion from sympathetic governments such as the USSR in the nineteen twenties and Germany during World War II[35]—these pacts were spasmodic and hesitant. More often than not, they were prompted by short-term difficulties and remained peripheral to strategic considerations; indeed, the IRA tended to act as if the outside world did not exist. The classic example was probably the 1938–39 bombing campaign in England, when neither the possibility of an improvement in Anglo-Irish relations because of the 1938 agreements nor the impending European war entered into the IRA's calculations.[36]   At other times, an excessive preoccupation with internal differences meant that the IRA lost opportunities to achieve their objectives.

The IRA's contempt for diplomacy has been matched only by its scorn for politics; that is to say, for any form of compromise with what it regards as collaborationist Irish governments. Although at times the organisation has had personal relationships with prominent policy-makers, the opportunities for fostering 'behind-the-scenes' influence have generally been wasted by a failure or an unwillingness to accept the constraints on governmental action. Mr de Valera and the Fianna Fáil party entered constitutional politics after a characteristic internecine feud in the IRA, but when de Valera came to power in 1932, the republican movement failed to capitalise on their common past; indeed it was Mr de Valera who capitalised on this situation by 'borrowing' the land annuities issue from the radical wing of the IRA and using it for his own ends. Even when Mr Seán MacBride, who had been a prominent IRA leader in the early nineteen thirties, was Minister for External Affairs, the IRA were not in a position to exert influence, for they were just recovering from the repressions which their activities of the previous decade had brought upon them.

Nonetheless, in spite of its failings, the IRA has on more than one occasion exerted a seriously negative influence on Irish foreign policy. The bombing campaign of the late nineteen thirties brought a halt to the (admittedly faint) prospects of further negotiations on partition

[35] IRA dealings with Germany are examined in E. Stephan, *Spies in Ireland* (Macdonald, London, 1963).

[36] See J. Bowyer Bell, *The Secret Army*, chapter 8. During the current phase of IRA activity, the most publicised contacts between the IRA and foreign governments have been with the revolutionary régime in Libya

between intermediaries of the British and Irish governments. But during World War II, what had been an irritant became a serious wound.[37] Further IRA activity, combined with even tentative German support, might have been sufficient provocation to bring about the collapse of the policy of neutrality. This prospect was sufficiently embarrassing to persuade Mr de Valera to severely repress IRA activists and thus avert the threat against his policy of non-intervention in the war.

When the IRA recovered from this set-back, their campaign of border raids from 1956 to 1962 proved an embarrassment to the government. Mr Costello's second coalition government was beleaguered by requests from the British government to act against the terrorists. Simultaneously, public support for the IRA was widespread. Forced to act against the IRA, and at the same time faced with serious economic difficulties, Costello's coalition collapsed because of the defection of the Clann na Poblachta party which had previously supported, though not participated in, the government.

However, it is one thing to be instrumental in removing a government, but quite another to ensure that a sympathetic government replaces it. As it happened, the new Fianna Fáil government was considerably more severe in its treatment of the IRA, and the movement's objectives remained as elusive as ever. There was, however, a residuum of embarrassment for the Irish government, since sporadic IRA activities—even as late as November 1961—led to representations by the British government. Embarrassment was also caused by the international publicity given to the process of interning IRA suspects without trial.[38]

From the time that the conflict in Northern Ireland erupted in 1969, the IRA has again become an important factor in Irish foreign policy, and especially in the (at times) strained relations between the Irish and British governments. Many of the movement's former characteristics are still evident: it is still prone to internal dissension

[37] ibid., chapters 9 and 11.
[38] The campaign during the nineteen fifties is discussed in ibid., chapters 15 and 16. See also T. P. Coogan's claim that it was a factor which delayed revision of the 1948 Anglo-Irish Trade Agreement: Coogan, op. cit., p. 340. For instances of British representations to the Irish government about the IRA, see *The Irish Times*, 19 July, 1958 and 15 November 1961.

(there is an 'official' and a 'provisional' IRA), and in spite of external liaisons, is still predominantly inward-looking. But the degree of support which it has received in Northern Ireland and its ability to maintain the initiative have never previously been as evident. It clearly has the capacity to thwart and disconcert both the British and Irish governments more acutely than at any time in the past; but it remains to be seen whether in the long term it will exert any significant, positive influence on the policy of either government.

Another new development is the fact that one main group in the IRA now plays an active role on issues removed from the irredentist question; in 1971, the official IRA's political organisation—the official Sinn Féin—dropped its policy of abstaining from participation in constitutional parliamentary politics. This decision facilitated the open participation of even the extreme nationalist groups in the political debate on Ireland's membership of the EEC. Because membership implied an amendment of the Constitution, a referendum was obligatory, and this, together with the fact that the formal negotiations were drawn out over a period of some eighteen months, resulted in a prolonged campaign to influence the electorate. This rare opportunity to exert influence at this decisive stage of the political process, before a *fait accompli* could be finalised in parliamentary or especially governmental institutions, mobilised almost every interest group in the state and several outside it, and may be interpreted as a classic (though far from typical) example of interest group activity.

The main brunt of the referendum campaign was borne by groups established specifically for that purpose, staffed by relatively few personnel but acting to some extent as 'umbrella organisations' in their attempt to include the participation of representatives from a wide range of other groups. Thus, the opposition to EEC membership was concentrated on the Common Market Study Group—a small number of speakers and pamphleteers—some of whom were also members of the Wolfe Tone Society which had been founded in 1964 in an attempt to broaden and radicalise the political basis of the IRA and its political wing, Sinn Féin. During the abortive attempt to renew membership negotiations in 1967, the Wolfe Tone Society had been the principal if not the only mouthpiece of opposition and it was hardly surprising to see its members again taking the lead through the CMSG.

Although the CMSG was early in the field and remained the focus of activity for anti-market opinion, it tried to supplement its efforts by creating a mass organisation which would have no obvious political associations and which would thus mobilise all opponents of EEC membership, no matter what their political allegiance might be. This was the Common Market Defence Campaign, launched in July 1971 under the patronage of a number of 'respectable' personalities active in public life. It is debatable whether this organisation achieved fully its intention to coordinate anti-market associations and avoid the waste of what relatively small resources the anti-marketeers could rely on, for in the final stages of the campaign the other participants often seemed to be operating on an individual basis. This may be a consequence of the association of the Northern Ireland issue with that of membership of the EEC: once the argument was put forward that EEC membership implied abandoning the claim to Irish unity, it was difficult to keep the differences of opinion on the irredentist issue out of the referendum campaign. Labour party spokesmen were often embarrassed by having to appear on the same platform as members of either Sinn Féin/IRA group, and the trade unions seemed to be taking some care to fight their own fight.

The case for EEC membership, on the other hand, was supported by both the government party, Fianna Fáil, and the main opposition party, Fine Gael, and had been an integral part of government policy since 1961. At that time, opposition to membership had been negligible —the extreme nationalists being neither willing nor able to contribute to public debate. The pro-EEC organisation, the Irish Council of the European Movement, had the field to itself and was active in putting the case for membership at public meetings and in the press. After the French veto of the first negotiations in 1963, the Council had the difficult task of keeping the government's attention on the long-term prospects for EEC membership; for example, in 1966 it was active in pressing for the appointment of a separate ambassador to the EEC. The Council was able to put its views in a variety of ways: in memoranda to the government, briefing journalists and arranging special visits to Brussels for them. Individual members of the Council could also use their political position to some effect. In spite of the fact that, on the whole, the Council was on the government's side,

20

its activities were not superfluous, for it acted as a source of information and a means by which supporters of the Irish EEC application could both stiffen the government's resolve and advise on the tactics to be followed.

When the EEC negotiations became a reality in the summer of 1970, the ICEM assumed responsibility for putting the case for membership to the electorate. In presenting the case, it worked with the government, especially the Department of Foreign Affairs, with the major parties and with national economic interest groups such as the Confederation of Irish Industries and the National Farmers' Association. Nevertheless, although these bodies contributed individually to the campaign, the ICEM, like its counterpart the CMSG, was undoubtedly the centre of activity. Indeed, the two groups between them provided teams of speakers which travelled around the country debating the issue with each other before public audiences. This political circus, touring from the autumn of 1970 up to the referendum itself in May 1972, was the backbone of the campaign.

However, the ICEM was operating under more favourable conditions than the CMSG. It received direct financial support from the government in addition to what it may have received from other backers, and when, in July 1971, the anti-marketeers felt it necessary to create a mass organisation (the Common Market Defence Campaign), the ICEM, confident that the electoral machinery of the Fianna Fáil party and probably that of Fine Gael could be utilised to counter such a development, was able to strengthen its central effort by appointing a full-time campaign director.

Thus, against a background of a parliament ill-equipped to deal with foreign policy issues, the indifference of many parliamentarians and the continuing public preoccuaption with the crisis in Northern Ireland, the Irish Council of the European Movement and the Common Market Study Group represented the main focus for the discussion of one of the most important foreign policy decisions in Irish history.[39] These groups continued their activities after the EEC referendum. The ICEM holds a watching brief over the development of Irish

---

[39] A leading participant in the ICEM even went so far as to maintain, in conversation with the author in 1971, that the ICEM worked so closely with the government that it was the main source of Irish foreign policy during the period of the negotiations.

participation in the European Community. So, too, from its different point of view, does the CMSG. However, in October 1972, the latter (and the associated Common Market Defence Campaign) were transformed into the Irish Sovereignty Movement: this is in effect a radical 'ginger group' and does not restrict itself to European affairs.

Many aspects of EEC membership were not discussed fully in the referendum campaign which, like any public debate, was prone to over-simplification and distortion. Not unnaturally, the debate centered on the economic consequences of entry, and the view of Europe was inevitably coloured by the mythology of the European movement and (perhaps more seriously) by a narrow, legalistic interpretation of the political possibilities. There was relatively little appreciation of the political concerns of the other European states or of how EEC membership would affect those aspects of Irish foreign policy which had to do with countries and international organisations outside western Europe. This rather narrow view of membership of the European Community reflected the absence of any group in Ireland whose main purpose was to promote an interest in foreign policy. A group of this type, which amasses and disseminates information on all aspects of foreign policy, may offer a broader perspective of the state's position in the world than is generally found in the policy-maker's domestic environment. Most west European states have one or more bodies of this kind, generally referred to as institutes of international affairs. It is perhaps a measure of the degree of Ireland's isolation that a similar institute has not yet established firm roots in Ireland.

The first attempts to create this type of organisation were made in the late nineteen thirties. The Catholic Association of International Relations was founded in 1937 but did not make a serious impact. The previous year, the Irish Institute of International Affairs had been established: this was modelled on the British Royal Institute of International Affairs. It did not enjoy official state support, and its subsequent fate illustrates some of the difficulties which can beset an endeavour to increase participation in the discussion of foreign policy. In 1944, the Institute invited representatives of some belligerent governments-in-exile to speak in Ireland, an invitation which was interpreted by the de Valera government as a provocative repudiation of its strict neutrality policy.

Jan Masaryk, Foreign Affairs Minister to the Czechoslovakian government-in-exile, was refused permission to speak to the Institute on the 3 November 1944, an action which was subsequently defended in the Dáil by an indignant Mr de Valera:

> I am charged with the responsibility for the conduct of the foreign relations of this State. I find a body of this kind carrying on propaganda against the declared policy of the country in a time like this by using a self-assumed title, suggesting that it has a status which it does not possess at all, inviting members of foreign Governments and foreign diplomats over here without the slightest reference to their own Government, thereby creating difficulties and most regrettable incidents between ourselves and other countries . . .[40].

In the difficult conditions of 1944, when Mr de Valera was under strong external pressure to abandon neutrality, his sensitivity towards the Irish Institute of International Affairs was perhaps understandable. But the controversy set an unhappy precedent; little more was heard of the IIIA and no replacement was subsequently established.

This lack of a focus for the public discussion of foreign policy is perhaps more serious than it would seem at first sight. Admittedly, the effect of the activities of bodies like the IIIA is limited by their general and non-partisan approach to policy and by their membership, which is the 'attentive minority' rather than the public at large. Nevertheless, it would be foolish to overlook their influence in providing information and encouraging discussion on international affairs. Nor should we overlook the fact that this attentive minority probably forms the immediate environment of the policy-maker in so far as it is composed of an educated *élite* with an interest in public affairs; constant discussion within such organisations can serve to stimulate and broaden the policy-maker's view of the alternatives open to him.

The civil servant, the politician, the academic, the businessman and the labour representative could discuss foreign affairs at an institute for international affairs in an atmosphere in which their primary

---

[40] Dáil Debates: 95, 932–3. Mr Masaryk was in fact allowed to address the public—on the same platform as Mr de Valera—but not under the auspices of the IIIA.

sectional or partisan roles need not be rigidly maintained. In this way, it would be possible for them to appreciate the overall objectives of foreign policy, as distinct from the specific, limited objectives with which they are most familiar. As a result, foreign policy might become more a synthesis of national aspirations than the collection of fragmentary and often contradictory aims which it often appears to be. At least the participants in this type of discussion would find it easier to inform themselves and, ultimately, to educate their colleagues in the government departments, in the parties and parliament and in the country at large.

On occasion, both the Irish Council of the European Movement and the Irish United Nations Association have tried to do this, but only in a very limited way. Neither group—and particularly the UN Association—can call upon sufficient resources to operate more than intermittently. A more serious limitation is the fact that neither group covers the whole range of foreign policy and naturally each tends to show a bias towards its own particular area of interest. But more serious still, in the long term, is the absence of any systematic and sustained intellectual tradition in the fields of foreign policy and international relations.[41] Without this tradition, any organisation with an interest in foreign policy will lack the commitment, continuity of effort and detachment from short-term political considerations which are necessary if it is to be effective.[42]

★   ★   ★   ★

The domestic environment in which Irish foreign policy is made remains in a fragmentary and relatively unstructured stage of its development. Irish political parties and the parliamentary institutions through which they operate have made even less impact on foreign policy than in most parliamentary democracies, and interest groups, while contributing to policy formulation, have not always encouraged the evolution of coherent policy guidelines. Thus, apart from the sensitive area of Anglo-Irish relations, it is fair to say that the policy-maker has, up to the nineteen seventies, been left largely to his own devices in meeting the challenge which the external environment represents.

[41] See above, pp. 176.
[42] See P. Keatinge, '[The] Study of International Relations', *Léargas/Public Affairs*. vol. 4, no. 5, January 1972.

POSTSCRIPT

IRELAND'S NEW DIPLOMACY

"If we do not attend to whatever foreign affairs we have, though they be relatively small, they will be attended to all the same, but not by us."

Desmond FitzGerald, 1925
(Dáil Debates: 11, 1415)

SINCE the inception of the Irish state, foreign policy has remained something of a mystery to the general public and to informed observers alike. In 1966, attempting to summarise Ireland's role in international politics, T. D. Williams commented on the difficulties of identifying any "long-term diplomatic tradition of the State".[1] Often underpinning the popular and somewhat cynical assumption that Ireland has no foreign policy is the implication that she does not need one. Although this assertion is exaggerated, it is perhaps understandable in view of the intermittent and confused way in which the principal characteristics of the state's role in international affairs have emerged since statehood was achieved in 1922.

The economic and constitutional aspects of the search for a satisfactory relationship with Ireland's neighbour, Britain, have been distorted by the harsh glare of a thwarted aspiration towards unity; too often, the real problems and possible solutions have been blurred, and other facets of the state's position in the world have remained in the shadows. It is true that Ireland, as a small power, has an interest in acting with other small powers, often through the medium of international institutions, to avoid or modify the consequences of great power conflicts. Nevertheless, this aim has not always harmonised with her consciousness of being partly engaged in great power

[1] T. D. Williams, 'Public Affairs, 1916–1966: 1. The Political Scene', *Administration*, vol. 14, no. 3, Autumn 1966, pp. 191–8.

conflicts, of being a 'christian' or 'western' state, obliged to rally together with like-minded states under a loosely defined ideological banner. Furthermore, the broad objectives—'independence', 'neutrality' —which are pursued if not always achieved, sooner or later find themselves in conflict with the more concrete material objectives which, in the context of European integration, have in recent years assumed a much greater significance.

Indeed, the only characteristics of Ireland's diplomatic tradition which are in any way clear are the obscurity of its existence on the fringe of public life and the dimly perceived contradictions inherent in it. To some extent, this is perfectly natural. Since Ireland has only marginally been a participant in the great issues of world politics, it is hardly surprising that world politics remain on the margin of Irish political life. Nevertheless, there is a danger in non-participation in so far as the temptation arises to treat international affairs, and particularly the state's foreign policy, in a casual and artless way. Unfortunately, the abstract, intangible nature of so many foreign policy issues makes it all the more difficult to avoid this temptation. Only too often, foreign policy is defined in a narrow sense, as something which is left over after economic and social policies have been considered—a question merely of diplomatic machinery and speeches in the United Nations General Assembly. The fact that "all that we can do, or can hope to do, in this country is materially conditioned by the state of the world in which we live"[2] is perceived in only a fragmented way; too rarely is it seen that the state's external policy impinges not only on certain limited, residual issues, but on the whole range of public policy and the very existence of the state itself.

Once Ireland had achieved a *modus vivendi* with Britain, and the indirect threat to the state during World War II had been circumvented, 'foreign policy' came to mean a limited range of activities, often of a purely symbolic or administrative nature, undertaken on the sidelines of governmental action. However, there is good reason to believe that this view of foreign policy will become dangerously unrealistic in the future, if indeed it has not already become so. From 1973, participation in the expanded European Community changed Ireland's

[2] James Dillon TD, in 1944 (Dáil Debates: 94, 1338).

external environment in a more fundamental way than has generally been realised. Irish foreign policy will henceforth be made in a very different diplomatic setting.

One aspect of this new diplomacy, which has already been perceived by the government and by many non-governmental groups throughout the state, is that membership of the EEC necessitates close diplomatic and political relations with the central bodies of the Community system—the Commission, the Council of Ministers and the European Parliament. But perhaps what is not so clearly appreciated is the fact that membership entails intensive contacts with all the governments of the other member states, for Brussels is still only the tip of the Community iceberg. Ireland has long had diplomatic relations with these states, but only with Britain can it be said that the relationship has been close and often demanding. Because of the Northern Ireland issue, Anglo-Irish relations are likely to be more demanding in future, but they will not assume the overwhelming predominance which they have previously enjoyed. The Irish government is now obliged to negotiate with Britain and with the other member states all policy decisions relating to the maintenance and advance of the existing economic arrangements within the Community, and although the problems encountered may not be altogether new, this means a good deal more work. But the Irish government will be obliged also to take a stance on many issues which hitherto it has been able to avoid: the problems of *détente* with eastern Europe, the sensitive question of the defence of western Europe, the relationship of the European Community with other states in western Europe and beyond, and the future development of the Community system itself. These are questions which will demand policies and decisions and a continuing review of those decisions as circumstances change.[3]

All of these new factors will make increased demands on Ireland's policy-making process, which more often than not has been able to run at half speed. The increased tempo of activity during the entry negotiations for the EEC between 1970 and 1972, a tempo which seemed exceptionally quick in relation to previous experience, pro-

[3] The changing substance of Irish foreign policy is reflected in the policy statement made in the Dáil on 9 May 1973 by the incoming Minister for Foreign Affairs, Dr Garret FitzGerald. See Dáil Debates: 265, 740–769.

vided an indication of the pace at which the diplomatic machine will be obliged to operate in the future. It is difficult to envisage a Minister for Foreign Affairs and his department waiting passively on the sidelines, merely reacting to the initiatives of other sectors of the political system and concentrating their efforts on a limited number of esoteric though important issues. Rather, will he find that he and his advisers are called upon to play an important administrative role in coordinating the separate efforts of other departments; consequently, the minister will be able to bring much weight to bear on the establishment of priorities between the demands of this department against that department, or between the economic and political views of particular problems. As principal representative of the government in the European Community's Council of Ministers (which remains— and may well remain for some time to come—the focus of EEC decision-making), the Minister for Foreign Affairs will have the opportunity, so rarely granted to his predecessors, of participating *continuously* in the formulation both of national policy and of European policy.

Unless there is significant strengthening of his supporting staff in the Department of Foreign Affairs, he will not be able to grasp this opportunity, and Ireland's role within the EEC will remain indistinct and ineffectual. The active and extended diplomacy arising from participation in the EEC suggests the desirability of more overseas missions and of more generous staffing of some existing overseas missions, in addition to the consolidation of the more important sections in the headquarters office. This process has started already, but it is likely to continue to be important, for the back-log is considerable, and experience inside the Community may raise problems as yet unforeseen.[4] The temptation to meet new demands at the expense of existing commitments, such as participation in the United Nations, or even at the expense of possible future commitments outside the immediate scope of the EEC, should be avoided. A new

---

[4] On 9 May 1973, Dr Garret FitzGerald referred to his department's previous development as being "for a long time unduly restricted, leaving them quite inadequately equipped to cope with the enormous expansion of work . . ." (Dáil Debates: 265, 769). He also spoke of the need for, "above all, adequate staff to consider and formulate proposals for longer-term developments in foreign policy—a task which has imposed excessive strain for some time past due to constant pressure of urgent matters." (Dáil Debates: 265, 768).

game demands an appropriate number of players and not merely the redistribution of the existing number of players.

More scope for specialisation may arise, for instance, in connexion with economic and legal developments within the Community, but at the same time, in view of the department's coordinating role and its expanded political horizons, most members of the Irish diplomatic service are likely to remain generalists rather than specialists. In either case, the need both for more officials and for more intensive training at all stages of the official's career may become more acute. Above all, it will be vital, in a foreign ministry which is growing rapidly both in size and in importance within the structure of central government, to ensure that officials have a clear appreciation of what they are doing in the present and what they hope to do in the future.

Ideally, the makers of Irish foreign policy should be better equipped to explain their activities to the public whom they serve, and more willing to do so than they have been at times in the past. The impediment to improved communications has lain not only with the policy-maker but in his domestic environment, particularly the casual attitude towards foreign policy which pervades all levels of public life. As we have seen, the channels of public opinion deal with foreign policy intermittently and in the most general fashion and nowhere is this more strikingly demonstrated than in the principal forum of public opinion—parliamentary and party politics. The infrequent attention generally given to foreign policy in the Dáil, the superficial and confused debates on the subject and the inability of the average parliamentarian to participate in discussion on it, all conduce to an environment which dictates that the policy-makers operate with a minimum of supervision and guidance from the public, in whose interests policy is made.

Thus policy may reflect—to a greater extent than is necessary—the objectives, the attitudes and the energy of the few individuals ultimately responsible for its formulation, the government. Where these individuals have been effective policy-makers, the credit must be given to their personal qualities rather than to the parliamentary environment from which they were drawn, and in which they have to operate. On the other hand, where they have a narrow and fragmented view of foreign policy, it is not surprising that the 'Irish diplomatic tradition' should remain an elusive quantity in public life, for Irish public opinion is poorly equipped to focus on the policy-makers' limitations and inconsistencies: "the absence of any real public discussion about the nature of an Irish diplomatic tradition is a major cause of impeded efficiency and importance".[5]

Faced with the challenge posed by membership of the European Community, it becomes a matter of urgency to encourage "real public discussion" of Irish foreign policy. The most immediate task is to make the parliamentary system more conscious of foreign policy as a broad and important area of public policy, by reorganising it in such a way that its members will find it difficult to regard the discussion of foreign policy as the occasion for an annual (or even a bi-annual) holiday. The formation of a special external affairs committee has been suggested as a means to this end.[6] The composition and powers of this committee could take a variety of forms; the essential characteristic of such a body, if it is to be anything more than a facade, is that its terms of reference should be broad and unhampered by a legalistic or compartmentalised view of its subject-matter. Its primary purpose should *not* be to extract confidential information from the government, although it might have powers to do this under certain conditions; rather it should serve to focus public attention on the information which is available but which, under the present system, is not considered in a systematic and comprehensive manner. This might appear to be a highly self-conscious approach to the discussion of foreign policy, but self-conscious discussion is a virtue when the alternative is hardly any discussion at all.

In the long term, the problem must be dealt with outside the confines of parliamentary institutions. The habit of looking at what is happening outside the boundaries of the state and of relating this to the values, objectives and resources which exist within the state is not a habit which has been developed in Ireland. Again, we do not need to learn solely from the (often bitter) school of experience. In most areas of public life, policy-making is aided (often indirectly and imperceptibly) by the measure of understanding and the systematic organisation of knowledge which is to be found in the study of and

[5] Williams, op. cit., p. 197.
[6] See above, pp. 233-246.

research into the relevant academic disciplines. That foreign policy is the sole exception to this has in the past been something of a curiosity; in the future, it could be a crippling weakness.

In addition to the commitment of the Irish university system to the study of international relations, the creation of a research institute in this field would provide a means of linking what might otherwise remain an unnecessarily theoretical academic pursuit to those individuals with a more practical and immediate interest in Irish foreign policy. Such an institute could provide the public discussion of foreign policy with the same focus, depth and continuity which a special committee would provide in the parliamentary context and which has hardly existed up to now. The fact that many representative democracies are increasingly aware of their failure to cater for adequate means of participation, consultation and explanation, makes such a body a modest necessity, rather than the luxury which it seems to be at first sight.

For fifty years, Ireland has defined and protected her identity as a member of the world community of nation states, by virtue of a combination of some good management by her leaders and a greater share of good fortune than that enjoyed by most states. There can be no guarantee that the latter element will remain indefinitely to counter-balance what is lacking in the management of her affairs. Ireland was fortunate in inheriting and being able to apply some of the most successful and equitable political and administrative traditions of the nineteenth century. Nevertheless, it is clear that the time has come to re-examine this inheritance in the light of the very different circumstances which now prevail.

SELECT BIBLIOGRAPHY

A PART from D. W. Harkness's study of Irish policy towards the evolution of the British Commonwealth from 1922 to 1932, there are no full-length works which deal exclusively with either the substance or the making of Irish foreign policy. The following bibliography is a selection of published books, articles and pamphlets which cover some aspects of the subject.

Asmal, K. *Irish opposition to Apartheid*. UN Department of Political and Security Council Affairs: Unit on Apartheid, notes and documents No. 3/71, February 1971

Bell, J. Bowyer. *The Secret Army*. Anthony Blond, London, 1970

Bell, J. Bowyer. 'Ireland and the Spanish Civil War 1936-1939'. *Studia Hibernica*, No. 7, 1969

Chubb, F. B. *The Government and Politics of Ireland*. Oxford University Press, London, 1970

Costello, J. A. *Ireland in International Affairs*. Dublin, 1948

Department of External Affairs (from 1971, Department of Foreign Affairs), *Ireland at the United Nations*. Browne and Nolan, Dublin, 1958 —

De Valera, E. *Peace and War: speeches on international affairs*. Gill, Dublin, 1944

De Valera, E. *Ireland's Stand: a selection of the speeches of E. de Valera during the war, 1939-45*. Gill, Dublin, 1946

Fabian, L. L. *Soldiers without Enemies*. The Brookings Institution, Washington D.C., 1971

Farrell, B. *Chairman or Chief? The role of Taoiseach in Irish Government*. Gill and Macmillan, Dublin, 1971

FitzGerald, G. *Towards a New Ireland*. Charles Knight, London, 1972

Hancock, W. K. *Survey of British Commonwealth Affairs. Vol. 1 Problems of Nationality, 1918-1936*. Oxford University Press, London, 1937

Harkness, D. W. *The Restless Dominion*. Macmillan, London, 1969

Harkness, D. W. 'Mr de Valera's Dominion: Irish relations with Britain and the Commonwealth, 1932-1938'. *Journal of Commonwealth Political Studies*, Vol. VIII, No. 3, 1970

Hillery, B. and Lynch, P. *Ireland in the International Labour Organisation.* Department of Labour, Dublin, 1969

Howard, C. 'Eire'. in A. J. Toynbee and V. M. Toynbee (eds.). *The War and the Neutrals.* Oxford University Press, London, 1956

Jones, T. *Whitehall Diary.* Vol. III: *Ireland, 1918-1925.* K. Middlemas (ed.). Oxford University Press, London, 1971

Keatinge, P. 'Ireland and the League of Nations'. *Studies*, Vol. LIX, No. 234, Summer 1970

Keatinge, P. 'Ireland and European Security'. *International Affairs*, Vol. 48, No. 3, July 1972

Keatinge, P. 'Ireland's journey into the unknown'. *Osterreichische Zeitschrift fur Aussenpolitik.* 12 Jahrgang, Nr 6, 1972

Keatinge, P. 'The foreign policy of the Irish coalition Government'. *The World Today*, Vol. 29, No. 8, August 1973

Lemass, S. 'Small States in International Organizations' in A. Schon and A. O. Brundtland. *Small States in International Relations.* John Wiley, New York, 1971

Lynch, J. M. 'The Anglo-Irish problem'. *Foreign Affairs*, Vol. 50, No. 4, July 1972

Lyons, F. S. L. *Ireland since the Famine.* Weidenfeld & Nicolson, London, 1971

Mansergh, N. *Survey of British Commonwealth Affairs: Problems of External Policy, 1931-1939.* Oxford University Press, London, 1952

Mansergh, N. *Survey of British Commonwealth Affairs: Problems of Wartime Cooperation and Post-War Change, 1939-1952.* Oxford University Press, London, 1958

Mansergh, N. 'Ireland and the British Commonwealth of Nations' in T. D. Williams (ed.). *The Irish Struggle, 1916–1926'* Routledge and Kegan Paul, London, 1966

Mansergh, N. 'Ireland: External Relations 1926-1939' in F. MacManus (ed.). *The Years of the Great Test 1926-39.* Mercier Press, Cork, 1967

Mansergh, N. 'Irish Foreign Policy, 1945-51' in K. B. Nowlan and T. D. Williams (eds.). *Ireland in the War Years and After, 1939-51.* Gill and Macmillan, Dublin, 1969

Mathisen, T. *The Functions of Small States in the Strategies of the Great Powers.* Universitetsforlaget, Oslo, 1971

Mulkeen, T. A. 'Ireland at the U.N.' *Eire/Ireland,* Vol. VIII, No. 1, Spring 1973

O'Brien, C. Cruise. *To Katanga and Back.* Hutchinson, London, 1962

O'Brien, C. Cruise. *Ireland, the United Nations and South Africa.* The Irish Anti-Apartheid Movement, Dublin, 1967

O'Brien, C. Cruise. 'Ireland in International Affairs' in O. Dudley Edwards (ed.). *Conor Cruise O'Brien introduces Ireland.* Deutsch, London, 1969

O'Brien, C. Cruise. *States of Ireland.* Hutchinson, London, 1972

O'Connor, B. J. *Ireland and the United Nations.* Tuairim pamphlet, Dublin, 1961

O'Sullivan, D. *The Irish Free State and its Senate.* Faber and Faber, London, 1940

Pakenham, F. A. *Peace by Ordeal.* Jonathan Cape, London, 1935

Pakenham, F. A. (Lord Longford) and O'Neill, T. P. *Eamon de Valera.* Gill and Macmillan, Dublin, 1970

Williams, T. D. 'A study in neutrality'. *The Leader,* January-April 1953

Diplomatic Missions	Date of Establishment	Ambassador	Chargé d'affaires	Minister-Counsellor	Counsellor	1st Sec.	3rd Sec.[1]	Misc.	TOTAL	Location
Great Britain	January 1923	1		1	2	3	4	2[3]	13	London
USA	October 1924	1			2	2[1]	2		7	Washington
Holy See	June 1929	1					1		2	Rome
France	October 1929	1			1	2	1		5	Paris
(also to OEEC/OECD (and UNESCO	September 1948) December 1961)									
Belgium	September 1932	1				1			2	Brussels
(also Luxembourg	April 1962)									
Spain	September 1935	1				1	1		2	Madrid
Italy	April 1938	1				1	1		3	Rome
(also to Turkey	October 1951)									
Canada	August 1939	1				1			2	Ottawa
Switzerland	October 1940	1				1			2	Berne
(also to Austria	March 1952)									
Portugal	February 1942	—	1						1	Lisbon
Sweden	July 1946	1					1		2	Stockholm
(also to Finland	June 1964)									
Australia	October 1946	1				1			2	Canberra
(also New Zealand	January 1966)									
Argentina	January 1948	1					1		2	Buenos Aires
Netherlands	February 1950	1				1	1		2	The Hague
West Germany	June 1951	1				1	1		3	Bonn
(originally accredited to the whole of Germany)	October 1929)									
United Nations Organisation	January 1956	1		1	1	1	1		3	New York
Nigeria	September 1960	1				1			2	Lagos
Denmark	July 1962	1				1			2	Copenhagen
(also to Norway* and Iceland	April 1950 1970)									
India	April 1964	1				1			2	New Delhi
UN (Geneva)	July 1965	1				1			2	Geneva
European Communities	October 1966	1			7[5]	7			15	Brussels
(originally combined with* mission to Belgium	December 1959)									

*formerly/covered from Sweden.

Total officials in diplomatic missions 76
Total officials in consular missions 9
— 85

Total officials serving overseas

N.B.: Total number of officials, foreign service and equivalent.

		(1967)
at home	= 74	(50)
abroad	= 85	(74)
	159	124

Notes
1. In some missions 3rd Secretaries are given a *nominally* higher rank i.e. "2nd Secretary" or "Secretary".
2. The Council of Europe has a non-resident representative, stationed in the headquarters office at Dublin.
3. 1 Local Advisory Officer in London and 1 Agriculture Trade officer in Liverpool.
4. 1 1st Secretary is attached to the New York Consulate as Press and Information Officer.
5. 1 Counsellor also serves as Agricultural Attaché in Bonn.
Sources: Information supplied by the Department of Foreign Affairs.

Consular Missions	Date of Establishment	Consul General	Deputy Consul General	Vice Consul	Total
USA: New York	1930	1	1		2
USA: Boston	1930	1		1	2
USA: Chicago	1933	1		1	2
USA: San Francisco	1933	1		1	2
Germany: Hamburg	1962	1			1
					9

Table 3

A SURVEY OF CAREER PATTERNS IN THE DEPARTMENT OF EXTERNAL AFFAIRS

Case	Date of Birth	Education: School	Education: University (1st degree)	Education: University (additional)	Experience outside Govt.: No. of Years	Occupation	Experience in other Govt. Depts.: No of Years	Departments	Stage of Govt. career	Age at Entry	Up to Ambassadorial rank: HQ	Overseas	Total	At Ambassadorial rank: Age at appt.	HQ	Over-seas	Total (1967)
1	1903	Blackrock	NUI (Dublin)	NUI (Dublin), Kings Inns	3	Barrister				26	9	8	17	43	6	15	21
2	1917	Blackrock	NUI (Dublin)	Kings Inns			6	Agriculture, Defence	Beginning	24	8	10	18	42		8	8
3	1904	Clongowes	Trinity College Dublin	Kings Inns			2	Industry & Commerce	'Middle'	25	7	2	9	34	12	13	25
4	1913	Rockwell	NUI (Dublin)	Harvard, Chicago			13	Agriculture, Supplies, Ind. & Comm.	Beginning	33	6	3	9	42		12	12
5	1908	Killarney, Athens, Rome	NUI (Cork)	NUI, Oxford						27	2	6	8	35	6	18	24
6	1909	Clongowes	NUI (Dublin)	NUI, Kings Inns	6	Barrister	4	Dept. Attorney General	Beginning	32	5	1	6	38	3	17	20
7	1909	(N.I.)	Glasgow	Oxford			8	Finance, Supplies	Beginning	32	5	0	5	39	5	14	19
8	1912	(N.I.)	NUI (Cork)	NUI (Cork), H.Dip Ed.						26	5	3	8	34	7	14	21
9	1918	CBS Synge St., Coiaiste Muire, CBS O'Connell Schools					11	Education	Beginning	28	9	9	18	46		3	3
10	1918	CBS O'Connell Schools	NUI				11	Revenue Com., Ind. & Comm.	Beginning	32	5	10	15	47		2	2
11	1921	CBS Dundalk	NUI (Dublin)	NUI (Dublin)						22	5	13	18	40		6	6
12	1915	Belvedere	London School of Economics				15	Pub. Works, Finance	Beginning	32	9	5	14	46		6	6
13	1916	(N.I.)	NUI (Cork)	(N.I.)	(N.I.)	(N.I.)	4	Ind. & Comm., Supplies	Beginning	28	2	8	10	38	6	7	13
14	1910	Castleknock	NUI (Dublin)	NUI (Dublin), Madrid	(N.I.)		(N.I.)	(N.I.)	(N.I.)	28	9	7	16	44		13	13
15	1923		NUI (Dublin)							24	3	13	16	40		4	4
16	1916	CBS (Dublin)	NUI (Dublin)	NUI (Dublin), Kings Inns			12	Ind. & Comm., Finance	Beginning	30	6	5	11	41	7	3	10
17	1916	Belvedere & Blackrock	NUI (Dublin)	NUI (Dublin), Kings Inns	8	Barrister	6	Local Gov. (Legal Adv.)	Beginning	38	8	0	8	46	2	3	5
18	1910		Trinity College Dublin	NUI (Dublin), Kings Inns			13	Land Comm. (Legal Adv)	Beginning	37	0	14	14	51		6	6
19	1917	(N.I.)	NUI (Cork)	NUI (Cork), Hochschule fur Politik (Berlin)						25	6	6	12	37	4	8	12
20	1911	High School Dublin	Trinity College Dublin				2	Finance	Beginning	24	6	1	7	36	2	23	25

Note: 1. 'Ambassadorial rank' includes all appointments above the rank of Counsellor
2. (N.I.) — No information available.

Sources: International Who's Who, International Year Book & Statesman's Who's Who and information supplied by the Department of External Affairs.

	Age at Entry	Up to Ambassadorial rank: HQ	Overseas	Total	At Ambassadorial rank: Age at appt.	HQ	Over-seas	Total (1967)
Average	28.8	5.8	6.2	12.0	41.0	4.8	13.1	17.9
Range	22 to 38	0 to 9	0 to 14	5 to 18	34 to 51	0 to 12	7 to 23	10 to 25

Of those with at least

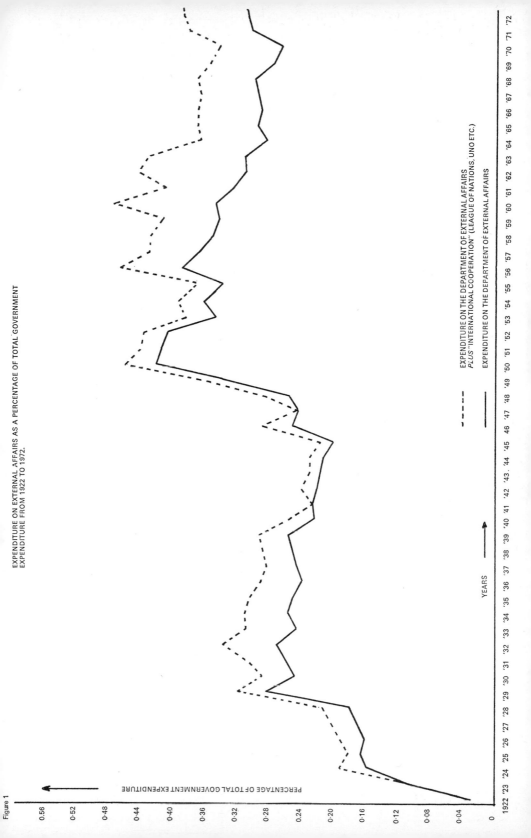

Figure 1

EXPENDITURE ON EXTERNAL AFFAIRS AS A PERCENTAGE OF TOTAL GOVERNMENT
EXPENDITURE FROM 1922 TO 1972.

EXPENDITURE ON THE DEPARTMENT OF EXTERNAL AFFAIRS
PLUS "INTERNATIONAL COOPERATION" (LEAGUE OF NATIONS, UNO ETC.)

EXPENDITURE ON THE DEPARTMENT OF EXTERNAL AFFAIRS

YEARS

PERCENTAGE OF TOTAL GOVERNMENT EXPENDITURE

0·56 0·52 0·48 0·44 0·40 0·36 0·32 0·28 0·24 0·20 0·16 0·12 0·08 0·04 0

1922 '23 '24 '25 '26 '27 '28 '29 '30 '31 '32 '33 '34 '35 '36 '37 '38 '39 '40 '41 '42 '43 '44 '45 '46 '47 '48 '49 '50 '51 '52 '53 '54 '55 '56 '57 '58 '59 '60 '61 '62 '63 '64 '65 '66 '67 '68 '69 '70 '71 '72

Figure 2

DEPARTMENT OF FOREIGN AFFAIRS, HEADQUARTERS ORGANISATION, JUNE 1972

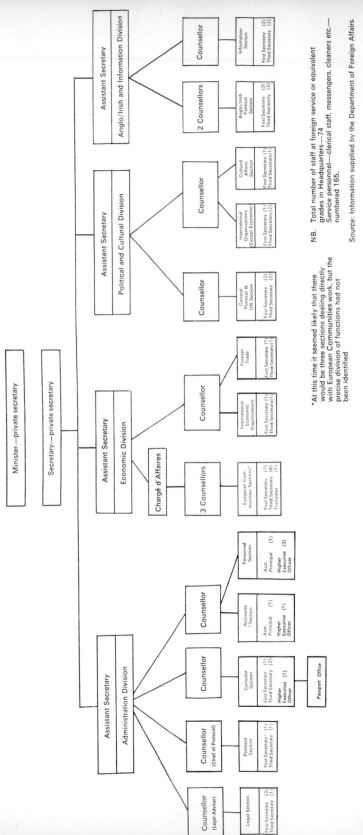

NB. Total number of staff at foreign service or equivalent grades in Headquarters—74 Service personnel—clerical staff, messengers, cleaners etc.—numbered 165.

Source: Information supplied by the Department of Foreign Affairs.

*At this time it seemed likely that there would be three sections dealing directly with European Communities work, but the precise division of functions had not been identified

Figure 3

DEPARTMENT OF FOREIGN AFFAIRS, HEADQUARTERS ORGANISATION, JUNE 1967

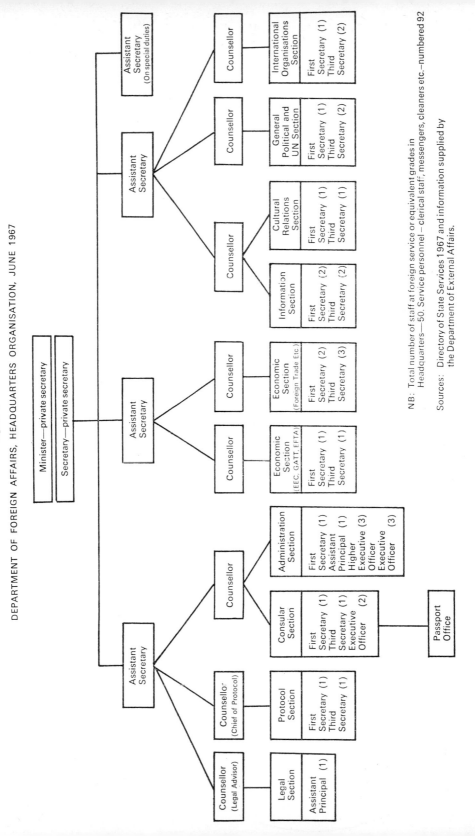

NB: Total number of staff at foreign service or equivalent grades in Headquarters—50. Service personnel – clerical staff, messengers, cleaners etc.–numbered 92

Sources: Directory of State Services 1967 and information supplied by the Department of External Affairs.

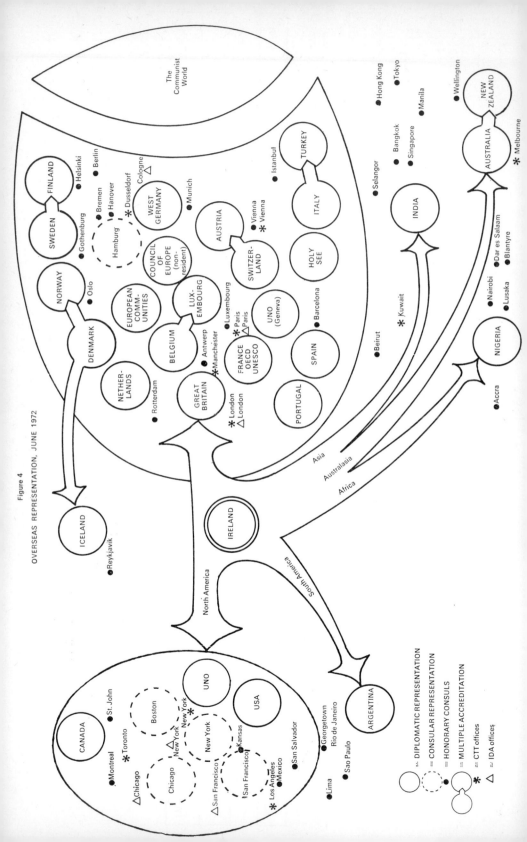

Figure 4

OVERSEAS REPRESENTATION, JUNE 1972

= DIPLOMATIC REPRESENTATION
= CONSULAR REPRESENTATION
= HONORARY CONSULS
= MULTIPLE ACCREDITATION

* CTT offices
△ IDA offices

INDEX

Adenauer, Konrad 55n
Advisory Committee on Cultural Relations, 113, 119–120
Africa, 121n, 217n
Agriculture, Department of, see Department of Agriculture
Agriculture, Minister for, see Minister for Agriculture
Aiken, Frank, 31, 50, 51, 59, 60, 73, 74, 93, 94, 95, 96, 151, 202, 206, 209, 223, 229, 237, 273, 282; as foreign minister, 84–89; and Irish policy in the United Nations, 32–34
Ancient Order of Hibernians (AOH), 285
Anglo-Irish Agreements, 1938, 22, 56–57, 111, 235, 252–253
Anglo-Irish Free Trade Agreement, 1965, 35
Anglo-Irish free trade area, 67
Anglo-Irish relations, 97, 117, 142, 164, 172–173, 296, 297; and constitutional legislation, 198–199; and Dáil deputies, 215, 228, 230–231; and the Department of Foreign Affairs, 120; and Eamon de Valera, 56; and elections, 249–254, 258; historical development, 1–2, 5, 13–16, 18–22, 26–29, 35–36; and the IRA, 285–288; and Seán MacBride, 80–81; and public opinion, 174. See also: Economic war; Northern Ireland, policy towards
Anglo-Irish Trade Agreement, 1948, 287n
Anglo-Irish Treaty, 1921, see Treaty
Anti-apartheid attitudes, 172, 283–284
Anti-communism, 175, 259, 279, 280, 281–282
Anti-Partition Leagues, 285
Aontacht Eireann, 260, 268n
Arab-Israeli war, 1967, 278n
Argentine, 108, 111, 121, 141
Army, 66, 84–85, 175
Attorney General, 62, 80, 128
Australia, 15, 48, 52, 55n, 111, 121, 123, 124, 164; diplomatic training procedures, 153: foreign affairs committee, 243
Austria, 124

Baldwin, Stanley, 53
Barcroft, Stephen, 24n, 57n
Baxter, Patrick F., 218
Belfast, 36, 272
Belgium, 110, 136
Belton, Patrick, 171, 172, 252, 281, 283
Biafra, 183, 282
Binchy, Daniel A., 138
Bipartisan approaches to foreign policy, see Parties, political
Blackrock College, 154
Blaney, Neil, 48, 97
Blowick, Joseph, 270
Boland, Frederick H., 33, 118, 127
Boland, Gerry, 263, 264
Boland, Kevin, 260
Bonn, 121, 123
Booth, Lionel, 224, 273
Bord Fáilte, 152
Boston, 110, 122
Boundary Commission, 14, 16, 53, 76
Brennan, Robert, 140
Briand-Kellogg Pact, see Treaty for the Renunciation of War, 1928
Bristol, 1
British Empire League, 138
British monarch, 190, 191, 199, 200
British parliament, 189
Browne, Noel, 80, 163, 168, 191, 218, 226, 248, 260, 261, 266, 277, 282, 283
Brussels, 114, 133, 289, 297
Burke, Edmund, 212, 227

Cabinet, see Government, the
Canada, 15, 48, 52, 55, 63, 111, 121
Canberra, 121
Castleknock College, 154
Catholic Association of International Relations, 291
Catholic Church and foreign policy, 164–165, 171–172, 278–283
Caulfield, Mr, 108
Cean Comhairle (Chairman of the Dáil), 200, 201
Censorship, 85
Chamberlain, Neville, 25, 57n
Chicago, 110, 122

pean Parliament, 193, 225, 241, 297; and the European affiliations of Irish parties, 265–266; and Fianna Fáil 289–290; and Fine Gael, 289–290; and Garret FitzGerald, 90; formulation of Irish policy towards, 130–131; and Patrick Hillery, 89–90; impact of membership on diplomatic service, 142; and information in the Dáil, 208; and Ireland's application for membership, 1961, 34–35; Ireland joins, 1969–1972, 36–37; Irish diplomatic representation in, 114, 122–123; and Irish interest groups, 275, 288–291; and the Labour Party, 277; and Seán Lemass, 67–68; and the National Progressive Democratic Party, 256; and opinion polls, 175–176; questions in the Dáil in 1961, 201–202; and the referendum of May 1972, 167–168, 257–258, 288–291; responsibility for Irish policy towards, 93–94, 98; and the Senate, 193, 241–242; and special parliamentary committees in member states, 241–242; Taoiseach's role in negotiations to join, 51

European Defence Community, 61
European Progressive Democrat Group (European Parliament), 266
European recovery programme, 81, 113
European Free Trade Area, 237
Executive Authority (External Relations) Act, 1936, 20, 27–28, 64, 191, 198, 231, 252, 253
Executive Council, 43, 216. *See also* Government, the
External Affairs, Department of, *see* Department of External Affairs
External Affairs, Minister for, *see* Minister for External Affairs
External association, 19–22, 27–28, 45, 56, 59, 230–231, 252

Facts about Ireland, 87, 205
Farmers' Party, 276
Federated Union of Employers (FUE), 276
Federation of Irish Industries, 275
Fenians, 272
Fianna Fáil: attitudes towards Britain in 1932, 18; attitudes towards international politics, 258–259; and diplomats, 138–139; and elections, 251–259 *passim;* formation, 250; and *The Irish Press,*

178; and the IRA, 286, 287; and membership of the EEC, 289–290; and the Northern Ireland crisis, 48, 264; party committee on foreign policy, 264–265; party organisation and foreign policy, 261–266 *passim;* party spokesmen on foreign policy, 222–224; and proposals for a committee on foreign affairs, 243. *See also* Parties, political
Figgis, Darrell, 43, 55, 109
Finance, Department of, *see* Department of Finance
Finance, Minister for, *see* Minister for Finance
Fine Gael: attitudes towards international politics, 258–259; and the Catholic Church, 281–282; and elections, 251–259 *passim;* and membership of the EEC, 289–290; and neutrality, 254–256; opposes Irish policy in the UN, 33, 83, 86, 256; party organisation and foreign policy, 261–266 *passim;* and party spokesmen on foreign policy, 222–224; and proposals for a committee on foreign affairs, 240, 243. *See also* Cumann na nGaedheal; Parties, political
Finland, 124
FitzGerald, Desmond, 17, 44, 52, 54, 62, 73, 74, 79n, 90, 91–92, 96, 101, 102, 108, 139, 140, 141, 223, 234, 295; as foreign minister, 75–77
FitzGerald, Garret, 73, 74, 87, 98, 121n, 131, 223, 241n, 297n, 298n; becomes foreign minister, 90
Flanagan, Oliver J., 72n, 211
Food and Agriculture Organization (FAO), 119, 275
Foreign Affairs, Department of, *see* Department of External Affairs
Foreign Affairs, Minister for, *see* Minister for External Affairs
Foreign policy: bipartisan consultations, *see* Parties, political, bipartisan approaches to foreign policy; and civil servants, 101; coordination of policy-making and administration, 124–128; division of governmental responsibilities, 35, 49, 91–94, 131; economic aspects, *see* Economic policy; and elections, 248–249; and the foreign minister, 71–72; the government's predominance in, 41–47; and government solidarity,